Partnering to Prepare Urban Teachers

"As you begin to experience the rich intellectual content of this important volume, be prepared for a compelling, hopeful, and sobering encounter with some of the most challenging circumstances imaginable on the part of teacher education to meet the needs of learners. You will be presented with honest reports of comprehensive and determined efforts to understand and respond to the realities of urban schools. You will read of programs that address the complexity of urban settings that influences teacher preparation and retention and, ultimately, student achievement. These experiences present in powerful terms one of the most significant challenges to the professional efficacy of the teacher education enterprise that exists today. That challenge is one that teacher educators cannot—must not—ignore. This book could not be more timely, nor its call to action more critical.... The contributors make one point very clear: urban teaching is not missionary work but work that is possible only when it is grounded in a personal and professional commitment to the mission of social justice."

—Excerpt from the Introduction by Sharon P. Robinson

"As someone who has become increasingly suspicious, indeed downright weary, of calls to activism that do not give the reader any tools for the activism, I found *Partnering to Prepare Urban Teachers* a refreshing change. For those of us whose professional lives are immersed in the preparation of urban teachers, this book is an invaluable guide. It is both a call to action and a repository of examples of good curriculum and best practices. And, for anyone who cares about the teachers in the city schools of the twenty-first century—be they teacher educator, teacher, parent, policy-maker, or concerned citizen—the passionate yet practical call to activism embedded here is essential reading."

—Excerpt from the Conclusion by James Fraser

Partnering
to Prepare
Urban
Teachers

PETER LANG
New York • Washington, D.C./Baltimore • Bern
Frankfurt am Main • Berlin • Brussels • Vienna • Oxford

Partnering to Prepare Urban Teachers

A Call to Activism

Francine P. Peterman, EDITOR

Serving Learners

PUBLISHED FOR THE AMERICAN ASSOCIATION OF COLLEGES FOR TEACHER EDUCATION

PETER LANG
New York • Washington, D.C./Baltimore • Bern
Frankfurt am Main • Berlin • Brussels • Vienna • Oxford

Library of Congress Cataloging-in-Publication Data
Partnering to prepare urban teachers:
a call to activism / edited by Francine P. Peterman.
p. cm.
Includes bibliographical references and index.
1. Education, Urban—United States.
2. Teachers—Training of—United States.
3. Community and school—United States.
I. Peterman, Francine P.
LC5131.P37 370.71'11732—dc22 2007046369
ISBN 978-1-4331-0117-5 (hardcover)
ISBN 978-1-4331-0116-8 (paperback)

Bibliographic information published by **Die Deutsche Bibliothek**.
Die Deutsche Bibliothek lists this publication in the "Deutsche
Nationalbibliografie"; detailed bibliographic data is available
on the Internet at http://dnb.ddb.de/.

The paper in this book meets the guidelines for permanence and durability
of the Committee on Production Guidelines for Book Longevity
of the Council of Library Resources.

© 2008 Peter Lang Publishing, Inc., New York
29 Broadway, 18th floor, New York, NY 10006
www.peterlang.com

Printed in the United States of America

Table OF Contents

Preface: A Call TO Activism, A Call TO Hope

FRANCINE P. PETERMAN

Cleveland State University

Six years before this book went to press, at a Memphis meeting of the Urban Network to Improve Teacher Education (UNITE), formerly a special interest group of the Holmes Partnership, three teacher educators met for breakfast to discuss where we might go with the work we were doing in partnering to prepare urban teachers. UNITE provided us with triennial opportunities to meet not only with our partnership teams from our universities, local school districts, and their unions, but also with teams from urban settings across the United States. UNITE brought together teams of bright, energetic, innovative, and sometimes exasperated teachers, teacher educators, and administrators, who—like us—found renewal and inspiration in the organization's ongoing, collaborative professional development. Furthermore, in UNITE, we found each other and most of the other contributors to this volume—a core of mentors, allies, and friends who were engaged in similar struggles toward particular aims—each partnering to prepare teacher activists who would be successful and remain in urban classrooms for the long haul.

Dennis Shirley, Peter Murrell, Jr., and I met that morning in Memphis to talk about the political nature of preparing teachers as social activists in university and school settings, where such work was not always explicitly embraced or advanced. At several conference presentations at the annual meetings of the American Educational Research Association (AERA) and the American Association of Colleges for Teacher Education (AACTE), where drafts of most of these chapters were previously presented, our discussants, Kenneth Zeichner and Jeannie Oakes, helped us think critically and historically about our work, situating it in the context of both urban settings and political activism. To expand our network and advance social activism as integral to urban teacher education, we made a commitment to publish a compendium of chapters theoretically and practically detailing the layers and conundrums, tribulations and triumphs, contexts and voices of the challenges facing urban teachers, teacher educators, and administrators who work collaboratively to prepare and support teachers as social activists. On a paper napkin, we detailed an outline for the book, including colleagues whose work advanced a social justice perspective on partnering to prepare urban teachers and presented a variety of perspectives on the work. Thus began the effort that led to this book, *Partnering to Prepare Urban Teachers: A Call to Activism*—a book that chronicles university-school partnerships dedicated to preparing and retaining urban teachers—a book about hope.

This book is comprised of three sections that focus on (a) theoretical and historical underpinnings of partnering to prepare urban teachers as social activists; (b) stories from the field, explored through the voices and actions of students, families, teacher educators, and preservice and in-service teachers; and (c) a critical analysis of our work. Rather than detail the contents of each chapter, I invite you to use the following questions to guide your reading and help you think about this crucial work—work that is situated in settings that mirror those across the United States and that represents partnerships in Boston, Chicago, Cleveland, Los Angeles, and Wilmington.

The first section of this book provides both context and theory for urban teacher preparation that are situated in defining urban settings, socioculturally refining our notions of teacher development, and reviewing community organizing as a means to promote social justice through participatory democracy. It prompts you to explore several questions: What does it mean to be *urban*? What are the implications of *urban* for preparing teachers? How do teachers engage in circles of co-practice to support their development in high-needs urban schools? What can teachers learn from community organizing to foster and support teachers (and teacher educators) as social activists?

The second section of this book details the work of partnering to prepare urban teachers from a variety of perspectives. The narratives therein delineate the layers of the social contexts in which the important work of being a student, partnering with families, becoming a teacher educator, learning to teach, and teaching in urban settings takes place. It poses and examines the following questions: How do students talk about schooling? How do teachers support families' social activism? What dilemmas face teacher educators as they become *urban* teacher educators? How can new urban teacher-activists be sustained?

The third section of this book provides a critical analysis of the contributors' efforts at partnering to prepare urban teachers as it addresses these questions:

How do we as teacher educators catalyze activism in partnering to prepare urban teachers? How can we sustain such collaborative efforts? How do we create contexts that support this work? In this section, our esteemed critical friend James Fraser of New York University's Steinhardt School of Culture, Education, and Human Development, situates his analysis in his extensive experience and knowledge of urban teacher preparation and activism. He reminds us that this work is difficult yet critical to making a difference in urban communities, schools, and universities.

Despite the best intentions of its founders to legislate equity, high levels of achievement, and accountability in public schools, when enacted in urban settings, the No Child Left Behind Act has frequently resulted in districts' bureaucratic demands for drill-and-skill test preparation and scripted curriculum rather than for the kinds of reforms our partnerships have shown make a difference in the lives and education of children and families—such as cultural competence, challenging coursework, caring, and social activism. As I indicated earlier, this is a book about hope. Most of all, we want the tales from the field that we have included in these pages to engender the kind of hope that each of us, through our work, has nurtured in ourselves, in each other, in our partners, and in other folks we have met along the way. Thus, in a time and in places where accountability masquerades as a call for excellence, this hope fuels our quest to heed the call to activism in partnering to prepare urban teachers.

Francine Peterman
Cleveland State University[1]

NOTES

1. The editor/author acknowledges the support of Cleveland State University under grant #P336C020018, awarded by the U.S. Department of Education, Office of Postsecondary Education, Teacher Quality Enhancement Programs.

Introduction

As you begin to experience the rich intellectual content of this important volume, be prepared for a compelling, hopeful, and sobering encounter with some of the most challenging circumstances imaginable on the part of teacher education to meet the needs of learners. You will be presented with honest reports of comprehensive and determined efforts to understand and respond to the realities of urban schools. You will read of programs that address the complexity of urban settings that influences teacher preparation and retention and, ultimately, student achievement. These experiences present in powerful terms one of the most significant challenges to the professional efficacy of the teacher education enterprise that exists today. That challenge is one that teacher educators cannot—must not—ignore. This book could not be more timely, nor its call to action more critical.

As *Partnering to Prepare Urban Teachers'* impressive cadre of contributors points out, *not* pursing the topic of this volume is not an option for those of us in teacher preparation today. The United States is presently a largely urban nation—indeed, 57% of its population is located in urban areas—and it is continually becoming more so, as each new demographic report attests. Population surges in the nation's metropolitan areas are expected to continue throughout the coming decades. We are fast becoming a multiracial, multiethnic, highly mobile global society; 45% of U.S. children under the age of five years are members of minority groups. All preparation institutions, whether urban or rural, must be able to produce large numbers of increasingly mobile teachers who are capable of engaging the diverse types of learners who presently attend our public schools. Schools, colleges, and departments of education are increasingly entering partnerships with PK–12 (pre-kindergarten through 12th grade) schools and their surrounding communities not only because it is the right thing to do, but also because it is the *only* prospect available if teacher education is to be relevant, useful, and successful in preparing teachers for the global village in which we now live.

It is fortuitous that this volume begins with a discussion of what is meant by the term *urban* when it is used to describe school settings and that it examines, from the outset, the mental images many of us hold of schools in urban communities. There is nothing easy about this image; visions of poverty, crime, and disorganization of families and social institutions usually come to mind. Although the authors of the chapters that follow note the impact of such perceptions regarding the urban communities in which they worked, they also report findings of opportunity and responsibility. In every instance, their research provides theoretical and practical analyses of the programmatic attributes that are essential for the preparation of competent urban educational professionals.

Readers may be shocked by the tough-love, tell-it-like-it-is nature of this volume, yet that aspect not only makes for easy page turning, but also provides an absolutely critical view of reality that all teacher educators and teacher candidates need to experience. This reading may be the first such experience (albeit vicarious) for some. In that regard, *Partnering to Prepare Urban Teachers* can be seen as a valuable tutorial. But it is also a wake-up call for teacher preparation programs, as many of the accounts presented herein point out institutional inadequacies in addressing the very substantial complexities and challenges presented by urban schools. Notwithstanding, these shortcomings are ones that urban teachers must overcome to succeed and, indeed, to survive.

The impetus to activism is a clarion call for schools, colleges, and departments of education to develop educators for urban settings who are equipped with the skills essential both for student success and for professional fulfillment. Urban teacher education is highly culturally contextualized, requiring special sensibility and a broad repertoire of professional skills to educate diverse learners. These skills include the capacity to enact standards-based teaching that provides ongoing feedback to students, as well as a variety of opportunities for them to enhance their understanding and communicate what they have learned. Urban educators must also develop the capacities to use student groupings and assessments that fit the needs of all learners; to engage culturally responsive pedagogy that not only establishes relevance for students, but also encourages their further effort on behalf of worthwhile goals and aspirations; and to apply theories of language development and metacognitive strategies that result in English proficiency while valuing language diversity. With skills such as these, professional urban educators will be better able to act in ways that create school environments that are free of threat, respectful of the communities in which they are situated, and prepared to address the inequities that might limit student achievement.

This volume also tackles the myriad challenges of cultural incongruence that teachers should expect to encounter among the diverse political, educational, social, and cultural networks to be found in urban communities. The contributors make one point very clear: Urban teaching is not missionary work but work that is possible only when it is grounded in a personal and professional commitment to the mission of social justice. That commitment to social justice must be evidenced in all partners, from the university-based faculty and staff who bring their knowledge of and skills in organizational development and community organizing, human resources and professional development, design of content and clinical experiences, and pedagogy and politics; to the urban teacher candidates in programs of teacher education; and to the teachers already serving in urban settings.

Partnering to Prepare Urban Teachers: A Call to Activism should become essential, required reading for discussion and action by every teacher educator in the nation. It describes work that is long past due. Fortunately, as the book's contributors variously attest, that work is now ongoing in many communities. Their chapters describe the exciting future that is here and now, all around us, and not to be ignored. Their insights compel us to relish and embrace our urban destinies with curiosity, reverence, and concern for the magical variety of human beings that presently constitute the global village that is right here at home. Their stories detail the plain hard work of doing what must be done in the interest of students in urban communities. Their conclusions and recommendations are not romantic exhortations but actual tools for addressing the barriers of tradition, language, and culture that confront urban teachers and their teacher educators.

Their message: Be inspired, and be prepared to act!

Sharon P. Robinson
President and Chief Executive Officer
American Association of Colleges for Teacher Education

What's *Urban* Got TO DO WITH It? The Meanings OF *Urban* IN Urban Teacher Preparation AND Development

VICTORIA CHOU

STEVEN TOZER

University of Illinois at Chicago

In teacher preparation and development, as in all educational endeavors, we take for granted that context makes a difference and that situated knowledge is essential. Yet, we do not often enough share with one another precisely *how* we believe context makes a difference. Work in high-stakes urban contexts, in particular, demands that we make our assumptions about the term *urban* as explicit as possible, for the modifier *urban* in *urban education* frequently creates tension of understanding and communication. For example, *urban* is often a coded marker for conditions of cultural conflict grounded in racism and economic oppression. The term may also be used in a self-congratulatory manner, as in, "I teach in an urban school," which is a variant of the more obvious statement, "I teach in the inner city." Such assertions often indicate a we-they demarcation, where *they* are viewed as different, confined to a challenging and perhaps deficient space in which *we*, who are not so confined, choose to help.

While we are mindful of the baggage that the term *urban* carries, we are also mindful of the challenges to educators who seek to become more effective allies of parents who want the best education for their children but are having a difficult time finding it in city schools. The obstacles to successful teaching and learning in urban environments are several, as we will discuss, and the record is clear that some teachers and schools have learned better than others how to address those obstacles (Designs for Change, 2005). This chapter attempts to make explicit—from our perspective as urban teacher educators—what we believe to be *urban* about urban teacher preparation and development and how these understandings affect the ability of partners invested in teaching and learning to achieve their goals.

Though *urban* and *nonurban* are often treated as disjunct categories, we begin our discussion with Weiner's observation (2000) that the quality of being urban exists on a continuum:

> Urban-ness is best understood as existing on a continuum. … the structural characteristics of urban school systems, their size and bureaucracy, are the most salient factors because they frame the interaction of the other elements. Size and bureaucracy intensify the contradiction between teaching and learning as personal, human activities, on the one hand, and the standardization that is intended to make urban schools efficient, fair, and impartial. (pp. 370–371)

Size and bureaucracy, however, are only a part of the story and possibly are not the more important part. It is tempting, for example, when witnessing the failure of so many high-rise apartment buildings of late 20th-century public housing, to conclude that the source of the problem is size and bureaucracy: too many people located in too small a space for the organized delivery of services. But, as well-to-do neighborhoods demonstrate the contrasting success of even larger high-rise apartment buildings and condominiums, we realize that other variables matter, too—namely, racism and segregation, inequitable distribution of resources, and human resistance to conditions that are perceived as demeaning or unfair.

To size and its concomitant bureaucracy, therefore, we add the variables of ethnic and economic heterogeneity of people and the infusion of cultural politics in school reform to arrive at our definition of what is distinctively challenging about the urban education environment. Cutting across these three dimensions are dynamics of race, resources, and resistance. The interaction among all of these variables and dimensions, we argue, helps define what educators need to understand if we wish to serve *all* of the nation's school children well. In the following sections, we clarify what we mean by each variable.

MATTERS OF SIZE AND SCALE

Clearly, not all uses of the term *urban* are coded judgments. The word can simply mark an attempt to distinguish city areas from noncity areas, however those are defined, and the distinction can be a useful and even necessary one for thinking about the real conditions that affect learning in the nation's schools. Even so, a range of meanings crops up. Some are quantitative, though still not definitive. The U.S. Census Bureau (2004) classifies *urban* as "all territory, population, and housing units located within an urbanized area (UA) or an urban cluster (UC)." *Urbanized areas* and *urban clusters* are further defined as "core census block groups or blocks that have a population density of at least 1,000 people per square mile" and "surrounding census blocks that have an overall density of at least 500 people per square mile," respectively.

This flexibility of definition, applied to understanding schooling in the United States, places most public school students in urban systems. Of over 46 million PK–12 students, more than 33 million live in the following four urban categories used by the U.S. Office of Education: central city of large metropolitan statistical area (i.e., an MSA with a population greater than 400,000), central city of midsize MSA, urban fringe of large MSA, and urban fringe of midsize MSA. The remaining students are in large and small towns and rural areas. Thus, one, and by no means the only way to think about the extent of *urban education* in this volume is to assume that it includes three-quarters of the nation's students.

To illustrate the significance of size in matters of educational quality, we will use an example from our local context. We began this chapter by observing that context matters, and situated knowledge is essential, and we will refer often to Chicago, as it is the urban environment that we know best. To illustrate the importance of district size, consider the second largest high school district in Illinois: District 214, just northwest of Chicago. Over 12,000 high school students and 800 teachers present a considerable challenge for school improvement efforts—but a manageable one. If the superintendent of District 214 wants to effect significant improvement, he or she can bring the principals of the six high schools of the district into the central office and develop a shared strategy with considerable confidence that these six administrators understand and can implement it. With only six principals in this relatively large district, the superintendent can have considerable confidence in their quality as instructional leaders. Each time a principalship opens, the applications pour in from qualified candidates, and the position is offered to a person whose proven record of leadership stands up well against strong competition.

Contrast this with the situation of the largest school district in Illinois, Chicago Public Schools (CPS), with some 80 high schools. School reform is a continuing challenge among Chicago's secondary schools. A new Office of Principal Preparation and Development was created because there are not enough qualified principals available to put a qualified leader in each school, and the stresses of school leadership in a large urban district are such that turnover is high. Instead of hiring one or two principals every few years, as in the state's second largest high school district, the system must hire eight to ten secondary school principals each year. When the chief executive officer (CEO) of Chicago Public Schools seeks to make an improvement in CPS high schools, it will not typically be the result of shared deliberation among them but an edict that some principals will incorporate, some will not fully understand, some will not have the skills to implement, and some will ignore because they are retiring and cannot bring themselves to make the necessary investment. Chicago's high schools are part of a district with an additional 500 elementary and middle schools, and it is expected that the system will need a minimum of 50 principals a year for the next several years (district-wide, over 80 principals were hired for the 2005–2006 school year, elementary and secondary schools combined). The sheer size of CPS, with 28,000 teachers and 437,000 students, affects how change is brought about and how likely it is to succeed (Chicago Public Schools, 2005).

This example illustrates quite a bit about the significance of scale in the urban environment. One dimension of that might be called the *human capital* dimension: the quality of personnel that an urban system is able to attract and retain. Another dimension is the organization of resources: how those personnel and other resources are effectively organized into professional communities that support student learning. Together, these two dimensions interact.

However, the numbers by themselves do not tell a complete story. Conditions among large school districts can vary considerably. For example, of the 10 largest school districts in the nation, 5 have child poverty levels of 30% to 39%. These districts—New York, Los Angeles, Chicago, Houston, and Detroit—differ in significant ways from the 2 districts with less than 15% child poverty. Hawaii's one-state school district and Nevada's Clark County do not have the same configuration of urban characteristics as the other districts that are among the nation's 10 largest, though the matter of scale applies to all. Likewise, some of the districts ranking 91 to 100 among the top-100 largest districts illustrate the interaction of scale and economics. For example, though Buffalo, New York, and Plano, Texas, are similar in size (46,000 and 45,000 students, respectively), Buffalo's 45% child-poverty rate is more than 10 times Plano's 3.7% rate, and the concerns of each district can be expected to differ accordingly (U.S. Census Bureau, 2004). To understand the challenges these districts face, it would be important to understand issues of human capital and district organization—and how these interact with the challenges of attracting, developing, and organizing talent on a large scale.

Scale and Human Capital

The need to replace large numbers of teachers and administrators annually in large districts with a variety of organizational stresses helps define the causes of urban teacher shortages. Discussions about whether a teacher shortage actually exists or whether the problem is retention are moot when applied to hard-to-staff schools in these regions. The Southeast Center for Teaching Quality (*Recruiting Teachers*, 2002, p. 3) defines *hard-to-staff schools* as meeting the following criteria:

- 50% or more of students are below grade level
- 50% or more of students are eligible for free and reduced-price lunch in elementary schools (40% for high schools)
- annual teacher turnover rate of 15% to 18%
- 25% or more of teachers have provisional licenses; are lateral entry (up to 5 years to earn full licensure), emergency, or temporary; or are probationary.

Urban educators are familiar with precisely these conditions, which lead to what Wise and Levine (2002) term "the parade of teaching temps" (p. 38). In Chicago, for example, an October 2001 audit of low-performing schools revealed a school where 11 of 25 teachers lacked full teacher certification (Gewertz, 2002). Prior to the advent of the No Child Left Behind Act of 2001 (NCLB) legislation, well over 500 bilingual education teachers in Chicago were working on provisional certificates. A recent analysis of the latest federal Schools and Staffing Survey revealed that the problem of out-of-field teaching is worst at the middle school level (Jerald, 2002). Such schools as these have the hardest time meeting the NCLB mandate that every classroom be staffed by a "highly qualified" teacher by the end of the 2005–2006 school year. For a small district to locate and replace a handful of underqualified teachers is a challenge with some promise of success. For a large district to do so for hundreds of teachers requires something more extraordinary. Partly due to scale, therefore, urban schools have difficulty providing qualified teachers for each child and qualified administrators for each school.

Organization of Resources in Large-Scale Urban Systems

It has become commonplace to observe that teachers leave urban districts in large numbers partly due to the sense of teaching in out-of-control environments. This is partly a scale issue, in that district size relates to the organizational structures that have evolved to deal with massive numbers of students, teachers, staff, school buildings, and other district resources. The sheer size of urban school districts typically means that decision making must be centralized and invested in authorities that are often both physically and conceptually removed from the teachers and students affected. Even if the per-child funding of the district is not egregiously low compared to the funding of other districts in the state (as is Chicago's), organizing resources effectively is a long-standing challenge to urban districts. We note that the 20th century was marked by centralization of decision making to organize and allocate resources efficiently, despite discouraging results and despite the array of activist stakeholders found in urban environments, often pushing for a significant community voice in school reform and policy making. These include the teachers' unions, local advocacy and reform groups, organized business groups, philanthropic foundations, and higher education, among others. At the school level, Payne (1998) talks about patterns of contestation among the principal, teachers, local school councils, and parent groups, often leading to a pattern of stalemated power.

The persistent failures of urban school systems have largely fed the centralization impulse that results in top-down mandates for standardized curriculum, instruction, and assessments—whether or not sufficient funding is provided for these mandates to succeed. What teachers perceive to be remote, top-down decision making with insufficient resource allocations leads, in turn, to problems with the social infrastructure in schools, argues Payne (1998). These problems are found in distrust and lack of social comfort among adults; low mutual expectations; tensions pertaining to race, ethnicity, and age cohort; and, in some schools, a predisposition to factions. The communication problems that result then lead, in turn, to various patterns of withdrawal as a major coping strategy. One of these patterns, of course, is withdrawal from the district or from the profession altogether. We are well aware that teacher attrition is a much greater problem in urban environments than in middle-income suburban environments. Ingersoll (2001, 2003) showed that 20% of teachers at high-poverty schools, which are disproportionately located in urban systems, departed teaching or transferred to other schools in 1999, compared to 12.9% of teachers in low-poverty schools.

The picture that Ingersoll, Weiner, Payne, and others portray goes beyond municipal population figures to show how the sheer scale of urban districts can translate into low-performing schools through the challenges of human capital and organization of resources when the structure of support for improving either situation is largely absent. Payne (1998) observes that urban districts are characterized by a failure to organize time, including time for retraining, shared planning, and reflection. A narrow base of resource support leads to an inappropriate pace and scale of change, partly due to inadequate leadership. Even something as basic as the absence of quality substitute teacher support can affect efforts in staff development, as can the chronic instability of key administrative personnel. These are compounded, in turn, by an absence of mechanisms for ongoing, accurate assessment of innovations, an absence of follow-through, and an inability to make midcourse corrections. External demands for results, which are annually fueled by newspaper printings of results of student test scores, lead to reactive solutions that sometimes delay, interfere with, or even abrogate prior initiatives. It should be noted, however, that large urban school district centralization is not necessarily a black-and-white, good-or-bad matter. A 2002 study by the Council of the Great City Schools and the Manpower Demonstration Research Corporation (MDRC) found that clear and consistent centralized policies that focused on measurable goals and the provision of sufficient support to attain the goals did, in fact, lead to improved academic achievement and reductions in the achievement gaps between different racial groups.

Significance for Teacher Educators

Partnering effectively with such school districts to provide exemplary training for prospective teachers is difficult, even for teacher education programs whose faculty seek to be agents of positive change in the urban school system. Serious tension exists between *small-scale* and *to-scale* approaches to educational change. While big-city school administrators seek system-wide change as quickly as possible, teacher educators seek to develop and evaluate model programs that, in contrast, affect a very few teachers in a very few schools. How can one model program influence the system to accommodate its small percentage of teachers? The challenge is how to avoid model efforts that have no genuine theory of large-scale change other than the hope that others will copy a good model and follow its exemplary lead. This hope, however, is no substitute for a change theory, and it has proven to be a vain one in urban education. There is no lack of fine models—the problem is one of large-scale change. Can teacher educators seriously address systemic change as part of their teacher development agenda when teacher development is such a small part of the wider urban ecology? Or are teacher educators left with a different alternative: abandoning systemic change in favor of finding pockets of excellence in urban school systems, where teacher candidates can be educated, even if those schools are not where the majority of new teachers will be hired?

The late 20th-century failure of teacher education to demonstrate that it can prepare sufficient numbers of teachers who are both committed to the highest-need urban schools and qualified to teach the highest-need subjects in those schools has created a market niche for alternative teacher certification programs. The chief asset of such programs, from the point of view of urban districts, is that they supply substantial numbers of teachers for hard-to-staff schools and subjects. In short, they meet the district's needs. In Chicago, for example, all the 15 alternative teacher certification programs currently partnering with Chicago Public Schools are designed specifically for placements in hard-to-staff schools, and nearly all of them are designed to fill subject shortages such as middle grades math and science, secondary school math and science, and special education (Chicago Public Schools, 2005).

In an important sense, the primary client for such alternative certification programs is not the candidate who wishes to teach, but the school system and its specific needs. The alternative certification program provider shapes a partnership with the school system, and the candidate's professional preparation needs are met only if they are compatible with the district's needs. This stands in contrast to the standard model of admissions to teacher education programs, where the primary client is the prospective teacher. The prospective teacher's career interests may not coincide at all with the needs of urban districts, and he or she may have no intention at all of teaching in an urban school. To conceive of the district and its children as the primary client would require that most teacher education programs change their program goals, program admissions, and program content.

Challenges to a Theory of Urban Teacher Preparation

A number of theoretical challenges emerge from this discussion of scale, of which two stand out. One is that a theory of change is essential. Without it, teacher education programs cannot articulate how their practices are likely to improve student learning at the scale and pace that urban districts find necessary. In the absence of a compelling account of the relationship between teacher education practices and significant urban school improvement, there is little reason for urban districts to look to teacher education providers as partners. The second challenge is the potential theoretical shift in identifying school districts (instead of teacher education candidates) as the primary client and targeting teacher education programs to meet that client's needs. In Chicago, this is what alternative certification programs have done. The result is the establishment of partnerships between alternative certification programs and the district, bringing district resources to the provider—in terms of tuition and internships—and large numbers of teachers for high-need areas to the district.

CULTURAL HETEROGENEITY AND CULTURAL CAPITAL

It is commonplace to remark that the United States is a nation of immigrants. Less often remarked is that the history of urbanization in this country is a history of cultural heterogeneity and conflict. This has been played out in schools in successive waves of immigration and migration, from the Irish in the 1830s to post–Civil War African American migration to turn-of-the-20th-century eastern European immigration to late 20th-century immigration and migration of Latino communities (Tozer, Violas, & Senese, 2002). African American, Latino, Asian American, and other non-Anglo groups have settled disproportionately in large cities, where education and the labor market have interacted with ethnicity to produce much higher rates of poverty than in nonurban areas. The contrasts between Chicago and the rest of Illinois, for example, are startling, despite Illinois having a number of other midsize cities such as Peoria, Aurora, Rockford, Springfield, and East St. Louis (see Table 1). Table 1 is based on data presented in *Left Behind: Student Achievement in Chicago's Public Schools* (Education Committee of the Commercial Club of Chicago, 2003).

Chicago students represent about 21% of statewide school enrollments, but it should be clear that the sheer size of the district is inseparable, as a challenge to educators, from the realities of poverty and ethnic difference. In contrast to the rest of the state, the cultural capital of middle-class teachers with college educations and of schools as institutions is not the same cultural capital brought by the majority of students to schools. When home language or knowledge conflicts with the approved institutional knowledge of schools and standardized tests, the institutional capital of the school trumps the cultural capital of the home. Weiner (2000) writes the following:

> The most salient aspect of urban teaching then is that urban teachers must be able to accommodate the greatest diversity of student needs under conditions that continually subvert their efforts to personalize and individualize education. … Urban teachers often work detached from the community and family resources that would help them to understand their students' lives, needs, and interests, a problem compounded by procedures and regulations designed to make education impersonal and anonymous. (p. 371)

Table 1. Poverty and Ethnic Difference: Illinois School District Characteristics

Student Characteristics	Student Enrollment (Median Figures)	
	Illinois, Outside Chicago (Percent)	Chicago Only (Percent)
Low income	21.3	85.3
African American	1.1	50.8
Latino	1.6	36.1
White non-Latino	95.2	9.6
Asian American	0.6	3.3
Mobility	12.4	24.8
Limited English-language proficiency	0	14.3

Note. Data are from *Left behind: Student achievement in Chicago's public schools*, by Education Committee of the Commercial Club of Chicago, 2003, Chicago: Civic Committee of the Commercial Club of Chicago. Adapted with permission.

Urban schools serve a highly diverse student population, including high concentrations of students whose orientations toward schooling are different from and in conflict with that of mainstream orientations toward schooling. Urban environments are characterized not just by ethnic and language diversity but also by patterns of sharp ethnic and economic segregation, and these are reflected in the schools. A recent analysis by Orfield (2001) reveals that, despite the U.S. Supreme Court's desegregation ruling in 1955, the 1990s saw a decade of resegregation. The strong pattern of resegregation, Orfield asserts, is accompanied by a growing gap in the quality of schools attended by White students and schools attended by African American and Latino students.

Chicago Public Schools provide an illustrative case of how segregation is a more illuminating construct than diversity. The communities CPS serves are highly segregated and predominantly poor, the norm for millions of students in large cities and rural areas (College Entrance Examination Board, 1999). Nearly half of CPS schools (46%) are 90% to 100% African American in enrollment; another 7% of CPS schools are 60% to 90% African American. Seven percent of CPS schools are 90% to 100% Latino in enrollment, and 15% of CPS schools are 60% to 90% Latino. Fifty-six percent of the schools, then, are over 90% Black or Latino, and 78% of CPS schools are either predominantly Black or predominantly Latino.

This segregation reminds us of an old and tragic lesson: Where separateness prevails, inequality is rarely far behind. Roth, Brooks-Gunn, Linver, and Hofferth's (2003) findings are by now familiar: "Our data illustrate the racial and economic inequality in America's schools: Poorer minority children do not have the same opportunities as richer White students" (Discussion section, para. 3). The heterogeneity, segregation, and inequities of urban districts can be found in high proportions of learners of English as a second language, special education students, and poverty-level children and youth. These factors interact, in turn, with other race and ethnicity differences in many schools, including differences between the majority of urban school children and their teachers, such that predominantly White, female, and middle-class teachers are educating predominantly minority, poor students. The persistent difficulties of race and racism in the wider society—coupled with extremes of wealth and poverty and concomitant disparities in per-pupil expenditures—are concentrated in city schools, where they are part of how teachers and students interact on a daily basis.

Those interactions are conditioned in part by what many teachers might perceive as so-called unmotivated or misbehaving students, but what educational theory suggests may be better understood as student resistance to demeaning experiences. Over 20 years ago, in *Theory and Resistance in Education*, Giroux (1983) alerted educators to an evolving body of theory grounded in the work of

Freire, Willis, Aronowitz, Apple, Bourdieu, and others, in which "the notion of resistance points to the need to understand more thoroughly the complex ways in which people mediate and respond to the interface between their own lived experiences and structures of domination and constraint" (p. 106). Stated differently, when people (including students) see their identities and experiences devalued by those in authority over them, they resist that authority. It seems clear that some teachers—and schools as organizations—are more adept than others at helping students learn mastery of new cultural codes without demeaning the cultural capital students bring to the school.

Significance for Teacher Educators

Infused in all of the recent teacher quality recommendations is recognition that teacher preparation models nationwide must address the cultural heterogeneity of students in schools. This is not new information. The National Commission on Teaching and America's Future summarized this view in its 1996 report:

> In short, to meet the needs of the 21st century, schools must successfully reach many more students from much more diverse backgrounds. And they must help them master more challenging content many times more effectively than they have ever done before. This means that teachers must understand students and their many pathways to learning as deeply as they comprehend subjects and teaching methods. It means that teachers need to understand how students of different language backgrounds and cultures can be supported in learning academic content and how those with a range of approaches to learning can be met with a variety of teaching strategies. It also means that schools must reorganize themselves to enable more intensive kinds of learning, supported by close, personal relationships as well as new technologies. (p. 13)

We must point out the irony of talking about growing diversity when, at the school level, tomorrow's schools might be even more segregated than they are today. Kozol (2005) powerfully describes today's de facto apartheid in his book, *The Shame of the Nation*. However, whether or not schools are going to be diverse in the future is beside the point. Urban schools are systematically failing to educate poor and minority students today, with no promising remedy in sight. Warnings about growing diversity in schools seem typically to be made to say to suburban residents that, "You too should care about this because it's coming to your neighborhood soon." Even if that were not true, we are not addressing the racist and inequitable distribution of resources that pervade state school systems today.

Hollins (1997) reminds us that urban districts serving predominantly minority students frequently base their curriculum, instruction, and expectations on European American culture. This is not likely to decrease in the NCLB era of standards-driven assessments and high-stakes accountability to test scores based on the cultural capital of the European American middle class. These dynamics stand at odds with culturally responsive models of pedagogy and assessments of students' intellectual work—models taught in many teacher education programs.

Teacher educators understand that teachers need insight into how their students' past experiences have shaped their current knowledge (e.g., Howey, 1996). Even when they are told, for example, that doing well in school will ultimately bring tangible social and economic rewards, young people from historically oppressed groups are not apt to believe it because they generally know few adults for whom school has served as a path to a better life. Seeing no value in school knowledge for themselves, these students can become resistant to learning environments that are marked more by failure than success (Villegas & Lucas, 2002).

The concepts of culturally relevant or culturally responsive pedagogy, which, for some, are quite different from "just good teaching," require greater explication and unpacking if teachers are to be widely in command of the practical implications of such ideas. Erickson (1987) writes that culturally responsive pedagogy

> … is not the only route to establishing and maintaining trust and legitimacy between teacher and students, however. If children and their parents believe very strongly in the legitimacy of school staff and in the content and aims of a school program, as in the case of a black Muslim school (or in the case of some immigrant minority students and their parents as they encounter an arbitrary American public school), then even if the cultural style of classroom interaction is very discontinuous with that of the children's early childhood experience, they may well learn the new cultural styles without setting off a chain reaction of resistance and cultural schismogenesis. (p. 354)

The dimensions of cultural heterogeneity considered here—differences in cultural capital based on race, ethnicity, and economic class—are intimately related to ideals of equity and social justice. If we in higher education are not aiming at and thoughtful about preparing teachers for the schools that most need excellent teachers for students, then we remain encapsulated in the ivory tower. We fail the very students who are usually implied by the phrase "all children," as it is used in the expression "meeting the needs of all children" or "no child left behind." The case of our own university experiences in the context of the Chicago Public Schools illustrates the need for more research on the *interactions* of moderate to large urban school districts and their partnering universities in the preparation of quality urban teachers.

Although barely over one-fifth of CPS schools include populations where no one racial-ethnic group predominates, the University of Illinois at Chicago (UIC) has been placing roughly 40% of its teacher candidates in these so-called diverse schools for field experiences, including student teaching. We place another 43% in schools with predominantly Latino student bodies, while we place only 10% of our teacher candidates in schools that are 90% to 100% Black. Why? Faculty members supply various understandable reasons: long-standing relationships with particular schools; mentor teachers whose knowledge, skills, dispositions, and pedagogy are congruent with those of the teacher educators; standards-based school programming; strong instructional leaders; geographic proximity; and exposure to a diverse student body (integrated rather than segregated). They are trying to avoid or mitigate some of the more deleterious effects of scale and cultural conflict in urban schools.

Asking teacher candidates to succeed in hard-to-staff urban schools, where instructional approaches often do not match those taught by the university faculty, importantly requires teacher educators who are committed to examining their own beliefs and actions and who are committed to working with more challenged schools to address the gap between culturally responsive theory and prevailing school practices. This implies specific priorities in faculty hiring and development, including creating a professional learning community that respects the knowledge and experiences of all of its members. This further implies that a critical mass of faculty members either is knowledgeable or must become knowledgeable about the day-to-day realities of teaching and learning in those schools that Chicago's teachers find most challenging, in part by learning from the teachers with whom faculty members work (e.g., Madsen & Mabokela, 2000). Ladson-Billings (1999) points out the need for institutional incentives to encourage faculty to take on such learning:

> How institutions respond to issues such as increasing the diversity of their faculties, administrators, and student population, as well as the need to reexamine their curricula and course requirements, campus climate, and reward structures, all signal the level of commitment and value placed on cultural diversity. (p. 102)

Supporting teacher candidates in low-performing schools with large populations of children of color may require, on the part of the university in partnership with schools and communities, Murrell's (2001) "humility of practice"—the recognition that we have much to learn from those we purport to serve and a commitment to "accessing knowledge from those who have it" (p. 31). For Murrell, the challenge is to develop teachers who recognize, understand, and successfully negotiate the "complexities of urban communities that impact children's learning and development" (p. 32). One concrete suggestion he offers is requiring field experiences in nonschool, community-based settings. These field experiences allow students to experience teaching and learning in community contexts so they can begin to understand the community's interests, needs, and requirements for good education before becoming too quickly immersed in the traditional routines and practices of school life. Murrell argues that those traditional practices may or may not support the community's interests and needs and are best experienced after students develop the critical interpretive lenses with which to interrogate them. He further calls for "a critical redefinition of what the establishment considers good teaching," if teachers are to learn how best to address the learning needs of low-income African American children and youth (p. 62).

Challenges to a Theory of Urban Teacher Preparation

A number of theoretical issues emerge from this discussion of cultural heterogeneity and cultural capital. One is that the catchword *diversity* is itself a homogeneous term that obscures the many different kinds of diversity within an urban district—unless the term is understood in specific contexts and for its dire consequences for student learning differences. The diversity of city schools can reside in cultural differences at the school level—for example, some immigrant communities in Chicago may have over 20 different language groups in one school. A different kind of diversity might reside at the district level because the majority of schools are almost exclusively one ethnic group or another. It also resides in cultural capital differences between teachers and students in both of those instances. Furthermore, in a historically racist society, it is unreasonable to believe that teachers' (and teacher educators') biases and preconceptions about race and ethnicity are not themselves at play. This is further exacerbated by high-stakes testing that holds the majority of Chicago schoolchildren accountable to a codified body of cultural capital that is in many ways different from their parents'. Together, these conditions contribute to various forms of student resistance that teachers and administrators may misread as lack of ability, lack of motivation, or any of a number of deficiencies that obscure the realities of student responses to schooling.

For teachers to negotiate these challenges effectively on behalf of their students requires that they understand the multiple cultural and socioeconomic sources of student learning differences and how to address those differences effectively. They must help students get from where they are to where they need to be in the face of district accountability policies, their own limited cultural knowledge and preexisting biases, and schools that are typically not organized as effective professional learning environments for adults. This is an enormous challenge for teacher preparation and professional development programs. Moreover, it is an organizational challenge for schools because underresourced schools that foster good professional learning are not plentiful. How do higher education and school districts work together to support the development of culturally responsive teaching practices that also result in strong student performance on standardized exams and other measures? This remains a theoretical and practical challenge.

THE CULTURAL POLITICS OF URBAN SCHOOL REFORM

Intersecting the scale and cultural heterogeneity of large urban environments is the cultural politics of school reform. It is reasonable to believe that it takes different shape in each large urban community because the cultural and political histories are so dramatically different in, for example, New York, Chicago, Los Angeles, San Diego, and Houston. The civic and advocacy groups, the local business elites, the ethnic power bases, and the histories of educational and civic reform are distinct in each setting, as recent research illuminates (see, for example, treatments of San Diego and Chicago schools in Hess [2005] and Lipman [2004]). While educational researchers and curriculum theorists have called for a more culturally responsive pedagogy in urban environments, municipal governments have increasingly made such theorizing appear to be irrelevant to actual practice. Usdan and Cuban (2002) recently wrote an article titled "Powerful Reforms with Shallow Roots: Educational Change in Six Cities" (also the title of their book), documenting how city governments have assumed control of large urban school systems in Baltimore, Boston, Chicago, Philadelphia, San Diego, and Seattle.

Although the increased involvement of municipal governments in urban school governance has taken different forms, it has been triggered by years of frustration with the slow pace of educational improvement. Usdan and Cuban note that urban systems like Baltimore and Philadelphia are also subject to state takeover. In Chicago, it took an act of the state legislature to hand control of the public schools to the mayor.

Usdan and Cuban indicate that the municipal control of urban schools has not been all bad news for schools and students. Among the positive developments they include the following:

- Linking to existing political structures leads to increases in standardized test scores, partly because noneducationist managers, linked to urban political structures, are more efficient and effective at achieving measurable outcomes.
- Buy-in from business and political community has produced at least a temporary stability for reform efforts.
- Accountability to measurable standards will continue to be a driving force (which is good when this focuses efforts on student learning and staff development, and bad when it leads to iatrogenic problems such as increased failure rates, dropouts, and teacher alienation).
- These linkages have brought with them at least the potential for greater collaboration among schools, health services, social services, mental health services, and related agencies.

However, Usdan and Cuban indicate that these positive developments are accompanied by a range of concerns about the sustainability of early, fragile successes in school reform through city government intervention:

- In the seesaw of centralization, decentralization, and recentralization, the "search for structural panaceas will continue" (p. 40).
- The fragility of urban politics makes sustainability of reforms questionable, in part because the top-down nature of the reforms makes them regime dependent, and practitioners are alienated by feeling not included. For example, teachers' unions in San Diego and Chicago have expressed resistance to what they perceive as top-down control, and, without these groups, sustainability of reform is still more fragile. It is difficult for large urban districts to focus limited resources on sustained systemic change over several years without the support of the rank and file who have learned over time that "this, too, shall pass."
- Higher education has also felt alienated due to lack of inclusion of colleges and universities in the reform process. This might not matter so much were it not for the strong sense among college and university educators that the top-down solutions implemented often fly in the face of what they know about good teaching and learning (e.g., strong staff development, engaged student learning, and enlightened assessment approaches). While, in the short term, funding may be showering the schools from several directions—foundations, business, and state sources—there are serious concerns about the coherence of the initiatives that these short-term funds support. In the Chicago environment, it is so common to see the most underresourced, lowest-performing schools festooned with programs and initiatives that the term *Christmas tree schools* is now widely recognized in describing this phenomenon. Such programs may ornament but do not fundamentally change the school in terms of sustainable improvements in student learning.
- Sustainability of reform is also compromised by backlash against disempowerment of school boards.

Significance for Teacher Preparation

The business connection that is so central to the ascendancy of municipal governance of the schools involves a commitment of efforts and resources to market-metaphor solutions such as charter schools, school choice, and the aforementioned alternative routes to teacher education, leadership preparation, and staff development. For teacher educators, the market metaphor is somewhat ironic, because alternative teacher education programs tend to be so expensive they must be subsidized by federal grants, foundations, and urban school districts. Many in higher education have developed alternative routes to teacher certification that turn out to be more expensive models for teacher preparation than standard programs. We are left to imagine what could be achieved if the standard teacher education programs were funded at levels comparable to alternative routes.

The market metaphor is not entirely off target, however, because the subsidies are motivated by a market of urban school staffing needs and student learning needs that are not being adequately addressed by standard teacher preparation programs. Urban districts seeking ways to meet those needs have moved aggressively to diversify the sources of their teachers and the models of schools that will serve students: from charters to contract schools, from International Baccalaureate schools to magnet schools. Usdan and Cuban (2002) report the following:

> The postsecondary sector has not been a particularly relevant or influential participant in urban governance issues. Unless there is much more responsiveness to urban school realities on the part of higher education, staff-development activities increasingly will fall under the purview of local school systems and new leadership and teacher-development academies that are divorced from traditional postsecondary education. (p. 40)

As a consequence of the municipal power over urban schools, school systems have the political power to announce targets for the number of alternatively certified teachers they will seek to hire from year to year. When Chicago Public Schools announced last year that they hoped to hire 500 teachers from alternative certification programs, the market was redefined. Higher education is left in the position of either yielding teacher education to other providers, who are creating their own alternative programs, or finding another way to be relevant to the district's needs.

Lipman's recent book, *High Stakes Education* (2004), is one of the few to provide an in-depth, critical assessment of the cultural politics of municipal governance of urban schools. Her analysis portrays this new development as a hegemonic move by the urban business/government elite to respond to new global economic opportunities while appearing to be focused on student outcomes. In this analysis, teacher educators are simply not relevant to an elite decision-making process that directs so-called urban school reform.

Challenges to a Theory of Urban Teacher Preparation

This final part of the discussion has addressed the politics of governance in urban school reform: Who gets to call the educational shots? Who gets to sit at the reform table? As part of the educational establishment that has failed to educate poor urban students for decades, teacher educators cannot be surprised to have had limited (if any) influence in major educational policy decisions being made by city governments controlling urban schools. One challenge to theorizing about the impact of municipal control of schools is the relative dearth of literature on this new development. Such treatments as Lipman's, however, do not provide cause for optimism. They suggest that teacher educators will have no choice but to prepare teachers for school environments over which teacher educators have little or no influence and that teachers who do not fit those environments will not be welcome. Theorizing about teacher education under such circumstances must take into account the question of how teacher educators can achieve their goals of disrupting the reproduction of an inequitable social order when that social order seems more firmly and directly in control of schools than ever before.

CONCLUDING COMMENTS

If the first section of this chapter addressed urban scale, while the second addressed urban ethnicity, and the third addressed the politics of urban school governance, then the intersection of these three dimensions suggests that teacher education as it now exists cannot long endure—at least not teacher education for urban schools. From the perspective of urban school leadership, teacher education practitioners offer no theory of institutional change to address the massive scale of the needs of urban districts; they seem unable to bridge the gap between theories of culturally responsive pedagogy and the hegemony of cultural capital that forms the basis of high-stakes testing and school curriculum; and they are perceived as having little to offer in the conference rooms where the decisions about urban school reform are made. The work culture in an immense urban school bureaucracy, subject to powerful political and economic forces that affect how an ethnically and economically heterogeneous student body will be served, is qualitatively different from the relatively cloistered work culture of a school of education, which is typically neither immense, nor economically powerful, nor culturally very diverse. Any one of the three variables alone might render difficult the development of partnership infrastructures that foster trusting learning communities and support coherent instructional programming; with the three operating together, the challenge becomes all the more daunting. What incentives exist for urban districts to partner with teacher educators on any terms but the district's? How can teacher educators have a significant impact on urban schools without such partnerships? The stakes have never been so high for the children and youth targeted by President Bush's No Child Left Behind Act.

REFERENCES

Chicago Public Schools alternative certification programs. (2005). *Chicago Public Schools.* Retrieved February 22, 2006, from http://firstclass.cps.k12.il.us/

College Entrance Examination Board. (1999). *Reaching the top: A report of the National Task Force on Minority High Achievement.* New York: The College Board.

Designs for Change. (2005, September). *The big picture: School-initiated reforms, centrally initiated reforms, and elementary school achievement in Chicago (1990 to 2005).* Retrieved February 22, 2006, from http://www.designsforchange.org

Education Committee of the Commercial Club of Chicago. (2003, July). *Left behind: Student achievement in Chicago's public schools.* Chicago: Civic Committee of the Commercial Club of Chicago.

Erickson, F. (1987). Transformation and school success: The politics and culture of educational achievement. *Anthropology and Education Quarterly, 18,* 335–356.

Gewertz, C. (2002, September 11). City districts seek teachers with licenses. *Education Week, 22*(1), 14–15.

Giroux, H. A. (1983). *Theory and resistance in education: A pedagogy for the opposition.* South Hadley, MA: Bergin and Garvey.

Hess, F. M. (2005). *Urban school reform: Lessons from San Diego.* Cambridge, MA: Harvard Education Press.

Hollins, E. R. (1997). Directed inquiry in preservice teacher education: A developmental process model. In J. E. King, E. R. Hollins, & W. C. Hayman (Eds.), *Preparing teachers for cultural diversity* (pp. 97–110). New York: Teachers College Press.

Howey, K. R. (1996). *The Urban Network to Improve Teacher Education: A final report. Preparing teachers for inner city schools.* Columbus, OH: Urban Network to Improve Teacher Education.

Ingersoll, R. (2001). Teacher turnover and teacher shortages: An organizational analysis. *American Educational Research Journal, 38,* 499–534.

Ingersoll, R. (2003). *Is there really a teacher shortage?* Philadelphia: Consortium for Policy Research in Education and the Center for the Study of Teaching and Policy.

Jerald, C. D. (2002, August). *All talk, no action: Putting an end to out-of-field teaching.* Washington, DC: The Education Trust.

Kozol, J. (2005). *The shame of the nation: The restoration of apartheid schooling in America.* New York: Crown.

Ladson-Billings, G. (1999). Preparing teachers for diversity: Historical perspectives, current trends, and future directions. In L. Darling-Hammond & G. Sykes (Eds.), *Teaching as the learning profession: Handbook of policy and practice* (pp. 86–123). San Francisco: Jossey-Bass.

Lipman, P. (2004). *High stakes education: Inequality, globalization, and urban school reform.* New York: Routledge Falmer.

Madsen, J. A., & Mabokela, R. O. (2000). Organizational culture and its impact on African American teachers. *American Education Research Journal, 37,* 849–876.

Manpower Demonstration Research Corporation. (2002, September). *Foundations for success: Case studies of how urban school systems improve student achievement.* Washington, DC: The Council of the Great City Schools.

Murrell, P. C., Jr. (2001). *The community teacher: A new framework for effective urban teaching.* New York: Teachers College Press.

National Commission on Teaching and America's Future. (1996). *What matters most: Teaching for America's future.* New York: NCTAF.

Orfield, G. (2001, July 17). *Schools more separate: Consequences of a decade of resegregation.* Retrieved February 22, 2006 from UCLA, The Civil Rights Project Web site: http://www.civilrightsproject.ucla.edu/research/deseg/separate_schools01.php

Payne, C. (1998). *So much reform, so little change: Building-level obstacles to urban school reform.* Unpublished manuscript.

Recruiting teachers for hard-to-staff schools: Solutions for the Southeast and the nation. (2002, January). Chapel Hill, NC: The Southeast Center for Teaching Quality.

Roth, J., Brooks-Gunn, J., Linver, M., & Hofferth, S. (2003). What happens during the school day?: Time diaries from a national sample of elementary teachers. *Teachers College Record, 105*(3), 317–343. Retrieved February 22, 2006, from http://www.tcrecord.org

Tozer, S. E., Violas, P. C., & Senese, G. (2002). *School and society: Historical and contemporary perspectives* (4th ed.). Boston: McGraw-Hill.

U.S. Census Bureau. (2004, September 30). *Census 2000 urban and rural classification.* Retrieved February 22, 2006, from http://www.census.gov/geo/www/ua/ua_2k.html

Usdan, M., & Cuban, L. (2002, February 22). Powerful reforms with shallow roots: Educational change in six cities. *Education Week,* pp. 37, 40.

Villegas, A. M., & Lucas, T. (2002). Preparing culturally responsive teachers: Rethinking the curriculum. *Journal of Teacher Education, 53,* 20–32.

Weiner, L. (2000). Research in the 90s: Implications for urban teacher preparation. *Review of Educational Research, 70,* 369–406.

Wise, A. E., & Levine, M. (2002, February 27). The 10-step solution: Helping urban districts boost achievement in low-performing schools. *Education Week,* pp. 38, 56.

CHAPTER TWO

Defining Standards THAT Respond TO THE Urban Context: A Call TO Activism

FRANCINE P. PETERMAN

CLEVELAND STATE UNIVERSITY

with KRISTY C. SWEIGARD

Teaching is a complex task—one that is complicated by the sociocultural dimensions of the context in which it occurs. In America's urban communities, context means poverty, diversity, bureaucracy, cultural incongruence, and often violence and hopelessness. These defining characteristics exponentially increase the demands placed upon urban teachers, who—like all other early 21st century American teachers—are under the local and national microscope of accountability. Parents, civic leaders, local media, and politicians want to know, "Are our children meeting high standards of achievement?" And, if not, "Why?" One response continues to focus on the quality of our teachers relative to generic competencies set at the national and state level. Such standards focus mostly on what goes on inside the classroom and how the teacher teaches. They are set to apply across settings, with little attention to the differentiating characteristics of large, diverse, economically depressed urban communities, where the achievement gap is greatest. To be best prepared for urban settings, however, we posit that teachers must meet not only generic standards for professionally planning, teaching, reflecting, and collaborating but also contextually responsive standards that represent the distinguishing characteristics of urban communities, schools and classrooms, and their students. Therefore, this chapter will provide a content analysis of definitions of *urban* included in research situated in these settings and will suggest standards that are responsive to the ecology of teaching urban schoolchildren.

BACKGROUND

In the American milieu of standards-based teaching, learning, and teacher preparation, many organizations have set forth standards and outcomes to guide the evaluation of teacher candidates, novices, and seasoned teachers. A majority of the United States have adopted, adapted, or replicated Praxis criteria created by the Educational Testing Service or Interstate New Teacher Assessment and Support Consortium (INTASC) standards as measures of teacher performance required for initial and/or professional teaching licenses. Consequently, these standards are mirrored in those set to guide and assess teacher preparation programs and their graduates' preparedness for teaching and licensing. Even when states and institutions invent their own standards, a content analysis generally reveals similar expectations for teacher performance during entry to a career in teaching. Similar standards are promoted for more experienced teachers (e.g., Danielson, 1996) and extended to address student learning, professional development, and ongoing reflection to improve teaching and learning (e.g., National Board for Professional Teaching Standards, 2002).

As a response to these standards, especially those of INTASC, several professional organizations and individuals have created new sets of standards that address specific concerns such as the social foundations of education, diversity, and technology. Mirroring the format and language of the INTASC standards, the International Society for Technology in Education (ISTE) established their national Educational Technology Standards to define the knowledge, skills, and dispositions for using technology in educational settings. Similarly, the Council for Social Foundations of of Education (1996) defines a set of knowledge, skills, and dispositions required for understanding the historical, political, economic, and sociological foundations of American education. In her latest book, Irvine (2003) delineates a set of standards that extend INTASC's to focus on the diversity of learners in today's classrooms—especially those in urban settings—by using culturally relevant pedagogy.

Each of these new sets of standards takes a particular political or theoretical stance:

1. All teachers must adequately use and apply technology in teaching and learning.
2. All teachers must understand and apply principles from the social foundations of education to teaching and learning.
3. All teachers must address the needs of culturally, racially, and ethnically diverse learners in their classrooms.

Such standards are established to address a variety of classroom settings across a varied educational landscape and to ignore context as an important determinant in what a teacher must know, be able to do, and express as values, attitudes, beliefs, or dispositions. Thus, standards are generally based upon the assumption that a teacher in any setting will succeed in the classroom—that is, his or her children will achieve—if he or she can demonstrate proficiency in the established standards. The premise of this chapter is that context matters. Specifically, urban teachers require context-based knowledge, skills, and dispositions that go beyond those delineated in the current sets of standards that guide teacher preparation and licensure, particularly the INTASC standards. To support this premise, we will (a) define *urban* through an extensive review of educational and sociological studies situated in such settings and (b) propose a set of context-bound standards for urban teacher preparation.

REVIEW OF THE LITERATURE

To define the urban context, we reviewed educational and sociological studies that had been conducted in urban settings and were published as books or in refereed journals within the last 12 years. To establish that the research was situated in an urban setting, we included studies that used the word *urban* in the title, descriptors, and/or abstract to distinguish the setting of and/or participants in the study. In all, we reviewed 112 books and articles—82 from educational journals and 30 from sociological ones. We examined sociological studies to expand our view and to determine whether the sociological literature defined *urban* in ways that our educational literature did not. As we reviewed each text, we noted descriptions of the settings and the subjects that were used to distinguish them as urban and then conducted a content analysis of these descriptions.

In general, we found that urban contexts were defined by (a) the communities in which they are located, (b) the inadequacies of their schools, and (c) their impact on their students. Though *poverty* was used most frequently as a descriptor of urban communities, other prevailing social and economic conditions depicting unstable, incongruent infrastructures and supports were defining characteristics. More than any other factor, the achievement gap and other measures of student achievement distinguished urban schools—as did the quality of the teachers who serve them. Both levels of achievement, including attending and completing school, and types of diversity described the students. Overall, the studies were embedded in rich descriptions of diverse students attending underresourced schools within beleaguered communities. Such an ecological framework—students situated in schools located in urban communities—guided this review of the literature and provided a rationale for distinct urban standards for teacher preparation.

Describing Urban Communities

Most frequently, authors describe urban communities by the level of poverty or number of low-income households found there. More than 75% of the studies describe the setting by its levels of poverty or by equivalent descriptors, such as low socioeconomic status (SES), poor, or low-income. In addition to levels of poverty, size, and location, urban communities are distinguished by social and economic factors, including (a) violence and crime; (b) the nature of families and the local economy, including the lack and quality of housing and public services; and (c) isolationism and racism.

Almost every setting is defined as a large, central or inner-city location with a population ranging between 50,000 and 430,000—most frequently, more than 150,000 and distinguished by the predominance of African American and Latino families, although many studies indicated an increasing number of immigrants. Almost one-third of the studies identify violence and/or crime, including drug and alcohol abuse and gangs, as endemic to urban settings. Twenty-two authors describe crime rates as high or increasing, 15 denote characteristics of local violence, 16 detail prevailing drug and alcohol sales and/or addictions, and 9 depict these as prevenient to the presence of gangs.

In at least eight studies, urban families are distinguished as "mostly female-headed single parent families" (Yeo, 1997, p. 8). According to the studies, many urban families live in overcrowded (Phillips & Straussner, 1997), substandard (Hadley, Simmerman, Long, & Luna, 2000; Lewis, 1999; Stanford, 1997; Yeo, 1997) housing. In describing urban families, authors discuss transience, child abuse and neglect, drug and alcohol addiction, homelessness and joblessness, work hours (including those of children who work to support their families), and parents' strained relationships with schools. Unstable, diminishing economies—often the result of lost manufacturing bases—demarked urban unemployment and dilapidation (Chazdon, 1998). According to Chazdon (1998), "This economic downturn has resulted in increased problems with crime, racial intolerance, small business decline, decreased homeownership, and increased transience" (p. 287). Several studies indicate the lack of and increasing need for health care (Cook, 2000; Gorman-Smith, Tolan, & Henry, 2000; Hammrich & Slesaransky-Poe, 2001; McClafferty, Torres, & Mitchell, 2000; Vail, 2003), including "limited access to medical care and increased exposure to violence and crime" (McClafferty et al., 2000, p. 111). As well, authors note not only the "increasing inability of lower-skilled workers to gain employment at decent wages" (Wolman & Agius, 1996, p. 25) but also "growing inequality in the distribution of wealth, income, and opportunity" (A. O'Connor, 2001, p. 1) as indicators of institutionalized racism characterized by a "massive disinvestment in the city's urban core" (Durr, Lyons, & Lichtenstein, 2000, p. 76). Thus, urban dwellers are viewed as experiencing decreasing businesses, resources, and services within cities that have "lost population, jobs, and a sense of community" (Keating, Krumholz, & Star, 1996, p. 1). Punctuated by empty storefronts, this lost sense of community is posited to contribute to urban dwellers' sense of isolation, alienation, despair, and hopelessness (Anderson, 2001; Anyon, 1997; Bettis, 1996; Hill & Celio, 1998; Keating, et al., 1996; Keith, 1996; A. O'Connor, 2001; Stanton-Salazar & Spina, 2003; Weis & Fine, 2000), which are exacerbated by "access to or lack of power in poor and working-class urban dwellers" (Green, 2001, p. 10).

Yeo (1997) punctuates the impact of economics on urban life while noting the role of race and power in sustaining current conditions:

> The apartheid-like economics of the ghetto translate into high crime (50 percent of black males will have been arrested at least once by age fifteen), unremitting poverty, dilapidated housing projects, mostly female-headed single parent families, rampant alcohol and drug addiction, proliferating liquor stores and crack houses, graffiti and gangs. (p. 8)

Through language not nearly as shameful as "apartheid-like" (Yeo, 1997, p. 8), 28 authors portray the urban setting as politically inequitable, too complex, and resource poor to address the concerns of all constituencies (Davis, 2002; Keith, 1996; Kirshner, Strobel, & Fernandez, 2003; McClafferty et al., 2000; Rose & Gallup, 2003; Shanklin et al., 2003; Weiner, 2000; Wolman & Agius, 1996) and its inhabitants—especially people of color, who are viewed as powerless (Green, 2001; Keith, 1996; McClafferty et al., 2000; Rogers, 2002). Using terms like "the stigma of race" (Anderson, 2001, p. 135), "discrimination" (Maxson et al., 2000, p. 40; Oakes, Franke, Quartz, & Rogers, 2002, p. 228; Phillips & Straussner, 1997, p. 5), "racial segregation, economic marginality, and institutionalized racism" (Stanton-Salazar & Spina, 2003, p. 233), "income inequality" (Shirley, 1997, p. 2), "culture war" (Haberman & Post, 1998, p. 96), and "deep issues concerning race and social and cultural factors" (Roth & Tobin, 2002, p. 177), many authors identify racism as a problem in urban politics, economics, government, and decision making (Bettis, 1996; Chazdon, 1998; Durr et al., 2000; McClafferty et al., 2000; Meyer & Northrup, 1997; A. O'Connor, 2001; Weis & Fine, 2000; Yeo, 1997; Yeo & Kanpol, 1999). Several write about community activists fighting for more community control (Chazdon, 1998; McClafferty et al., 2000) and programs that support community renewal (Groth, 1998; Hill & Celio, 1998).

Delineating the Inadequacies of Urban Schools

Urban schools are defined over and again by their inadequacies: (a) complex, highly bureaucratized systems of management; (b) quality, retention, and expectations of teachers; (c) limited resources and dilapidated facilities; (d) cultural incongruence; and (e) the achievement gap. In addition, measures of student achievement (perhaps an artifact of the times) most frequently demark urban schools and their students. Surprisingly, especially given an ongoing academic conversation about the highly bureaucratic nature of urban schools, only 10 studies define these settings by their organizational pattern, size, and complexity (Bettis, 1996; Groth, 1998; Hill, Guin, & Celio, 2003; Keith, 1996; Knapp & Plecki, 2001; Maxson et al., 2000; Metzger, 2003; Shanklin et al., 2003; Weiner, 1999, 2000). Four researchers distinguish urban districts from rural and suburban ones not solely by their size but also by their complexity and intensity (Keith, 1996; Knapp, 1995, Metzger, 2003; Shanklin et al., 2003)—a characteristic that Weiner (1999, 2000, 2002) declares the most critical for urban schools. Too often, one study notes, the scope and intensity of the urban school bureaucracy leads to crisis-response leadership and mixed messages (Peterman, 2005). Several authors assert that the highly bureaucratic structure of urban schools inhibits systemic change, especially that which relates to the distribution of resources or creation of curriculum to support student learning and achievement (Groth, 1998; Hill et al., 2003; Knapp & Plecki, 2001; Maxson et al., 2000; Weiner, 1999). They further contend that these bureaucracies make decisions that are politically and culturally incongruent with the values and beliefs of the communities, families, and students they serve (Groth, 1998; Weiner, 2000)—reinforcing the sense of isolation already prevalent within urban communities.

Sixteen studies refer to the quality, retention, and expectations of teachers as distinguishing characteristics of urban districts (Darden, 2003; Fuhrman, 2002; Garbarino, 1992; Groulx, 2001; Henig, Hula, Orr, & Pedescleaux, 1999; Hill et al., 2003; Hollingsworth & Dybdahl, 1995; Hunter & Donahoo, 2003; Keith, 1996; Llg & Massucci, 2003; McClafferty et al., 2000; Oakes et al., 2002; Roth & Tobin, 2002; Shanklin et al., 2003; Tobin, Roth, & Zimmermann, 2001; Weiner, 2002). Four studies note the shortage of teachers (Fuhrman, 2002; Roth & Tobin, 2002; Shanklin et al., 2003; Tobin et al., 2001); three note problems with teacher retention (Keith, 1996; McClafferty et al., 2000; Weiner, 2002); and one notes teachers' low expectations for urban students (Groulx, 2001). The authors who address teacher quality write about "poorly trained educators" (McClafferty et al., 2000, p. 111), the "prevalence of low teacher expectations for ethnic minorities and inner-city students" (Groulx, 2001, p. 61), "teachers … [who] try to make a difference in the lives of the urban poor" (Hollingsworth & Dybdahl, 1995,

p. 168), and "relatively high rates of attrition and absenteeism" (Keith, 1996, p. 48). As represented in the literature, ongoing federal funding, and states' legislation for alternative licensure, the shortage of quality teachers is critical in urban settings (Roth & Tobin, 2002; Tobin et al., 2001). Recent research, however, indicates that the more significant problem is retention, as large numbers of new urban teachers leave the profession within five years—or move to another district (Weiner, 2002). In urban schools, the quality and retention of the teaching staff is complicated by the No Child Left Behind Act of 2001, in which all sorts of measures have been devised to identify "highly qualified teachers."

As Weiner (1999, 2000, 2002) and others frequently note, urban schools are often defined by their lack of resources and inadequate facilities. In describing urban schools and school districts, researchers note the "structural foundations of the school and its surrounding neighborhoods ... [as] part of an unstable economic and social landscape" (Bettis, 1996, p. 108) with limited resources (Hollingsworth, 1994; Kirshner et al., 2003; Knapp, 1995; Knapp & Plecki, 2001; McClafferty et al., 2000; Norman, Ault, Bentz, & Meskimen, 2001; Rose & Gallup, 2003; Tobin et al., 2001)—often with less resources than suburban schools (Bettis, 1996; Knapp & Plecki, 2001; McClafferty et al., 2000; Norman et al., 2001) and complicated by the need "to provide an adequate program for special needs students" (Hammrich & Slesaransky-Poe, 2001). Inadequate facilities (Knapp, 1995) are specifically portrayed as "crumbling" (Darden, 2003, p. 34), "decaying" (Shanklin et al., 2003, p. 357), "unusable because of the shattered glass that carpets the broken concrete surface" (Garbarino, 1992, p. 140), or dilapidated. Yeo and Kanpol (1999) provide a description of such dilapidated urban school facilities:

> The windows in my room are broken, the door needs painting to cover gang signs and references to sex and drugs, light fixtures are broken, desks have taped up legs or are balanced on a stack of books, and the stucco walls are adorned with faded charts falling off as the tape wears out. (p. 131)

Such images create a metaphor for the lack of resources not simply to do the art of schooling but also to cross the sociocultural and political divides that exist in some settings.

Fifteen authors comment on the cultural incongruence that permeates urban schools. The "significant social and cultural distance between educators, students, and the students' communities" (Keith, 1996, p. 48) creates a complex political climate (Keith, 1996; McClafferty et al., 2000) in which the school "bureaucracy ... is politically isolated from communities" (Weiner, 2000, p. 370) and "cut off from the communities they are supposed to serve" (Weiner, 1999, p. 14). Such institutions are educationally distanced from "students ... whose cultural model of schooling is often different from, and in, conflict with that of the dominant cultural model" (Weiner, 2000, p. 370) and whose preferences are not "reinforced in the organization of schooling" (Tobin et al., 2001, p. 943). As Weis and Fine (2000) write,

> For many urban youth, racial, sexual, class and cultural markers prevent them from experiencing affirmation or engaged recognition in any "public space"—schools, buses, parks—or in the eyes of police, teachers, strangers, ministers, and sometimes family. (p. 1)

Furthermore, as Voltz (1998) notes, "home-school relationships ... have been characterized as particularly strained and [as demonstrating] a paucity of parental involvement" (p. 212). Such incongruence has been described as "ethnic and racial discrimination and tension" (Maxson et al., 2000, p. 40), "racial, socioeconomic and cultural tensions" (Shanklin et al., 2003, p. 357), and "deep issues concerning race and cultural factors" (Roth & Tobin, 2002, p. 178). Sometimes, this tension manifests as curriculum and instruction that is based upon culturally incongruent theories of learning and teaching (Weiner, 2000). "Teachers and students are caught in a system that undercuts their efforts to allow individuals to learn in the ways that are best for them" (Weiner, 1999, p. 14). Yeo and Kanpol (1999) note the incongruities another way:

> In what is perhaps one of the most divisive contradictions of our society, the public seems to want on one hand to discern and label any possible source of ethnicity or cultural diversity, whereas on the other hand it wants to claim to promote integration and cultural homogenization to deny differences. Thus, urban schools have become pedagogical creatures of assimilation, representative of educational rhetoric frozen in baleful promises of success and totally irrelevant curriculum. (p. 6)

Haberman and Post (1998) describe urban schools as "the battleground of a culture war" (p. 96), where "administrators and teachers often engage in their own dances of authority and resistance, knowledge and power, and cultural hegemony" (Shanklin et al., 2003, p. 375). In any case, such incongruities deliver "a mediocre product that sells their students short" (Henig et al., 1999, p. 11), especially students "who are not particularly well versed in the art of 'doing school'" (Knapp & Plecki, 2001, p. 1095); moreover, incongruities make it "more difficult for either group [of teachers and students] to succeed in school" (Hunter & Donahoo, 2003, p. 5).

Perhaps another artifact of cultural incongruence among teachers, students, and their communities is the achievement gap (Norman et al., 2001, p. 1102). Nine authors used the gap in White and African American students' achievement as a descriptor of urban schools. Other authors wrote generally about "low-achieving schools" (Smith, 2001, p. 301) or more specifically about students' science achievement and its decline "relative to their peers internationally" (Songer, Lee, & Kam, 2002, p. 129). Thus, researchers reported that urban schools "fall short" (Henig et al., 1999, p. 11) and attain "consistently substandard" (S. O'Connor, 2001, p. 175) and "low levels of results" (Keith, 1996, p. 48), including failing "to meet national goals" (Kamps et al., 2003, p. 212), "low test scores" (Maxson et al., 2000, p. 40), and "academic underachievement" (Voltz, 1998, p. 212).

Cultural incongruities and achievement—prevalent in descriptions of urban schools—also define urban students in the literature. In a standards-driven environment, it is easy to see why 28 researchers described schools and/or their students by their levels of achievement. Some simply noted the "achievement" of students and/or schools (Gonzales, Tein, Sandler, & Friedman, 2001; Henig et al., 1999; Lewis, 1999; Norman et al., 2001; C. O'Connor, 1999; S. O'Connor, 2001; Pandey & Zhan, 2000; Smith, 2001; Songer et al., 2002; Welch, Combs, Sigelman, & Bledsoe, 1997). For instance, Fuhrman (2002) describes urban students as having "low achievement—generally significantly lower than suburban districts" (p. 1). Other authors use test scores (Bettis, 1996; Henig et al., 1999; Maxson et al., 2000; McPartland, Bealfanz, Jordan, & Legters, 1998; S. O'Connor, 2001) or their abilities (Gilbert, 1997; Levin, 1998; McClafferty et al., 2000; Middlebrooks, 1998) to point out the lower achievement of urban students. Others label urban students "at risk" (Gilbert, 1997, p. 88; McClafferty et al., 2000, p. 3; Teel, Debruin-Parecki, & Covington, 1998, p. 485; Weiner, 1993, p. 5) or claim that they fail (Kenny, Gallagher, Alvarez-Salvat, & Silsby, 2002), underachieve academically (Voltz, 1998; Weber & Longhi-Chirlin, 2001), "lag academically behind" (Gordon, Rogers, Gavula, & McGee, 2001, p. 171), or are "academically disadvantaged" (Goddard, 2003, p. 65)—citing factors related to "academic success" (Newman et al., 2000, p. 387; Scheurich, 1998, p. 452). Only Keith (1996) refers to the "quality of student learning" (p. 48). Vail (2003) very specifically states that urban children often "enter school less ready to learn and lag behind their more-affluent classmates in ability to use language to solve problems" (p. 48).

Characterizing Urban Students

In addition to their levels of achievement, urban schoolchildren are defined by their (a) diversity (e.g., race, ethnicity, class, and language); (b) behavior and attendance (including suspension, retention, and transience); and (c) psychological and physical health (e.g., pregnancy, depression, anxiety, lack of hope, attention span, antisocial behavior, addiction, and abuse).

Diversity. Seventy-five researchers describe urban students in terms of their diversity. The term *diversity* encompassed several descriptors such as race (60 studies), ethnicity (37 studies), language (13 studies), and special needs (5 studies). Typically, authors delineate the urban student population as composed of Caucasian or White, African American or Black, Asian American, and Latino or Hispanic American children (Anderson, 2001; Astone, Schoen, Ensminger, & Rothert, 2000; Bettis, 1996; Carger, 1996; Chazdon, 1998; Davis, 2002; Durr et al., 2000; Edwards, Gilroy, & Hartley, 2002; Fairbanks, 1998; Gandara, Gutierrez, & O'Hara, 2001; Gilbert, 1997; Ginwright, 2000; Goddard, 2003; Gordon et al., 2001; Gorman-Smith et al., 2000; Hadley et al., 2000; Hewson, Kahle, Scantlebury, & Davies, 2001; Johanson, Duffy, & Anthony, 1996; Malecki & Demaray, 2003; Mason, 1999; McIntyre, 2001; Middlebrooks, 1998; Mintz & Yun, 2001; Moore-Hart, 2002; Norman et al., 2001; C. O'Connor, 1999; Plank, McDill, & McPartland, 2001; Rodriquez, 2001; Rogers, 2002; Roth & Tobin, 2002; Roxburgh, Stephens, Toltzis, & Adkins, 2001; Rushton, 2003; Settlage & Meadows, 2002; Teel et al., 1998; Weber & Longhi-Chirlin, 2001; Weis & Fine, 2000); however, many identify eastern European American (Bettis, 1996) and Arab American (Bettis, 1996) children as well. Ethnicity and nationality are often used simultaneously—as if one and the same (Bettis, 1996; McIntyre, 2001; Meckna, 1999). Several give no more specificity than to say that urban students are ethnically and/or racially diverse (Bettis, 1996; Gonzales et al., 2001; Groulx, 2001; Henig et al., 1999; Hollingsworth, 1994; Kenny et al., 2002; McClafferty et al., 2000; Metzger, 2003; Rymes, 2001; Shanklin et al., 2003; Sheppo, 1994–1995; Sobel, French, & Filbin, 1998; Stone, 1998; Weiner, 1999; Weis & Fine, 2000; Yeo & Kanpol, 1999) or simply "of color" (Chazdon, 1998, p. 288; Lewis, 1999, p. 12; McClafferty et al., 2000, p. 111; Moje, 2000, p. 659; Scheurich, 1998, p. 452; Weis & Fine, 2000, p. 1). The use of the term *minority* is complicated because in most urban settings the minority population is White; yet, when using the term, authors are most often referring to a large number of African American students (Bullough et al. 2002; Groulx, 2001; Hunter & Donahoo, 2003; Kenny et al. 2002; Middlebrooks, 1998; Newman, et al., 2000; Rodriquez, 2001). Only two authors report solely on nationality (Carger, 1996; Wong, 2001).

Linguistic diversity is represented by the phrases "bilingual" (Fairbanks, 1998, p. 190; Gilbert, 1997, p. 88; Hewson et al., 2001, p. 1134; Middlebrooks, 1998, p. 20), "dominant in their home language … and therefore in need of instruction in English as a second language" (Weber & Longhi-Chirlin, 2001, p. 24), "English is a second language" (Sheppo, 1994–1995, p. 82), "speak English as a second language" (Bullough et al. 2002, p. 70), "have difficulty speaking English" (McClafferty et al., 2000, p. 11), "limited facility with English" (Oakes et al., 2002, p. 228), and "limited English skills" (Fuhrman, 2002, p. 1). In some ways, these definitions represent subtle differences in approaches to and attitudes toward linguistic differences. There is a long history of bilingual versus English as a second language (ESL) instruction, as well as culture wars represented by equating having English as a second language with having difficulty speaking English. Current politics, for instance, dictate the term *English-language learners* to differentiate students whose primary language is not English—placing no emphasis on, and not even naming, the primary language.

Learning disabilities (Sheppo, 1994–1995), special needs (Johnson, 1997), and special education (Hammrich & Sleasarnanky-Poe, 2001; Hewson et al., 2001; Malecki & Demaray, 2003) were only mentioned five times in the research studies reviewed. This is surprising, given that there is evidence in the literature of inordinate numbers of urban students—especially African American males—being identified as learning disabled (Artiles, 2003).

Attendance and behavior. Forty-one studies make reference to students' behavior and/or attendance, including violence, crime, drop-out rates, suspension, and transience. Fourteen researchers note concerns about violence (Anderson, 2001; Christenson & Serrao, 1997; Cook, 2000; Garbarino, 1992; Harris, 1996; Maxson et al., 2000; McClafferty et al., 2000; Meyer & Northrup, 1997; Moses, 1999; Phillips & Straussner, 1997; Rogers, 2002; Stanford, 1997; Tobin, et al., 2001; Voltz, 1998); 14 discuss crime (Chazdon, 1998; Durr et al., 2000; Green, 2001; Groth, 1998; Hollingsworth, 1994; Hollingsworth & Dybdahl, 1995; Levin, 1998; McClafferty et al., 2000; Moje, 2000; Phillips & Straussner, 1997; Rogers, 2002; Shirley, 1997; Stanton-Salazar & Spina, 2003; Yeo, 1997); and eight studies mentioned gangs (Chazdon, 1998; Kirshner et al., 2003; Moses, 1999; Phillips & Straussner, 1997; Stanford, 1997; Voltz, 1998; Yeo, 1997; Yeo & Kanpol, 1999). Six researchers note student behaviors such as conduct (Gonzales, et al., 2001), discipline (Darden, 2003; Maxson et al., 2000; Voltz, 1998), behavioral problems (Kenny et al., 2002), and resulting suspension (Bettis, 1996). Six authors mention below-average attendance rates and above-average drop-out rates (Bettis, 1996; Keith, 1996; McPartland et al., 1998; C. O'Connor, 1999; Voltz, 1998; Weiner, 1993); eight, including those who discuss student attendance and truancy, also note above-average drop-out rates (Rymes, 2001; Vail, 2003). Transience—though more frequently mentioned as a characteristic of urban dwellers—was used to describe students in seven studies (Bullough et al. 2002; Chazdon, 1998; Fuhrman, 2002; Johanson et al., 1996; Keith, 1996; Knapp, 1995; S. O'Connor, 2001; Voltz, 1998).

Health. Three researchers mention poor health experienced by children and their families (Haberman & Post, 1998; Levin, 1998; Vail, 2003), yet six indicate the frequency of teenage pregnancy as a distinguishing characteristic of the urban student population (Cook, 2000; Kenny et al., 2002; Levin, 1998; Rymes, 2001; Vail, 2003; Voltz, 1998). In two instances, researchers link teen pregnancy with drug abuse (Cook, 2000; Levin, 1998). The studies further note urban students' struggles with abuse and neglect (Garbarino, 1992; Voltz, 1998) and drug and alcohol addiction (Anderson, 2001; Cook, 2000; Garbarino, 1992; Levin, 1998; Moore-Hart, 2002; Phillips & Straussner, 1997; Voltz, 1998). Moreover, they describe some urban students' antisocial behavior (Haberman & Post, 1998; Kenny et al., 2002) and psychological conditions such as low self-esteem (Levin, 1998), coping mechanisms (Kuo, 2001; Stanton-Salazar & Spina, 2003), boredom (Lewis, 1999), alienation (Anderson, 2001; Stanton-Salazar & Spina, 2003), motivation (Voltz, 1998), depression (Gonzales et al., 2001; Hollingsworth & Dybdahl, 1995; Levin, 1998), hopelessness (Anderson, 2001), and stress (Cook, 2000; Harris, 1996; Kenny et al., 2002).

Toward a Pedagogy of Hope

Very different frameworks distinguish the descriptions of urban communities, urban schools, and urban schoolchildren. Overall, researchers describe urban communities from a social justice framework: That is, they contend that inequities within communities lead to poverty, lawlessness, and hopelessness. This suggests (as was tried in the United States during the civil rights movement in the 1960s) that if we create social, political, and economic programs that address the inequities, then poverty, lawlessness, and hopelessness will abate. To complicate matters, researchers describe urban schools from a disorganization framework: Namely, they deem inequities as being based upon complex, highly bureaucratized, underresourced systems that are culturally incongruent to the communities they serve. Lastly, researchers describe urban students from a hopelessness framework—that is, inequities are based upon cultural incongruence that results in alienation and hopelessness. If such frameworks are actually in place (and we venture to say that, in many American urban settings, they are), the resulting cycle of hopelessness must certainly be addressed with a pedagogy of hope (Freire, 1998) and nothing less.

So, what do these distinguishing characteristics of urban contexts—their communities, their schools, and their schoolchildren—mean to urban teacher educators and teachers committed to working in urban settings? In today's parlance, standards seem the best way to translate this knowledge into action. To this point, we have described how researchers define *urban communities* in terms of these communities' demographics, social structures, economic conditions, isolationism, and racism; *urban schools* in terms of their complex bureaucracies, quality and retention of teachers, limited resources and dilapidated facilities, cultural incongruence, and achievement gaps; and *urban students* in terms of their achievement, diversity, behavior and attendance, and psychological and physical health. This examination reveals commonalities, incongruities, and consequences. In particular, urban communities, schools, and students share diversity, economic distress, and cultural incongruence among participants with power (politicians, administrators, teachers) and those without (community members, parents, and students). Such cultural incongruence manifests in inequity, hopelessness, and resultant gaps in achievement—failures that may not be about learning nor about teaching but require moving from the social justice framework of communities and the disorganization framework of schooling toward a pedagogy of hope. Thus, to prepare teachers for urban contexts, we must consider standards that represent a response to the culture of teaching urban schoolchildren and reduce the cultural incongruence and, concomitantly, the achievement gap within and across settings.

URBAN STANDARDS

To make a difference in the lives of their students, what is required of urban teachers? They must understand and respond to the nature of their communities—the diversity, poverty, isolationism, racism, and rich cultures found there. They must overcome and forebear the nature of their schools—the complex bureaucracies, limited resources, dilapidated facilities, and cultural incongruence with schoolchildren and their families. They must also attend to their students—their diversity, their cultural knowledge and literacies, and their achievement. Though many national standards suggest the importance of teaching diverse learners, including those with special needs, the needs that teachers encounter in urban classrooms are multiplied not simply in number but also in type and extent. Furthermore, language diversity has increased not only by the numbers of Hispanic Ameirican students replacing African Americans as the leading population in major cities throughout the United States but also by the numbers of Eastern Europeans immigrating to these metropolitan areas. The complexities and demands of urban settings, often enacted as crisis-based decision making, reinforce the cultural incongruities and inequities that lead to a hopelessness that is punctuated by violence and poverty. This review of the literature suggests that urban teachers must (a) examine identity formation, especially as it relates to race, social class, and culture; (b) practice standards-based, culturally responsive teaching that is based upon the diversity and needs of the learners served; (c) promote nonviolence; and (d) serve as advocates for schoolchildren and their families. To end the cycle of hopelessness, we propose refining and extending teacher preparation standards to include those that are contextually responsive to urban settings. To ensure high levels of achievement, the standards must include the following:

1. *Identity formation.* The teacher candidate creates a context in which identity formation, especially in relation to race, class, gender, age, language, and culture, is valued and advanced when interacting with students, their families, and other members of the school community (Anyon, 1997; Ginwright, 2000).

2. *Standards-based teaching.* The teacher candidate enacts standards-based teaching—that is, systematically assessing students' prior knowledge, experience, and achievement; expressing high expectations; and providing a variety of opportunities for learning, understanding, and communicating what has been learned.

3. *Culturally responsive pedagogy.* The teacher candidate promotes students' learning by using culturally responsive pedagogy (Villegas & Lucas, 2003).

4. *Special needs.* The teacher candidate uses a variety of strategies for meeting the special needs of students, including planning, teaching, grouping, and assessing in ways that are responsive to the diverse talents and needs of the learners.

5. *Linguistic diversity.* The teacher candidate applies theories of language learning and development and models metacognitive strategies to create instructional conversations that value linguistic difference while also developing English-language proficiency (Minaya-Rowe, 2002).

6. *Nonviolence.* The teacher candidate creates a classroom environment of nonviolence that promotes conflict resolution through mutual respect, boundary setting, and creative problem solving.

7. *Social justice.* The teacher candidate is a reflective, responsive teacher-leader who effectively addresses the inequities of policies, practices, and achievement related to race, class, gender, and linguistic differences.

8. *Community activism.* The teacher candidate demonstrates a strong commitment to urban schooling and community renewal by understanding social, political, and economic structures and collaborating to change resulting inequities through community activism.

9. *Resiliency, resistance, and persistence.* The teacher candidate addresses the bureaucratic complexities and demands of urban settings by responding appropriately with resiliency, resistance, and persistence to support teacher and student learning and development.

These standards are not intended as a panacea nor as a replacement for standards that focus on content, pedagogy, and professional development but rather are intended as an extension and critique of existing sets of standards. These standards make explicit the cultural complexities of urban settings that tend to reinforce existing inequities.

CONCLUSION

The complexities and demands of urban settings present an equally complex set of demands on urban teachers, not only to teach content and meet high standards of performance but also to come to understand themselves and others across cultural divides. Setting new standards that address the nature of urban schooling may provide the groundwork for addressing the incongruities and inequities that exist, but new teachers provide an even more important insight into the complexities and demands of becoming an urban teacher and the time, energy, engagement, collaboration, and reflection it takes to truly make a difference.

REFERENCES

Anderson, E. (2001). Going straight: The story of a young inner-city ex-convict. *Punishment & Society: The International Journal of Penology, 3,* 135–152.

Anyon, J. (1997). *Ghetto schooling: A political economy of urban educational reform.* New York: Teachers College Press.

Artiles, A. J. (2003). Special education's changing identity: Paradoxes and dilemmas in views of cultura and space. *Harvard Educational Review, 73,* 164–202.

Astone, N., Schoen, R., Ensminger, M., & Rothert, K. (2000). School re-entry in early adulthood: The case of inner-city African Americans. *Sociology of Education, 73,* 133–154.

Bettis, P. (1996). Urban students, liminality, and the postindustrial context. *Sociology of Education, 69*(2), 105–125.

Bullough, R. V. Jr, Young, J, Erickson, L, Birrel, J. R., Clark, D. C, Egan, M. W., Berrie C. F., Hales, V., and Smith, G. (2002). *Journal of Teacher Education, 53,* 68-80.

Carger, C. (1996). *Of borders and dreams; A Mexican-American experience of urban education.* New York: Teachers College Press.

Chazdon, S. (1998). Disillusioning tendencies: The challenge of civic education in an urban sociology course. *Sociological Imagination, 35,* 283–298.

Christenson, M., & Serrao, S. (1997). Cooperative learning in a hostile environment. *Teaching and Change, 4*(2), 137–156.

Cook, K. (2000). "You have to have somebody watching over your back, and if that's God, then that's mighty big": The church's role in the resilience of inner-city youth. *Adolescence, 35,* 717–730.

Council for Social Foundations of Education. (1996). *Standards for academic and professional instruction in foundations of education, educational studies and educational policy studies* (2nd Ed.). Retrieved September 17, 2007, from http://www.uic.edu/educ/csfe/standard.htm

Danielson, C. (1996). *Enhancing professional practice: A framework for teaching.* Alexandria, VA: Association for Supervision and Curriculum Development.

Darden, E. (2003). The race challenge. *American School Board Journal, 190*(12), 34–38.

Davis, K. S. (2002). Advocating for equitable science-learning opportunities for girls in an urban city youth club and the roadblocks faced by women science educators. *Journal of Research in Science Teaching, 39,* 151–163.

Durr, M., Lyons, T., & Lichtenstein, G. (2000). Identifying the unique needs of urban entrepreneurs: African American skill set development. *Race & Society, 3,* 75–90.

Edwards, A., Gilroy, P., & Hartley, D. (2002). *Rethinking teacher education: Collaborative responses to uncertainty*. New York: Falmer.

Fairbanks, C. (1998). Nourishing conversations: Urban adolescents, literacy, and democratic society. *Journal of Literacy Research, 30*, 187–203.

Freire, P. (1998). *Pedagogy of hope*. New York: Continuum.

Fuhrman, S. (2002). Urban educational challenges: Is reform the answer? *Perspectives on Urban Education, 1*(1), 1–10.

Gandara, P., Gutierrez, D., & O'Hara, S. (2001). Planning for the future in urban and rural high schools. *Journal of Education for Students Placed at Risk, 6*, 73–93.

Garbarino, J. (1992). *Children in danger: Coping with the consequences of community violence*. San Francisco: Jossey-Bass.

Gilbert, S. (1997). The four commonplaces of teaching: Prospective teachers' beliefs about teaching in urban schools. *The Urban Review, 29*, 81–96.

Ginwright, S. (2000). Identity for sale: The limits of racial reform in urban schools. *The Urban Review, 32*, 87–104.

Goddard, R. (2003). Relational networks, social trust, and norms: A social capital perspective on students' chances of academic success. *Educational Evaluation and Policy Analysis, 25*, 59–74.

Gonzales, N., Tein, J., Sandler, I., & Friedman, R. (2001). On the limits of coping: Interaction between stress and coping for inner-city adolescents. *Journal of Adolescent Research, 16*, 372–395.

Gordon, P. R., Rogers, A. M., Gavula, N., & McGee, B. P. (2001). A taste of problem-based learning increases achievement of urban minority middle-school students. *Educational Horizons, 79*(4), 171–175.

Gorman-Smith, D., Tolan, P., & Henry, D. (2000). Patterns of family functioning and adolescent outcomes among urban African American and Mexican American families. *Journal of Family Psychology, 14*, 436–457.

Green, C. (2001). *Manufacturing powerlessness in the black diaspora: Inner-city youth and the new global frontier*. Walnut Creek, CA: Altamira Press.

Groth, C. (1998). Dumping ground or effective alternative: Dropout prevention programs in urban schools. *Urban Education, 33*, 218–242.

Groulx, J. (2001). Changing preservice teaching perceptions of minority students. *Urban Education, 36*, 60–92.

Haberman, M., & Post, L. (1998). Teachers for multicultural schools: The power of selection. *Theory Into Practice, 37*, 96–104.

Hadley, P., Simmerman, A., Long, M., & Luna, M. (2000). Facilitating language development for inner-city children: Experimental evaluation of a collaborative, classroom-based intervention. *Language, Speech, and Hearing Services in Schools, 31*, 280–295.

Hammrich, P., & Slesaransky-Poe, G. (2001). Daughters with disabilities: Breaking down barriers. *The Electronic Journal of Science Education, 5*(4).

Harris, I. (1996). Peace education in an urban school district in the United States. *Peabody Journal of Education, 71*(3), 63–83.

Henig, J. R., Hula, R. C., Orr, M., & Pedescleaux, D. S. (2001). *The color of school reform: Race, politics, and the challenge of urban education*. Princeton, NJ: Princeton University Press.

Hewson, P., Kahle, J., Scantlebury, K., & Davies, D. (2001). Equitable science education in urban middle schools: Do reform efforts make a difference? *Journal of Research in Science Teaching, 38*, 1130–1144.

Hill, P., & Celio, M. (1998). *Fixing urban schools*. Washington, DC: Brookings Institution Press.

Hill, P., Guin, K., & Celio, M. (2003). The chasm remains. *Education Next, 3*, 52–55.

Hollingsworth, S. (1994). *Teacher research & urban literacy education; Lessons & conversations in a feminist key*. New York: Teachers College Press.

Hollingsworth, S., & Dybdahl, M. (1995). The power of friendship groups: Teacher research as a critical literacy project for urban students. *Advances in Research on Teaching, 5*, 167–193.

Hunter, R., & Donahoo, S. (2003). The nature of urban school politics after Brown: The need for new political knowledge, leadership, and organizational skills. *Education and Urban Society, 36*, 3–15.

Irvine, J. (2003). *Educating teachers for diversity: Seeing with a cultural eye*. New York: Teachers College Press.

Johanson, C., Duffy, F., & Anthony, J. (1996). Associations between drug use and behavioral repertoire in urban youths. *Addiction, 91*, 523–534.

Johnson, G. (1997). Teachers in the inner city: Experience-based ratings of factors that place students at risk. *Preventing School Failure, 42*(1), 19–26.

Kamps, D., Wills, H., Greenwood, C., Thorne, S., Lazo, J., Crockett, J., Akers, J. M., & Swaggart, B. (2003). Curriculum influences on growth in early reading fluency for students with academic and behavioral risks: A descriptive study. *Journal of Emotional and Behavioral Disorders, 11*, 211–224.

Keating, W., Krumholz, N., & Star, P. (1996). *Revitalizing urban neighborhoods*. Lawrence, KS: The University Press of Kansas.

Keith, N. (1996). A critical perspective on teacher participation in urban schools. *Educational Administration Quarterly, 32*, 45–79.

Kenny, M. A., Gallagher, L. A., Alvarez-Salvat, R., & Silsby, J. (2002). Sources of support and psychological distress among academically successful inner-city youth. *Adolescence, 7*(145), 161–182.

Kirshner, B., Strobel, K., Fernandez, M. (2003). Critical civic engagement among urban youth. *Penn GSE Perspectives on Urban Education, 2*(1), 1–20.

Knapp, M. (1995). *Teaching for meaning in high-poverty classrooms*. New York: Teachers College Press.

Knapp, M., & Plecki, M. (2001). Investing in the renewal of urban science teaching. *Journal of Research in Science Teaching, 38*, 1089–1100.

Kuo, F. (2001). Coping with poverty: Impacts of environment and attention in the inner city. *Environment and Behavior, 33*, 5–34.

Levin, M. (1998). *Teach me! Kids will learn when oppression is the lesson*. New York: Monthly Review Press.

Lewis, A. C. (1999). *Figuring it out: Standards-based reforms in urban middle grades*. New York: The Edna McConnell Clark Foundation.

Llg, T., & Massucci, J. (2003). Comprehensive urban high school: Are there better options for poor and minority children? *Education and Urban Society, 36*, 63–78.

Malecki, C., & Demaray, M. (2003). Carrying a weapon to school and perceptions of social support in an urban middle school. *Journal of Emotional and Behavioral Disorders, 11*, 169–178.

Mason, T. (1999). Prospective teachers' attitudes toward urban schools: Can they be changed? *Multicultural Education, 6*(4), 9–13.

Maxson, S., Wright, C., Wilson, J., Lynn, P., & Fowler, L. (2000). Urban teachers' views on areas of need for K-12/university collaboration. *Action in Teacher Education, 22*(2), 39–53.

McClafferty, K., Torres, C., & Mitchell, T. (2000). *Challenges of urban education: Sociological perspectives for the next century*. Albany, NY: State University of New York Press.

McIntyre, A. (2001). You should watch at least one show of Jerry Springer: Urban girls explore the meaning of feminism. *Feminism & Psychology, 11*(2), 157–161.

McPartland, J., Bealfanz, R., Jordan, W., & Legters, N. (1998). Improving climate and achievement in a troubled urban high school through the tale. *Journal of Education for Students Placed at Risk, 3*, 337–361.

Meckna, S. (1999). Teaching advanced placement European history in a multi-ethnic urban setting. *History Teacher, 32,* 249–258.

Metzger, C. (2003). Self/inner development of educational administrators: A national study of urban school district superintendents and college deans. *Urban Education, 38,* 655–687.

Meyer, A., & Northrup, W. (1997). What is violence prevention, anyway? *Educational Leadership, 54*(8), 31–33.

Middlebrooks, S. (1998). *Getting to know city kids: Understanding their thinking, imagining, and socializing.* New York: Teachers College Press.

Minaya-Rowe, L. (Ed.). (2002). *Training and effective pedagogy in the context of student diversity.* Greenwich, CT: Information Age Publishing.

Mintz, E., & Yun, J. (2001). *The complex world of teaching: Perspectives from theory and practice.* Cambridge, MA: Harvard Educational Review.

Moje, E. B. (2000). To be part of the story: The literacy practices of gangsta adolescents. *Teachers College Record, 102,* 651–690.

Moore-Hart, M. (2002). Creating a pathway to multicultural education in urban communities: Real-life experiences for preservice teachers. *Reading Horizons, 42,* 139–173.

Moses, A. (1999). Exposure to violence, depression, and hostility in a sample of inner city high school youth. *Journal of Adolescence, 22,* 21–32.

National Board for Professional Teaching Standards. (2002) *What teachers should know and be able to do.* Retrieved September 17, 2007, from http://www.nbpts.org/the_standards/the_five_core_propositio

Newman, B., Lohman, B., Newman, P., Myers, M., & Smith, V. (2000). Experiences of urban youth navigating the transition to ninth grade. *Youth & Society, 31,* 387–416.

Norman, O., Ault, C., Bentz, B., & Meskimen, L. (2001). The black-white "achievement gap" as a perennial challenge of urban science education: A sociocultural and historical overview with implications for research and practice. *Journal of Research in Science Teaching, 38,* 1101–1014.

Oakes, J., Franke, M. L., Quartz, K. H., & Rogers, J. (2002). Research for high-quality urban teaching: Defining it, developing it, assessing it. *Journal of Teacher Education, 53,* 228–234.

O'Connor, A. (2001). *Understanding inequality in the late twentieth-century metropolis: New perspectives of the enduring racial divide.* New York: Russell Sage Foundation.

O'Connor, C. (1999). Race, class, and gender in America: Narratives of opportunity among low-income African American youths. *Sociology of Education, 72,* 137–57.

O'Connor, S. (2001). Voices of parents and teachers in a poor white urban school. *Journal of Education for Students Placed at Risk, 6,* 175–198.

Pandey, S., & Zhan, M. (2000). Effect of urban poverty on parents' expectation of their children's achievement. *Advances in Social Work, 1*(1), 107–125.

Peterman, F. (Ed.). (2005). *Designing assessment systems for urban teacher preparation.* Mahwah, NJ: Erlbaum.

Phillips, N., & Straussner, S. (Eds.). (1997). *Children in the urban environment: Linking social policy and clinical practice.* Springfield, IL: Charles C. Thomas Publisher.

Plank, S. B., McDill, E. L., & McPartland, J. M. (2001). Situation and repertoire: Civility, incivility, cursing, and politeness in an urban high school. *Teachers College Record, 103,* 504–524.

Rodriquez, A. (2001). From gap gazing to promising cases: Moving toward equity in urban education reform. *Journal of Research in Science Teaching, 38,* 115–129.

Rogers, R. (2002). That's what you're here for, you're supposed to tell us: Teaching and learning critical literacy. *Journal of Adolescent and Adult Literacy, 45,* 772–787.

Rose, L., & Gallup, A. (2003). Urban dwellers on urban schools. *Phi Delta Kappan, 84,* 408–409.

Roth, W. M., & Tobin, K. (2002). *At the elbow of another: Learning to teach by coteaching.* New York: Peter Lang Publishing.

Roxburgh, S., Stephens, R., Toltzis, P., & Adkins, I. (2001). The value of children, parenting strains, and depression among urban African American mothers. *Sociological Forum, 16,* 55–72.

Rushton, S. (2003). Two preservice teachers' growth in self-efficacy while teaching in an inner-city school. *Urban Review, 35,* 167–189.

Rymes, B. (2001). *Conversational borderlands: Language and identity in an alternative urban high school.* New York: Teachers College Press.

Scheurich, J. (1998). Highly successful and loving, public elementary schools populated mainly by low-SES children of color. *Urban Education, 33,* 451–491.

Settlage, J., & Meadows, L. (2002). Standards-based reform and its unintended consequences: Implications for science education within America's urban schools. *Journal of Research in Science Teaching, 39,* 114–127.

Shanklin, N., Kozleski, E., Meagher, C., Sands, D., Joseph, O., & Wyman, W. (2003). Examining renewal in an urban high school through the lens of systemic change. *School Leadership & Management, 23,* 357–378.

Sheppo, K. (1994–1995). How an urban school promotes inclusion. *Educational Leadership, 52*(4), 82–84.

Shirley, D. (1997). *Community organizing for urban school reform.* Austin, TX: University of Texas Press.

Smith, R. (2001). Churches and the urban poor: Interaction and social distance. *Sociology of Religion, 62,* 301–313.

Sobel, D., French, N., & Filbin, J. (1998). A partnership to promote teacher participation for inclusive, urban schools: Four voices. *Teaching and Teacher Education, 14,* 793–806.

Songer, N. B., Lee, H.-S., & Kam, R. (2002). Technology-rich inquiry science in urban class-rooms: What are the barriers to inquiry pedagogy? *Journal of Research in Science Teaching, 39,* 128–150.

Stanford, G. C. (1997). Successful pedagogy in urban schools: Perspectives of four African American teachers. *Journal of Education for Students Placed at Risk, 2,* 107–119.

Stanton-Salazar, R. D., & Spina, S. U (2003). Informational mentors and role models in the lives of urban Mexican-origin adolescents. *Anthropology & Education Quarterly, 34,* 231–354.

Stone, C. N. (1998). *Changing urban education.* Lawrence, KS: The University Press of Kansas.

Teel, K., Debruin-Parecki, C., & Covington, M. (1998). Teaching strategies that honor and motivate inner-city African-American students: A school/university collaboration. *Teaching and Teacher Education, 14,* 479–495.

Tobin, K., Roth, W. M., & Zimmermann, A. (2001). Learning to teach science in urban schools. *Journal of Research in Science Teaching, 38,* 941–964.

Vail, K. (2003). The social challenge. *American School Board Journal, 190*(12), 46–52.

Villegas, A. M., & Lucas, T. (2003). *Educating culturally responsive teachers: A coherent approach.* Albany, NY: State University of New York Press.

Voltz, D. (1998). Challenges and choices in urban education: The perceptions of teachers and princi-pals. *The Urban Review, 30,* 211–227.

Weber, R.-M., & Longhi-Chirlin, T. (2001). Beginning in English: The growth of linguistic and liter-ate abilities in Spanish-speaking first graders. *Reading Research and Instruction, 4,* 19–50.

Weiner, L. (1993). *Preparing teachers for urban schools: Lessons from thirty-one years of school reform.* New York: Teachers College Press.

Weiner, L. (1999). *Urban teaching: The essentials.* New York: Teachers College Press.

Weiner, L. (2000). Research in the 90s: Implications for urban teacher preparation. *Review of Educational Research, 70*, 369–406.

Weiner, L. (2002). Evidence and inquiry in teacher education: What's needed for urban schools. *Journal of Teacher Education, 53*(3), 254–261.

Weis, L., & Fine, M. (2000). *Construction sites: Excavating race, class, and gender among urban youth.* New York: Teachers College Press.

Welch, S., Combs, M., Sigelman, L., & Bledsoe, T. (1997). Race or place? Emerging public perspectives on urban education. *Political Science and Politics, 30*, 454–458.

Wolman, H., & Agius, E. (1996). *National urban policy: Problems and prospects.* Detroit, MI: Wayne State University Press.

Wong, S. (2001). Depression level in inner-city Asian American adolescents: The contributions of cultural orientation and interpersonal relationships. *Journal of Human Behavior in the Social Environment, 3*(4), 49–64.

Yeo, F. (1997). *Inner-city schools, multiculturalism, and teacher education: A professional journey.* New York: Garland Publishing.

Yeo, F., & Kanpol, B. (1999). *From nihilism to possibility: Democratic transformations for the inner city.* Cresskill, NJ: Hampton Press.

CHAPTER THREE

Toward Social Justice IN Urban Education: A Model OF Collaborative Cultural Inquiry IN Urban Schools

PETER C. MURRELL, JR.

The increasing racial, cultural, and ethnic diversity among the populations attending urban schools poses a significant challenge to providing quality public education. Similarly, few would dispute that, in order to meet this challenge effectively, teachers must acquire the cultural competency for creating productive and inclusive learning environments, building academic capability among all students, and forging solid relationships with students' families and communities. Though this view has become an "official doctrine" among teacher educators, developing cultural competence in actual contexts consisting of urban schools and classrooms has proven a difficult challenge. This article explains a design for this work called Circles of Co-Practice as a system of practice and inquiry to develop cultural competency in partnership activity. The system design and application to the work of urban school-university-neighborhood collaboratives to improve urban education is illustrated with two case instances.

Few would dispute that the increasing racial, cultural, and ethnic diversity among the school populations attending urban public schools poses a significant challenge to providing quality education for all children (Sleeter, 2001a, 2001b). There also is little disagreement among teacher educators that successful urban teachers must develop cultural competency—the ability to work successfully and to build academic capability among all students in cultural, social, and linguistic settings unlike their own (Leigh, 1998; McAllister & Irvine, 2000). In the educational, health, and social welfare literatures, cultural competence refers to a professional's ability to function and communicate effectively in cross-cultural situations (Cross, Bazron, Dennis, & Isaacs, 1989; Davis, 1997; Sue, 1998). In teacher education, the notion of cultural competence (derived from multicultural education) additionally implies broader knowledge of social justice in practice and cultural context. Social justice here means a disposition toward recognizing and eradicating all forms of oppression and differential treatment extant in the practices and policies of institutions, as well as a fealty to participatory democracy as the means of this action. This knowledge of structural inequality in the social, historical, and political contexts of schooling is what enables teacher candidates from culturally mainstream backgrounds to create social learning environments among diverse student populations of children and youth (e.g., Henz, 2000; Murrell, 2002, in press; Tharp, Estrada, Dalton, & Yamauchi, 2000).

Over the past several years the Center for Innovation in Urban Education (CIUE) has addressed this need for comprehensive urban teacher competency by researching the partnership work of schools of education that are dedicated to improving the urban schools proximal to their universities. The core issue in our consultative inquiry concerned the development of cultural competency of individual teachers as well as how cultural competence is developed through systems of practice, where these systems include the participation of university clinical faculty, field-based instructors, school mentors, and practicing teachers. The focus question was: How do we create new systems of instructional and professional practice such that schools of education (SOEs) might simultaneously serve and learn from the most distressed, low-performing, and high-need city schools?

Through the Center for Innovation in Urban Education's field research, we found a shared view of the intractability of the problems facing urban schools and school systems. In the structured conversations we conducted with members of the professional networks of university, community, and school personnel in urban settings, we encountered many urban teachers who were experiencing the same struggles and issues of practice of three decades ago. These struggles were emblematic of the systemic and social-structural issues reminiscent of our eons-ago college reading Herbert Kohl's *36 Children* (Kohl, 1990), and Jonathan Kozol's (1970) *Death at an Early Age: The Destruction of the Hearts and Minds of Negro Children in the Boston Public Schools.* When we asked the more experienced teachers what have been the major innovations in advancing theory and practice that have actualized advantageous outcomes for urban schools in their area, the common sentiment reported was a variant of the aphorism "the more things change, the more they stay the same." The clear patterns of social injustice in American schooling have a daily demoralizing impact on the effect work of urban teachers.

One memorable meeting with an intrepid young white male is emblematic of this shared view. Teaching U.S. History in one of the most under-resourced high schools in Chicago, this young man explained that he entered teaching because he wanted to make a difference. He told us that he decided to teach in the same severely under-resourced high school where he did his student teaching the year before. The story of his first year was one filled with disillusionment, disappointment, and isolation. He spoke of how the anomie, hopelessness, and lack of commitment in the social environment as conditions that snuff out the initiative of young teachers. On the verge of tears, he spoke of how he was not able to plan for the next day of teaching most evenings because of frustration and exhaustion of the teaching day. He suffered in quiet desperation, struggling to maintain coherence in his teaching practice while receiving little encouragement or support. He spoke of how he vowed to leave teaching at the end of each week, and wonders why he keeps coming back on Monday mornings.

This kind of experience among urban teachers constitutes a timeless, pervasive and all-too-familiar narrative, one that has changed little over the past three decades. This common experience of futility suggests a reality of urban practice that seems not to factor into the way the issues of urban education are addressed either in the research literature or policy literature. The discourses of urban schooling in this era of accountability are dominated by a binary conception of achievement where there are just two kinds of schools: performing (those that meet their annual yearly progress criteria) and those that are underperforming. The contexts under which, and *with* which, urban teachers must struggle are rarely considered in the same conversations and deliberations on school performance. This reality put together with the "successful urban schools"phenomenon defines the challenge of our work as urban teacher-educator-researchers, as it has become the imprimatur of what constitutes quality in urban schooling.

The "successful urban school" phenomenon refers to those urban schools that get recognized as the "best" urban schools based upon such things as improved attendance statistics, the relative absence of discipline problems, a low teacher turn over, and a majority of the 8th grade or 10th grade classes meeting or exceeding national achievement test averages. But the sense of "best" is relative to the norm of schools in the district, and not typically "best" in the sense that everyone would want to send their children there. For example, an urban school may earn "best practices" status when there is a dramatic interruption in the decline of their achievement test scores. In every urban school district there are always a handful of schools that are recognized in this manner because they show some modicum of improvement in their statewide achievement test performance in a landscape of schools that are under-performing according to that measure. The implicit "gold standard" for the high-performing urban school has now become (under the No Child Left Behind Act, 2002) the accomplishment of having brought about improvement in its school-wide achievement test scores. This is a virulent, but hidden form of social injustice.

In short, the types of schools that are valorized as "successful urban schools" are typically not recognized as such by the quality of their teachers or the richness of the instruction, but rather by changes in aggregate test scores. This tendency has the unfortunate effect of extolling standards of school performance that most people think are good enough for urban schools but not worthy as standards of schooling for their own children. This is not to say that urban schools that demonstrate significant test score gains do not deserve credit. But it is clear there are other important measures of good practice that are not being applied to urban education, and that test-based benchmarks of good schooling would not be considered so in more affluent contexts. When aggregated test performance becomes the default indicator of "acceptable" or even "good" school performance, we consign a huge proportion of the children attending those schools to education that is neither "acceptable" nor "good." What happens to the majority of children in a school where the upper limit of aspirations for them is merely "average?" In many cases, those deemed "successful urban schools" are those in which few teachers would choose to work, much less send their own children to. These are schools from which few students go to college, or even earn a high school diploma. These are schools where too many children learn well their limitations and to recognize their small futures.

The mismatch between the test-based emblem of "the successful urban school" and the actual experiences of teachers and students is representative of many, perhaps most, central city urban public schools—in Boston, Cincinnati, Cleveland, Detroit, Chicago, and Los Angeles—where the experience of teaching is too often one of despair, hopelessness, and despondency. Many central city teachers we spoke with suffer quietly under regimes of mediocre and uninspired systems of practice. Too often, what is considered "good teaching" in these contexts is merely a matter of teachers "getting the students to do their work" under an uncomfortable détente with their students. In exchange for not being driven too hard in the daily routine of completing an endless litany of seatwork assignments and worksheets, students will "allow" the teacher "control" of the class, despite the fact that, secretly, many would prefer a teacher who pushed them to achieve. Nobody expects much from urban schools, even the "successful" ones.

It is this climate of despondency, low teacher morale, student apathy, and generally low scholastic expectations that places the development and training of teachers at the center of this social justice dilemma. This dilemma is one that SOEs must seriously consider as they begin to partner with the highest need and lowest performing urban schools. How will this entry take place such that SOEs do not merely become participants in a system that continues to relegate public school-goers to small futures and adds to the social injustice? A first step is adopting a critical awareness and analysis of the potential impacts—both positive and negative—for the community and school that partners with a university. There is an implicit emergency research agenda here—university people entering into partnership with high-need, low-performing urban schools must know (or quickly find out) what accomplished practice in these contexts looks like. Adding to this emergency is that the willingness and capacity for working with school people in a professional learning community often depends on whether collaboration offers any real results in terms of improved teaching, teaching conditions, and student performance gains.

This emergency creates a need for new cultural competence conceptualized as an ability that goes further than cross-cultural communicative skills of white mainstream teachers working with communities of color by encompassing the broader set of knowledge regarding institutions, policy, and the sociology of urban education. The dramatic underachievement of children and youth in big city public schools systems is not merely due to the lack of the multicultural competency of individual teachers. For example, African American and Latino students are disproportionately suspended, held back from matriculation and grade level completion, placed in special education programs, and underrepresented in programs for the gifted and talented (National Research Council, 2002). African American students are two to three times as likely to be suspended or expelled as other students (Skiba, Michael, Nardo, & Peterson, 2000). Dropout rates, low levels of academic skills, and school failure are higher for children and youth of color than their white, culturally mainstream, European American counterparts. These are systemic failures, linked to, and with implications for, improved practice of urban teachers. These systemic issues call for culturally-grounded knowledge for effective urban teaching, based on a working understanding of the systemic structural inequality extant in urban environments. Clearly, meeting the challenges to successful urban teaching is not simply a matter of working more effectively with children of color and poor children. It requires a critical understanding of how to effect change in the broader social, political, and historical context in which unequal schooling is constructed (Kozol, 2005). Cultural competency is more than the interactional and communicative skills of the individual teacher; it is also the teacher's capacity to interpret his or her practice as part of larger social and political systems and the related social justice issues that impact the school experiences of urban students. In addition to being able to structure academically, culturally, and socially enabling classroom environments, there are other abilities: productive collaboration, critical consumption of policy, and promoting the capacities of others with whom one works.

Although preparing preservice teachers to develop multicultural competency has become something of an official doctrine among teacher educators as the approach to elevate the quality of teaching in diverse and urban settings (e.g., Cochran-Smith, 1997; Irvine, 1997; Ladson-Billings, 1999; Melnick & Zeichner, 1997; Sleeter, 2001a, 2001b; Vavrus, 1994, 2002; Zeichner, 1996), it has been difficult to actualize in teaching practice—especially in urban contexts. Young people entering the profession of teaching are poorly equipped to deal with issues of race, culture, and identity (Sleeter, 2001a, 2001b). According to the National Education Association, 20% of new teachers leave the profession after three years, and in urban settings as much as 50% leave (American Federation of Teachers, 2000). Even so, the statistics do not begin to speak of the lack of care, the low morale, and the written-off status that black and Latino students experience in urban public schools. The prospect of a school of education partnering with a high-need, low-performance school has ethical and moral implications.

For SOEs to engage in collaborative partnership with the highest-need urban schools in ways that do not substantially improve the conditions of teaching and learning in those schools is ethically and morally problematic. Unless the collaboration with the university contributes to the improvement of school or pupil performance, it is questionable whether the added bureaucratic and time-resource strain should be permitted to further beleaguer the school. This is the ethical dilemma posed to an urban-focused SOE intending partnership with urban schools. Is it ethical to engage a partnership with an urban school without clear and likely prospects for improving school performance and achievement gains for students? We at the Center for Innovation in Urban Education think not, and consider this an important ethical matter.

As the community of urban teacher educators and researchers, we can either continue to work with those urban schools that are already over-endowed with "partners" and grants, or we can seriously consider what it takes to work with those school communities that suffer in quiet desperation and ignominy. In our work at CIUE, we have chosen the latter path and have been grappling with social and cultural challenges of schooling as they really exist in urban school settings. But this commitment entails another set of dilemmas and challenges—ones that neither school nor university partners are really prepared to address. A major challenge for the university partner is how to enter into partnership in ways that offer more immediate benefits to school performance, classroom practice, and student achievement. A major challenge for the school partners is whether they will be willing to critically and fundamentally examine their teaching and professional practices in the school in light of the social justice interests of university personnel. The remainder of this article describes the framework of the type of professional learning community designed to address the full array of challenges to urban education by describing instances of the model in use—one in Boston and the other in Chicago.

GENERAL THEORETICAL FRAMEWORK—COLLABORATIVE ASSESSMENT OF TEACHERS' PRACTICE

The interest in improving school performance through the development of professional learning communities has increased over the last decade (Marks, Louis, & Printy, 2000; McLaughlin & Talbert, 2001). Virtually every school reform model includes a component that focuses on building collaborative leadership within school communities. As noted above, the knowledge base for how this should take place in urban schools is difficult to come by. It is hard to run a school, improve the teaching practice of new faculty, engage in teacher training, and then "research" it as a community development enterprise all at the same time. The first example of the framework illustrates the attempt to carry out this approach to teacher development—where novice and experienced teachers participate in an ecologically designed activity setting for simultaneous inquiry into practice and field-based teacher preparation. The unique feature of this immersion model of teacher development at Northeastern University is the dedication to create public spaces for democratic decision-making in the mode of deliberative democratic process (Fung, 2003; Polletta, 2002). The following features characterized this new professional learning community:

1. Situating learning practice *for* urban schools *in* urban schools by creating new professional learning communities, where participants in multileveled roles (e.g., field instructors, supervisors, mentor teachers, curriculum specialists, and novice teachers) collaborate on instructional innovation in the classroom settings;
2. Focus on the development of teachers through a consistent and systematic appraisal of practice in the new professional learning community;
3. Focus on the development of practice through the systematic appraisal of the achievement gains and proficiency development of students served;
4. Focus on developing the socially just human systems and democratic social practices (especially deliberative democratic practices) that makes the professional learning community work.

In this framework, the units of analysis always derive from the linkages between the appraisal of teacher quality and student achievement. More specifically, collaborative work in this framework always looks to identify ways of assessing teaching practice as a function of actual improvements in students' academic performance. The reformulation of assessment in field-based teacher preparation is not just about classroom skills; also at issue is whether teaching practice is really impactful. Performance assessment of teaching viewed in this light still has not fully embraced the idea of assessment in assessing teacher performance in terms of the gains in achievement outcomes results for pupils across multiple measures, and not just those gains that are measured by tests. The deliberative work of groups is continuously framed by the question: How can we appraise instructional and professional practice in terms of student achievement gains? This is particularly important, given the continuing climate of standards-based high stakes standard-ized tests of student achievement and the unbalanced priority they are given as a measure of successful education. Working groups (called circles of co-practice) attend to the appraisal of teacher quality in ways that fully consider how students develop scholastically, socially, and intellectually in school.

In the socio-historical approach that informs our theoretical framework, learning practices of pupils are coexistent with the teaching practices of teachers. The quality of teaching practices is determined by the quality of learning practices among students—whether instruction results in their capacity to reason more powerfully, write more persuasively, and research more deeply. This relationship between learning practices and teaching practices is at the core of our framework for the assessment of instructional practice. This dialogic relationship is a way of appraising the quality of teaching practice in terms of student achievement. We therefore focus our work on the ability of teachers to create an environment for the context that will maximize learning and development. In sociocultural terms, the consequence of instructional practice is the joint development of teacher practice (pedagogy) and learner practice (learning achievement proficiency) occur-ring in settings of activity. We develop this idea as a system for the way urban university schools of education work toward the development of accomplished practice for teachers in conjunction with gains made by pupils and their teachers, particularly in diverse urban settings. The circle of co-practice is a concept of the professional learning community that informs the center's work. Based in schools, it is designed to address school performance and student achievement in conjunc-tion with the current arrangements of social and professional relationships in the school that might be appropriated as a system for the induction of new teachers, interns, and student teachers. This will encourage reflection on practices that are organic with the pre-existing practices in school settings. This circle of co-prac-tice arrangement includes what anthropologists call a participation structure for parents and other community stakeholders.

CIRCLE OF CO-PRACTICE AS THE NEW
PROFESSIONAL LEARNING COMMUNITY

Almost everyone in education is familiar with the idea of a "learning commu-nity." It is, however, more than just a charming vision and engaging metaphor for classroom life or rich professional interaction. It represents a system of organizing practice where the members of working groups are diverse in their professional roles, knowledge, and interests, and come together in a joint enterprise—such as when you bring together teachers, parents, teacher educators, and college faculty. What would a "learning community" be like if it were specifically designed to promote the achievement and academic development of real learners in real school communities? That is the aim of the circles of co-practice design: to offer a model for a professional learning community that develops teacher practice as a process of improving instruction. Let us turn now to two settings—one based at Northeastern University (NU) in Boston, and the other based at the University of Illinois—Chicago (UIC) in Chicago—that illustrate this framework.

A major component of the NU practice-based teacher preparation is that the center of the program activity is in an urban community school. Too often teacher candidates feel disconnected from what they learn in their teacher preparation courses and what they need to know as teachers. The cliché of student teaching is that ubiquitous lament that the "real world" experience of actually being in the classroom vastly outweighs what is learned in classroom coursework. The decision to situate professional learning on-site is, therefore, more than symbolic. When teacher candidates are learning about literacy theories, it is helpful for them to be in a classroom where the walls are covered with student compositions and an assortment of children's literature. The field instructors, a practicing teacher paired with a university professor, make use of the classroom and the school to examine literacy through grade levels and across the curriculum. Teacher candidates see how an urban school organizes literacy instruction in its classrooms and in school-wide events, rituals, and activities with families and the community.

Another component of this field-based design is that teachers in the school are engaged in teaching at the university. Teachers from the community school are hired to teach classes, such as special education inclusion, literacy, pre-K curriculum class, and student teaching seminar. One exemplary teacher, who has been a cooperating teacher and instructor with our program, supervises student teachers on-site in the partnering urban elementary school. The university contributes to her teacher salary and provides a graduate intern for her class. This site also hosts teacher preparation students at all levels of teacher readiness. All coursework in the teaching programs at the university require fieldwork. Teacher candidates are assigned 20–30 hours each semester to observe a classroom teacher and to work with individual or small groups of students through their literacy and math/science methods classes. Specific tasks are assigned, and teacher candidates write and reflect on the theory and practice with real students.

If you look into a classroom in the NU school-based program, you will see a teacher of record; an intern or student, teaching; and one or two early field students, observing or working with individual students. The principal may walk into the classroom in the role of instructional leader of the school, as a field-consultant, or as a field instructor. Parents are welcomed, and the school frequently hosts other principals, community members, and others who want to learn about a community of practice. Teachers use their planning and development time to analyze student work and jointly plan curriculum. Is this disruptive to the students attending the school? Not at all. Based upon the sociocultural-historical activity theory framework (e.g., Cole, Engeström, & Vasquez, 1997), we know that the most powerful and lasting forms of learning occur in a shared, vibrant, and engaging activity. Learners and teachers feel part of a larger community that recognizes that many people are committed to the success of everyone. Learners are not dependent on one person, and they recognize that there are many people who have something to offer the enterprise of learning and growth. Teacher candidates also recognize that they are not dependent on a single mentor teacher or cooperating teacher, and they are participants in the community of teachers in the school.

The model we are describing here began in a highly successful urban community school. The school culture has been well established by an exemplary principal and a strong stable faculty. The challenge now is to move this arrangement of practice to work in high-need, low-performing schools. In addition to working to develop exemplary building leadership and faculty, we think this will entail three additional principles or design features: (1) expanding the work of clinical field work to incorporate a focus on improving practice, not just on validating the student teacher or intern; (2) focusing on assessing teaching practice in terms of demonstrable gains in student achievement and scholastic development; and (3) finding the right mix of people in the new circle of practice to build a network of new professional learning communities within a school. We think this model is ready to replicate in high-need urban schools. The next example of co-practice is a project of inquiry into urban practice at the University of Illinois at Chicago.

As has been argued, the reflective and deliberative appraisal of teaching practice needed to elevate teaching and learning in high-need urban schools must necessarily extend beyond clinical supervision as it is traditionally done. The supervision arrangement needs to generate more "pedagogical mileage" out of the joint observation of the teacher candidate as is done in the clinical triad mode of field experience (Murrell, 2001). It also has been argued above and elsewhere (Murrell, 1998, 2002) that it is necessary for the inquiry into practice to extend beyond those participants in the clinical triad (i.e., teacher candidate, university supervisor, and cooperating/mentor teacher) if there is going to be improvement in instructional and professional practice in the school setting. The School of Education at the University of Illinois—Chicago has created a system for doing just that in a collaboration with the Chicago Public Schools (Berne & Mosak, 2004; Chou, 2003).

The model concept is depicted in Figure 1 and is predicated on the above-mentioned principles of teacher assessment that mold our approach—the community teacher (Murrell, 2001).

The model illustrates the principles of the approach (Berne & Mosak, 2004). First is the socio-culturally informed principle that improving teaching is not just a matter of changing the activity of the individual teacher. Therefore, rather than focusing on the teacher candidate per se, the focus is on the activity setting as the unit of analysis. This is shown in the diagram in that the ministrations of the field instructor and consultants are not focused solely on either the beginning teacher (BT) or the teacher candidate (TC) but on the practice. Critical attention is focused on the instructional activity setting when the field instructor (FI) and the field consultants (FC) are observing a teacher candidate (TC) in a clinical observation. The subsequent debriefing with the TC focuses critical attention on the professional activity setting by involving each participant on the key issue of how to elevate the quality of teaching and learning (Berne & Mosak, 2004).

The second principle of teacher assessment in this approach is that all appraisals of teaching performance are based upon demonstrable gains in student achievement and scholastic development. This is the idea that the efficacy of teaching practice can never legitimately be determined independently of student performance outcomes. The concept depicted in the figure is a circle of practice that

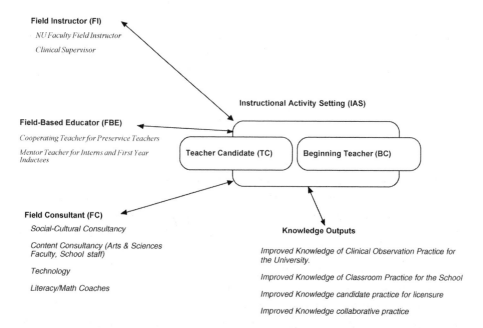

Figure 1. Circles of achievement practice—COAP.

enables the collaboration of clinical faculty and school faculty in the task of stewarding the development of teacher candidates and beginning teachers in the clinical triad. The model advocated here is an expanded circle of practice, a team that includes not only teachers and education professors, but also liberal arts and sciences faculty and others legitimately involved in the systematic inquiry that undergirds improvement of instructional practice, professional practice, and student development.

We have long known the limitation of the clinical triad—it is not the arrangement through which inquiry into practice beyond that of the individual candidate can take place. But finding a productive mix of people and procedures has been elusive for a number of reasons. Not the least of these is the difficulty of constituting a group for which additional participants (other than those in the clinical triad) can participate with legitimate and credible roles for engaging in serious inquiry into practice. This design creates legitimate participatory roles for arts and sciences faculty who would like to become more involved in school-partnership work but are not ready to do clinical supervision and would like to build their involvement gradually. Moreover, their initial participation as a Field Consultant allows them to develop their research participation and contribution as they become more accustomed to working in urban school environments.

The model illustrates how the circle of practice is expanded beyond the limited scope of reflection and observation offered by the clinical triad. The circle of co-practice design makes it possible for observers to appraise the "figure" of teacher performance as well as the "ground" of the instructional setting and pupil response. As in the gestalt psychology notion of figure and ground, there is a classic way in which the perception of images is mutually constituted by the background and foreground. In the "face and vase" image for example, the figure (object or image of the face) and the ground (background visual context) together produce an image. Depending which field you key in on, your perception will be either the face-figure or the vase-figure. Another way that the "figure-ground" analogy applies is to the nature of clinical observation as the co-determination of teaching practice and learning outcomes. The actions of the teacher, the reactions of the students, and the interactions among all participants would be more deeply understood as the relation between activity and context. The "figure" is constituted by student and teacher behavior, and micro-level interaction is the "ground" created by the situational context of activity and interaction. In any case, the framework for a new circle of practice provides not only a way for effectively observing the figure and ground-aspects of teaching episodes but also a way for the observers to assemble deep interpretations of each into a single multi-perspective interpretation of practice in the teaching episode. We are developing here a methodology that gets at the deep structure of teaching and learning, one that is looking at more than the operational proficiency of a single teacher candidate or student teacher. The expansion of a clinical triad into a circle of practice (or observational team) would include at least two other roles—both of these in the capacity of a Field Consultant. One of these would be an Arts and Science faculty member with a legitimate role in advancing instructional practice through his or her content matter expertise and participation in the group's instructional inquiry. The other of these credible roles might be a cultural competence coach (Berne & Mosak, 2004). The Field Consultant's observational lens is different from that of the Field Instructor in that their observational and interpretative responsibility is the "field" or "ground" of instruction—the cultural, social, and material context of the setting. Though it might be tempting to use the term "clinical quadrad" with the inclusion of the FC role, we avoid doing that to underscore the idea that an effective circle of co-practice does not simply mean adding another set of eyes or arbitrarily creating an observer role. Rather, it means taking seriously the task of "deep sight," shared analysis and collaborative work in the appraisal of the quality of teaching practice.

It is the added role of the Field Consultant to the clinical triad that transforms it into a circle of co-practice, enabling the critical deep collaborative interrogation of teaching and learning practices in ways that elevates the learning and development of children. The FC role may include more than one person. Over the course of a semester the FC role may include any number of people selected and brought in as needed at the appropriate points in the development of the teacher candidate and according to the direction of the team-determined direction of the "inquiry into practice." Field Consultants also might be determined by interests of the school-site council or other leadership structure in the school to look at particular curricular, developmental, or social issues.

Adding a Field Consultant enhances the role of the university supervisor in charge of the field instruction. Rather than simply supervising the intern or student teacher in a clinical setting, the FC is in the position to assume an expanded role that organizes the focus of the team doing the observations of practice—something of a "principle investigator" for the inquiry-into-practice of the team. This role is important to both the research-into-practice work of the team and to the assessment of teaching. Traditional practice is dogged by the unfortunate tendency to view the teaching episode as the frame for evaluating quality teaching. The result often is a tendency to focus on the overtly observable choices and actions of the individual teacher in certain episodes—narrowing the domain of teacher practice to what can be seen in a single sitting, instead of evaluating the impact on student learning progress over time. This circle of co-practice is an arrangement more likely to circumvent this limitation to teacher assessment by contextualizing practice more broadly than a single lesson or teaching episode.

This design creates legitimate participatory roles for arts and sciences faculty who would like to become more involved in school partnership work but are not ready to do clinical supervision and would like to build their involvement gradually. The involvement of faculty from humanities and social sciences interested in such themes as critical pedagogy, critical race theory, the sociology of urban schooling, or democratic movements is of particular interest because of another feature of the model: the development of participatory democratic models of decision-making and collaboration. An important feature of this model is that of deliberatively and deliberately working on building democratic and socially just social and professional environments in schools. This work ought to proceed with a focus on race and racism as powerful forms of structural inequality that persist in schools. Using recent works that expose the racialized discourse as embedded social practice (see for example, Bush, 2004; Lewis; 2003; Pollock, 2004; Van Ausdale & Feagin, 2001) the Field Consultant in the role of a cultural consultant will lead building-level inquiry into racialized cultural practices in schools. This is our next step in the evolution of work across boundaries drawn by race in schools with a predominance of white teachers and a predominantly African American student body.

Before beginning this redesign, we drew on survey research of how cooperating teachers performed in partnership schools (Abt Associates, 2003), summarized in Table 1 below. We determined that the host teachers of urban partnership

Table 1. Data from Abt Associates Survey

How capable is this individual of	n ($N = 237$)	Percent perceived as extremely capable or capable
Three most capable		
Recognizing students as individuals with particular skills and abilities	197	83.1%
Recognizing students as individuals with diverse social and cultural experiences	192	81.0%
Knowing the content/subject for her or his teaching assignment in the school	186	78.5%
Three least capable		
Persuading students that their individual and collective job is to learn	150	63.3%
Structuring learning activities so students can construct their own understanding	149	62.9%
Helping student arrive at their own understanding	148	62.5%

Rated by respondents on a scale of 1 ("Extremely capable") to 5 ("Incapable").

schools give teacher candidates in the field and interns high marks (averaging 80% agree or strongly agree) for doing the usual "teacherly things" in the traditional notions of teaching expertise, like recognizing students as individuals with particular skills and abilities and with diverse social and cultural experiences, and knowing the content/subject for her or his teaching assignment in the school. However, when it came to expertise related to organizing learning communities and ensuring achievement results of pupils, the host teachers gave teacher candidates in the field lower marks (averaging 63% agree or strongly agree) on abilities, such as "persuading students that their individual and collective job is to learn," "structuring learning activities so students can construct their own understanding," and "helping students arrive at their own understanding."

CONCLUSION

This chapter proposed a design for organizing a new professional learning community, specifically for urban schools of education that seek to engage in ethical, productive, and impactful work with high-need, low-performing urban schools. This framework, termed the circle of co-practice, is extending the framework of the community teacher (Murrell, 2001) toward realizing more democratically participatory models of community-oriented school-university partnership (Murrell, 1998). Real urban school improvement is vested in democratically expanding the circle of this practice-in-activity by organizing legitimate contributive roles for liberal arts and sciences faculty, parents, and others who might otherwise be peripheral to the work.

NOTES

"Toward Social Justice in Urban Education: A Model of Collaborative Cultural Inquiry in Urban Schools," copyright 2006 from Equity & Excellence in Education, 39: 81-90, by Peter C. Murrell, Jr. Reproduced by permission of Taylor & Francis Group, LLC., http://www.taylorandfrancis.com <http://www.taylorandfrancis.com>.

REFERENCES

Abt Associates, Inc. (2003). *Preliminary internal report to the Massachusetts Coalition for Teacher Quality and Student Achievement—Teacher survey on family and community support*. Cambridge, MA: Author.

American Federation of Teachers. (2000). Building a profession: Strengthening teacher preparation and induction. *Report of the K-16 Teacher Education Task Force*. Washington, DC: Author

Berne, J., & Mosak, E. (2004). Guide for field instructors and consultants (internal document). Chicago: College of Education, University of Chicago.

Bush, M. E. L. (2004). *Breaking the code of good intentions: Everyday forms of whiteness*. New York: Rowman & Littlefield.

Chou V. (2003). *Proposal document for Teacher Quality grant application.*

Cochran-Smith, M. (1997). Knowledge, skills, and experiences for teaching: Culturally diverse learners: A perspective for practicing teachers. In J. J. Irvine (Ed.), *Critical knowledge for diverse teachers and learners* (pp. 27–88). Washington, DC: American Association of Colleges of Teacher Education.

Cole, M., Engeström, Y., & Vasquez, O. A. (Eds.). (1997). *Mind, culture and activity: Seminal papers from the laboratory of comparative human cognition.* Cambridge, UK: Cambridge University Press.

Cross T., Bazron, B., Dennis, K., & Isaacs, M. (1989). *Towards a culturally competent system of care, Volume I.* Washington, DC: Georgetown University Child Development Center, CASSP Technical Assistance Center.

Davis, K. (1997). *Exploring the intersection between cultural competency and managed behavioral health care policy: Implications for state and county mental health agencies.* Alexandria, VA: National Technical Assistance Center for State Mental Health Planning

Fung, A. (2003). Deliberative democracy, Chicago style, grassroots governance in policing and public education. In A. Fung & E. O. Wright (Eds.), *Deepening democracy: Institutional innovations in empowered participatory governance* (pp. 11–143). London: Verso.

Henz. R. C. (2000). Leading for diversity: How school leaders achieve racial and ethnic diversity. Center for Research on Education, Diversity and Excellence. Retrieved March 1, 2005, from http://www.crede.org/research/pdd/rb6.shtml

Irvine, J. J. (Ed.). (1997). *Critical knowledge for diverse teachers and learners.* Washington, DC: American Association of Colleges of Teacher Education.

Kohl, H. (1990). *36 children.* New York: Penguin.

Kozol, J. (1970). *Death at an early age: The destruction of the hearts and minds of Negro children in the Boston Public Schools.* New York: Bantam.

Kozol, J. (2005). *The shame of the nation: The restoration of apartheid schooling in America.* New York: Crown. Ladson-Billings, G. (1999). Preparing teachers for diversity. In L. Darling-Hammond & G. Sykes (Eds.), *Teaching as the learning profession* (pp. 86–123). San Francisco: Jossey-Bass.

Leigh, J. W. (1998). *Communicating for cultural competence.* Prospect Heights, IL: Waveland.

Lewis, A. E. (2003). *Race in the schoolyard: Negotiating the color line in classrooms and communities.* New Brunswick, NJ; Rutgers University Press.

Marks, H. M., Louis, K. S., & Printy, S. M. (2000). The capacity for organizational learning: Implications for pedagogical quality and student achievement. In K. Leithwood (Ed.), *Understanding schools as intelligent systems* (pp. 239–265). Stamford, CT: JAI.

McAlister, G., & Irvine, J. J. (2000). Cross cultural competency and multicultural teacher education. *Review of Educational Research, 70*(1), 3–24.

McLaughlin, M. W., & Talbert, J. E. (2001). *Professional communities and the work of high school teaching.* Chicago: University of Chicago Press.

Melnick, S. L., & Zeichner, K. M. (1997). Enhancing the capacity of teacher education institutions to address diversity issues. In J. E. King, E. R. Hollins, & W. C. Hayman (Eds.), *Preparing teachers for cultural diversity* (pp. 23– 39). New York: Teachers College Press.

Murrell, P. C., Jr. (1998). *Like stone soup: The problem of the professional development school in the renewal of urban schools.* Washington, DC: American Association of Colleges for Teacher Education (AACTE).

Murrell, P. C., Jr. (2001). *The community teacher: A new framework for effective urban teaching.* New York: Teachers College Press.

Murrell, P. C., Jr. (2002). *African-centered pedagogy: Developing schools of achievement for African American children.* New York: State University of New York Press.

Murrell, P. C., Jr. (in press). *Race, Culture and Schooling: Identities of achievement in multicultural urban schools.* Mahwah, NJ: Erlbaum.

National Research Council (2002). *Minority students in special and gifted education.* Committee on Minority Representation in Special Education. Washington, DC: National Academy Press.

No Child Left Behind Act of 2001. (2002). Pub. L. No. 107–110, 115 Stat. 1425, 20 U.S.C. §§6301 et seq.

Polletta, F. (2002). *Freedom is an endless meeting: Democracy in American social movements.* Chicago, IL: University of Chicago Press.

Pollock, M. (2004). *Colormute: race talk dilemmas in an American school.* Princeton, NJ: Princeton University Press.

Skiba, R., Michael, R., Nardo, A., & Peterson, R. (2000). *The color of discipline: Sources of racial and gender disproportionality in school punishment.* Indiana Education Policy Center, Policy Research Report #SRS1.

Sleeter, C. E. (2001a). Epistemological diversity in research on preservice teacher education for historically underserved children. In W. G. Secada (Ed.), *Review of research in education,*(Vol. 6, pp. 209–250). Washington, DC: AERA.

Sleeter, C. E. (2001b). Preparing teachers for culturally diverse schools: Research and the overwhelming presence of whiteness. *Journal of Teacher Education, 52*(2), 94–106.

Sue, S. (1998). In search of cultural competence in psychotherapy and counseling. *American Psychologist, 53*(4), 440–448.

Tharp, R., Estrada, P., Dalton, S., & Yamauchi, L. A. (2000). *Teaching transformed: Achieving excellence, fairness, inclusion, and harmony* Boulder, CO: Westview.

Van Ausdale, D., & Feagin, J. R. (2001). *The first R: How children learn race and racism.* New York: Rowman & Littlefield.

Vavrus, M. (1994). A critical analysis of multicultural *Currents of reform in pre-service teacher education* education infusion during student teaching. *Action in* (pp. 133–175). New York: Teachers College Press. *Teacher Education, 16*(3), 45–57.

Vavrus, M. (2002). *Transforming the multicultural education of teachers: Theory, research and practice.* New York: Teachers College Press.

Zeichner, K. (1996). Educating teachers for cultural diversity. In K. Zeichner, S. Melnick, & M. L. Gomez (Eds.), *Currents of reform in pre-service teacher education* (pp. 133-175). New York: Teachers College Press.

CHAPTER FOUR

Promoting Participatory Democracy THROUGH Community Organizing

DENNIS SHIRLEY

Boston College

Participatory democracy, once a positively charged term in the arena of urban education, has fallen on hard times in the opening years of the 21st century. The phrase itself is straightforward enough—indicating a form of political decision making and action in which citizens are prime movers rather than passive observers—but the, at best, ambiguous, and, at worst, incontestably negative results of apparently democratic reforms in metropolitan areas in the recent past have led to skepticism about the idea of participatory democracy, not only from elite policy makers but also from urban parents and members of community-based organizations, the intended beneficiaries of democratic reforms. New York City's experiment in decentralization launched in the 1960s was recently described as a "textbook failure" in a *New York Times* article that described depressingly low academic achievement in the schools of Ocean Hill–Brownsville; New York subsequently centralized control of the schools in the mayor's office, rolling back reforms in place for almost a half a century (Traub, 2002). Chicago tried a radical form of participatory democracy beginning in 1988 in its public schools—extending to parents' representatives real power in the form of hiring and firing principals and staff—but, when research showed that subsequent academic gains were modest in the elementary schools (as an aggregate) and nonexistent in the high schools, the city turned to a corporate model of control, hiring a chief executive officer (CEO) with no prior experience in education to run the schools (Bryk, Sebring, Kerbow, Rollow, & Easton, 1998). Mayoral control has replaced appointed or elected school boards in Boston, Chicago, Cleveland, Detroit, and other smaller cities. Milwaukee, Philadelphia, and Baltimore have all experimented with voucher and choice models that either modify or reject the democratic facets of urban public school systems in favor of market-based solutions (Cuban & Usdan, 2003).

Could it be the case that recent political developments indicate that participatory democracy simply is not an effective strategy for improving city schools? Might it be true that urban schools are simply too troubled and that the urban political realities of which they are a part are too convoluted and opaque for working-class families to play a proactive role in shaping their children's educations on anything other than the model of the individual client brokering resources or favors for one's child? Clarence Stone, the leader of a large National Science Foundation–funded study of community "civic capacity" in 11 urban districts, wrote recently that "Citywide parent groups ... are a modest force in school policy at best" (Stone Henig, Jones, & Pierannunzi, 2001, p. 85). From the vantage point of Stone and his colleagues, parents are critical partners in enhancing civic capacity to improve urban schools; but at the same time that their contribution is critical, the realities of urban politics are such that parents are easily outmaneuvered by system insiders and rarely have the time and political capacity to organize to win victories on behalf of their children and their communities.

While democratically driven reforms appear to have stalled, a variety of market-driven reforms such as charters, vouchers, and public schools "contracted out" to private agencies are proving to be no elixir for the conundrums that face children from poor and working-class backgrounds in urban schools (Benveniste, Carnoy, & Rothstein, 2002).In many cases, these reforms simply reproduce the instability and low academic achievement of traditional public schools in a different organizational setting. Private foundations, which possess the potential to leverage change in urban schools, often seek to promote massive cultural changes based on relatively short intervals (at best, three- to five-year grants) and rarely understand the complexities of the problems of urban schools. By raising high expectations and failing to appreciate the complexity of issues at a building level, reformers can inadvertently reinforce an entrenched sentiment of fatalism about the prospects for improving urban education (Payne & Kaba, 2001).

These problems do not admit of an easy resolution. The discouraging results of decentralized, community-based reforms attempted in urban districts (such as those in New York City) in the past decades must be interrogated, and simplistic appeals for more democratic participation must be avoided, especially if learning outcomes for students of color in our nation's cities are modest (at best) under such reforms. Appreciating the complexity of the issues, I shall attempt in the following discussion to defend and revive the notion of participatory democracy in the current context.

I shall begin by recounting the origins of the term *participatory democracy* and articulating some of the most salient problems besetting participatory democratic practices in the United States today. These include the uneven distribution of political participation based on social class; the problems of building political capacity across group lines such as race and ethnicity; the increasing class stratification of American society; and the constraints on democracy in an era of economic globalization. I will then indicate how the tradition of community organizing—pioneered by Saul Alinsky and later enacted in the practices of the Alliance Schools initiative of the Industrial Areas Foundation (IAF) in Texas— provides one hopeful point of departure for increasing participatory democracy in urban education. No panacea shall be promised, for the IAF has encountered many of the same obstacles to reform as those encountered by legions of other school reformers, even though their anchoring in religious institutions provides a more authentic community base for their work than reformers focused solely on the internal dynamics of a school (Shirley, 1997, 2002). Next, my account will offer a critique of community organizing as practiced by the IAF and will argue for the development of a synthetic ensemble of practices based upon the full array of social movement, interest group, and coalition politics at our disposal. Finally, I will conclude with reference to intriguing recent developments in political theory and political science that have recognized the problems inherent in older concepts of participatory democracy and that seek to address those problems through a model of "empowered participatory governance" that aspires to maximize the benefits of grassroots reform while acknowledging the need for systems-level accountability systems to circumvent some of the more endemic problems in democratic deliberation (Fung & Wright, 2003). The overall effort here is to reconceptualize the work of school reform in the current context and to begin to articulate a more capacious and institutionally embedded form of community organizing for participatory democracy.

At the outset, it should be noted that the phrase *participatory democracy*— which originated with University of Michigan philosophy professor Arnold Kaufman—first entered the American lexicon with the publication of the *Port Huron Statement* by Students for a Democratic Society (SDS) in 1962 (Students for a Democratic Society, 1962; Kaufman, 1969; Miller, 1987; Isserman, 1987; Polletta, 2002). Of course, the notion itself has a much older pedigree, dating back to the Greek polis, in which citizens deliberated on political issues in a face-to-face community, and whose clearest exposition was Pericles' famous funeral oration during the Peloponnesian war (Thucydides, 1954). Yet the Greek polis, which excluded women, slaves, immigrants, and non-property holders from its deliberations, was but a modest foreshadowing of the form of civic engagement that the leaders of SDS articulated. Building upon a host of modern organizing strategies—such as those of labor unions, the Highlander Folk School, the civil rights movement, the peace movement, nondoctrinaire socialist parties, and an eclectic array of indigenous community-based organizations—SDS sought to bring all citizens, especially those hitherto disenfranchised by race or class, into democratic deliberation and action.

In many ways, the *Port Huron Statement* was a romantic and hopeful affirmation of the United States' potential as a nation with greater civic engagement and social equality. Yet as noted by Arnold Kaufman (1969) himself, the notion of participatory democracy contained within it aspirations that do not play out easily in the body politic. The description of a participatory democracy in the *Port Huron Statement* is, in and of itself, relatively innocuous. It contends "that decision-making of basic social consequence be carried on by public groupings," suggests that "politics be seen positively as the art of collectively creating an acceptable pattern of social relations," and asserts that "politics has the function of bringing people out of isolation and into community, thus being a necessary, though not sufficient, means of finding meaning in personal life" (Miller, 1987, p. 333). More problematic is the conviction that, if Americans had the opportunity to participate fully in the civic life of the nation, they would naturally evolve in a direction that supported SDS's anti-racist, pacifist, and egalitarian values (Matusow, 1984; Miller, 1987; Polletta, 2002). This evasion of the political complexities of American life reflected the youthfulness of SDS leaders, and SDS's subsequent ideological hardening—a consequence of the escalation of the war in Vietnam and the assassinations of Martin Luther King, Jr., and Robert Kennedy—led to the collapse of the organization in 1969.

Yet, the concept of participatory democracy was much greater than SDS, and the spirit of broad-based community organizing that it espoused perdured and took on a myriad of different forms. As alluded to previously, the notion of community control in school reform circles led to a dramatic shift in power in the New York City schools from the central office to local districts. Foundation officers began insisting that local stakeholders should not only be consulted by grant writers but also given leadership positions in school reform ventures as well as those ventures affecting the delivery of services in traditionally disenfranchised communities. The numerous Great Society programs launched in the 1960s, such as Title I of the Elementary and Secondary Education Act, specified roles for local community activists in program design and implementation. All of these different measures reflected the opening of democratic participation that was the hallmark of the 1960s and the more inclusive politics that brought African Americans, Latinos, and women more centrally into American civic life.

Many of these reforms transformed the United States in ways that would have been unimaginable to earlier generations and helped to fulfill the democratic promise for those who had previously been blocked by law and by culture from political participation. Given the magnitude of the historical injustices that confronted school reformers, it may have been naïve to expect that participatory democratic strategies, on their own, could upend decades of state-sanctioned segregation and the systemic miseducation of students of color. Larger social dynamics—perhaps underestimated by SDS and other 1960s activist groups—conspired against the kinds of social change envisioned in the *Port Huron Statement*. For reasons of brevity, I shall review only three of the more salient barriers to participatory democratic practices that have become clearer in the ensuing decades.

The first problem is that, when it comes to participating in the political arena, affluent Americans are far more experienced, engaged, and savvy than the poor. Political participation is very unevenly distributed in the United States. In 1989 political scientists conducted research that compared the civic engagement of wealthy Americans (those earning more than $75,000 per annum) with the poor (those earning under $15,000). They found that not only were the wealthy two-and-a-half times more likely to be affiliated with a political organization, three times more likely to be involved in community activities, and four times more likely to have done campaign work, but they were also more than twice as likely to have participated in protest activities (Verba, Schlozman, & Brady, 1995, p. 190). Those protest activities could take the form of a referendum against increased taxes, litigation against affirmative action, or the circulation of petitions against the provision of low- and moderate-income housing in affluent communities. The exact issue is less important than the overarching political import: When one turns to participatory democracy as a solution to the problems of urban education, one must acknowledge at the outset that the affluent have tremendous advantages in terms of their prior political work and their extant political networks.

This first problem leads to a second conundrum. To develop any reasonable clout, community organizers must do broad-based organizing: They must reach across race, class, and language barriers to develop a power base that commands the respect of influential decision makers in urban school systems. In the language of social capital theory, organizers must move beyond "bonding" social capital—which refers to strong social ties among individuals, similar to them in terms of categories such as race, gender, religion, or profession—to develop "bridging" social capital (Putnam, 2000, pp. 22–24). Yet to do so is exceptionally difficult. At the end of a careful review of 40 years of research on diversity in organizations, Williams and O'Reilly (1998) concluded that "the preponderance of empirical evidence suggests that diversity is most likely to impede group functioning. Unless steps are taken to actively counteract these effects," they warn, "diversity is more likely to have negative than positive effects on group performance" (p. 120). A host of educational analysts have confirmed that sociocultural dissonance, particularly in terms of relationships between White and Black Americans, complicates the work of urban educational reform (Anyon, 1997; Henig, Hula, Orr, & Pedescleaux, 1999; Orr, 1999; Payne & Kaba, 2001).

The point here is not to develop arguments against diversity in American political and social life, for diversity is, in many ways, one of the richest and most genuinely educational components of the American polity, when elaborated appropriately (Dewey, 1966). Rather, the point is a more simple political one: It is easier to organize individuals who can lay claim to a common ethnic or racial identity than it is to organize across group lines. In the second half of the 20th century, suburbanization transformed American culture to create a new pan-ethnic sense of "Whiteness" that has come to be culturally juxtaposed to the "national otherness" of people of color who are concentrated in cities (Goode & Maskovsky, 2001). Organizing across those boundary lines—which is absolutely essential to break out of the isolation of the inner-city poor (Wilson, 1999)—is much more difficult than organizing within them.

This second problem is not simply a reflection of unfortunate political choices, for it is rooted in a deeper set of structural relationships that have emerged and calcified in the last quarter century. The American power elite has, in many ways, withdrawn from arenas in which mixed-class encounters were once possible, leading to a phenomenon that Reich (1991) has characterized as the secession of the successful. Yet, the economic elite are not the only class to have erected barriers between themselves and their fellow citizens. Middle-class Americans have achieved a high degree of material homogeneity that is easily juxtaposed to poor and working-class urban dwellers of color, who are often spatially mismatched from new jobs that have been created in so-called "edge cities" in the suburbs (Goode & Maskovsky, 2001; Wilson, 1999;). The intensification of class stratification has made the establishment of bridging social capital across economic lines more difficult than in previous eras and complicates the creation of participatory democratic structures in which poor and working-class Americans can engage in political problem solving with their more affluent counterparts.

A third problem that must be confronted has to do with a certain naiveté about what community organizing can realistically accomplish. Although community organizations have launched a number of impressive agendas in the last quarter century in the arenas of school reform, crime prevention, health care, job training, and environmental protection, their net effect has been modest. The reason for this is relatively straightforward: Our current political economy is radically intertwined with increasingly global networks of production, exchange, and distribution. Community-based groups can possess tremendous reservoirs in terms of local knowledge but can be relatively powerless to affect economic cycles and the rapid pace of inventions in dynamic arenas like computer technology, telecommunications, and genetic engineering. Even when state courts support egalitarian educational policies in regards to school funding, as has been the case in a number of recent state supreme court decisions, elite and middle-class groups have been able to assert themselves to dilute or even mitigate altogether the results of the decisions (Anyon, 1997). For this reason, the cautions of sympathetic observers (e.g., Castells, 1983; Halpern, 1995) about the limitations of community organizing are well taken.

These impediments to community organizing for participatory democracy along the lines of 19th- or 20th-century labor unionism or the civil rights movement are daunting. Though one should recognize the many barriers to such organizing, it is also important to acknowledge the countervailing tendencies that are at work. Globalization, for example, has contributed to the widening gap between the rich and the poor in the United States, but computer technology, the internet, and telecommunications can also expedite the rise of global protest movements, as was evident in the recent peace movement against the invasion of Iraq, which crossed class lines. Diversity may by some measures, impede group functioning, but it also has the potential to contribute to a broader understanding of human commonalities as well as cultural richness, which can be profoundly educative. Although the stimulus was tragic, the evidence is clear that the events of September 11, 2001, produced a much greater sense of civic solidarity and purposefulness among Americans (Putnam, 2002). History is inherently unpredictable, cultures are dynamic rather than static, and politics continually provides opportunities for agency, negotiation, and purposeful coalition building.

In the arena of urban school reform, small victories have been garnered through numerous community organizing efforts in recent years; these initiatives provide opportunities to study successful organizing strategies, which can be adapted and disseminated in other settings. Two recent studies have identified over 200 community organizing groups that are now active in the arena of school reform, primarily in metropolitan areas in all regions of the country (Gold, Simon & Brown, 2002; Mediratta, Fruchter, & Lewis, 2002). These groups vary tremendously in size, organizing philosophy and strategies, and impact, and they deserve further study and analysis in terms of their potential for enhancing participatory democracy and academic achievement. Some of the better known groups are the Association of Communities Organized for Reform Now (ACORN), the People's Institute for Community Organizing (PICO), the Alliance Organizing Project (in Philadelphia), and the Logan Square Neighborhood Association (in Chicago). At this juncture, I shall turn to a description of what is arguably the most time-tested and powerful of such groups: the Industrial Areas Foundation (IAF). I shall describe the IAF's work in Texas, where it is most developed, and shall unpack some of the features that make its model of community organizing for participatory democracy and school reform especially alluring.

The Texas IAF has garnered considerable attention nationally because of its success not only in creating a network of roughly 130 Alliance Schools in poor and working-class communities, but also because the IAF has linked its school improvement work with a number of community organizing initiatives that have produced victories in the areas of job training, health care provision, environmental protection, and neighborhood safety. The Texas IAF has been working in urban schools for close to two decades, and though its educational activities have experienced some setbacks, the Texas IAF has generated enough successes to warrant national attention as one way in which community engagement contributes to academic achievement. All of its Alliance Schools are situated in communities of color characterized by concentrated poverty, and, given the obstacles to reform in such settings, the rises in test scores and other indicators of student achievement documented thus far indicate that, while no panacea has been identified, further collaboration and experimentation is surely warranted (Shirley, 1997, 2002). The Texas IAF's achievements have been described by numerous scholars who have found it to be a hopeful sign of a revival of civic engagement in an otherwise politically disconnected citizenry (Murnane & Levy, 1996; Osterman, 2002; Sarason, 2002; Sirianni & Friedland, 2001; Warren, 2001; Wilson, 1999).

How does the Texas IAF engage in community organizing? IAF strategies have evolved considerably since Saul Alinsky started the foundation in Chicago in 1940 and described his tactics in two books, *Reville for Radicals* (1946) and *Rules for Radicals* (1971). Alinsky worked with the urban poor to identify injustices, rally popular outrage, and attack political leaders. He happily personalized controversial issues, never hesitated to polarize the opposition, and loved flamboyant actions. One of his most famous gambits involved the threat of a mass occupation of all of the toilets at O'Hare International Airport for a day to force the city to meet the demands of working-class African Americans in the Woodlawn section of Chicago. Another involved purchasing numerous tickets for a performance of the Rochester Symphony Orchestra and literally creating a "stink-in" by hosting a massive bean dinner prior to attending a gala event. Both strategies were planned to force city leaders to improve conditions in northern ghettos, and neither strategy was actually ever carried through (Horwitt, 1992).

Amusing as such tactics were, they were primarily of value in terms of individual protest actions and attracting attention to Alinsky himself, who became a highly sought-after media celebrity in the 1960s. Charisma has its price, however, for when Alinsky died in June 1972, the IAF was little more than a handful of organizers operating on a shoestring budget. Ed Chambers, Alinsky's protégé and successor, then worked in a more focused and pragmatic way to give the IAF more of a solid foundation. He anchored the IAF in inner-city churches in African American and Latino neighborhoods, kept community leaders in the foreground and himself in the background in organizing actions, and sought to enhance the respectability, rather than the shock value, of IAF organizations. Actions undertaken by Alinsky and his colleagues that were sporadic and colorful Chambers sought to make strategic and long-lasting. Better than Alinsky himself, Chambers—whose skills as an organizer Alinsky describes in detail in *Rules for Radicals* but whom he never mentions by name—was able to build the IAF into a power organization that would perdure over time with a stable leadership core and training institutes to develop civic capacity.

IAF organizers today work with indigenous community leaders to identify grievances, conduct meetings across city boundaries and ethnic lines, and develop political solutions to community grievances. Part of this work has entailed the creation of an IAF nomenclature linked to specific components of community organizing. "One-on-one" meetings between organizers and community stakeholders; "research actions" with community members on problems afflicting a school, neighborhood, or congregation; and "accountability sessions" in which community members recruit civic leaders to endorse their agenda are part of a concerted campaign to develop the political capacity to build an organization that represents authentic community interests (Shirley, 1997; Warren, 2001). Fourteen IAF organizations are now active in Texas, encompassing all of the state's major metropolitan areas (Houston, Dallas, Fort Worth, San Antonio, El Paso, and Austin) as well as smaller cities (such as Beaumont, Port Arthur, Lubbock, and McAllen).

Community organizing for participatory democracy and school improvement is demanding work. Texas IAF organizers who first approached schools anticipated that teachers, principals, and parents would be most appreciative of assistance in academic matters, but they quickly learned that in communities of concentrated poverty the school was often viewed as a relatively stable and strong institution. Rather than issues pertaining to instruction and curriculum in the school, teachers and parents were concerned about neighborhood conditions such as a crack house across the street from the school, the lack of employment opportunities for youth and young adults, or the unavailability of affordable health care. These grievances then became points of departure for community organizing, but the novel twist on the IAF's work in these situations was the development of conjoint organizing practices that brought together teachers and school administrators, on the one hand, and parents and community leaders, on the other, to battle for improved conditions for a community's children.

In these political actions, the exact nature of a given grievance in a community generally has mattered little. Parents and teachers at one elementary school in Austin fought for a school-based health clinic; the school community affiliated with a middle school in Fort Worth shut down a nearby convenience store that was illegally selling alcohol to children and young adults; and parents and teachers united in many cities have fought for preschool and afterschool programs that will keep the children safe and educated while parents are working. The IAF is focused on developing community leadership, not programs. By linking the real needs of the youth to an integrating organizing strategy that takes the needs of the whole child seriously, the IAF has helped classroom teachers to engage in the world beyond the school boundaries and, at the same time, has served as a catalyst for developing more culturally responsive teaching (Shirley, 1997, 2002).

To carry out the organizing described above, organizers must ask themselves a number of strategic questions. What grievances do individuals (such as parents and teachers) have about which they are so concerned that they will not simply complain, but will also develop their capacity to act, even if time and money are scarce? What grievances can a community-based organization not only address but actually *win*, since a record of failure will quickly ruin an organization with a fragile financial base? What battles can an organization take on that will lead other congregations or voluntary associations to want to join the organization, not just in terms of vocal support but also in terms of dues?

IAF organizations exhort individuals to recognize and act on their self-interest, insist that compromise and negotiation are critical political tools, and follow their famous "Iron Rule": "Never do for others what they can do for themselves" (Shirley, 1997, p. 244). Because the organizations are based in inner-city churches, values embedded in the Judeo-Christian religious traditions are evident in their organizing efforts, although it should be emphasized that the IAF abstains from evangelical work and seeks to develop a broad "theology of organizing" that will include the broadest possible range of religious institutions (Warren, 2001, p. 40). The fact that the organizations are based in congregations that pay dues to support IAF organizers and their staff is important, not only because of the economic contribution but also because religious institutions play an especially important educational function in the contemporary United States for poor and working-class Americans in regards to civic engagement. Church activities provide their members with opportunities to learn skills like speech making, letter writing, committee leadership, and community advocacy, which can be translated into civic engagement (Verba et al., 1995). For African Americans and Latinos, church membership is a predictor of higher levels of civic engagement than for their nonchurched peers (Warren, 2001, p. 210).

There are nonetheless several criticisms that one can advance about IAF organizing. The IAF has been faulted for overemphasizing local (as opposed to national or international) issues, downplaying racial and ethnic differences, and concentrating on battles that can be won rather than those that should be fought on moral principle (Ganz, 2002; Warren, 2001). The IAF's emphasis on self-interest, though intending to demonstrate a spirit of tough-minded realism, might unintentionally erode the ethical sensibility that would appear to be not only a natural concomitant of its values-laden activities but also a highly desired outcome of its own ethical undertakings. The IAF's emphasis on self-interest, though intending to demonstrate a spirit of tough-minded realism, might unintentionally contribute to the kind of public apathy toward politics because it fails to appeal to our search for meaning and social justice (Shirley, 1997). Additionally, while there are strengths to the IAF's focus on congregationally based community organizing, there are also limitations, in terms of the large numbers of Americans who are either nonchurched or only attend religious institutions erratically. Finally, one should note that despite the many successes of the IAF over the past quarter century, it is precisely in this same time period that the class stratification of American society has intensified and that many indicators of civic engagement in our country indicate a worsening rather than an improvement of conditions. Given these problems, one can legitimately query whether IAF strategies really can be helpful in addressing these complex issues and enhancing participatory democracy for school improvement.

One potential rejoinder to these criticisms is related to a distinction that Sirianni and Friedland (2001) make between civic innovation in broad-based organizations like the IAF and social movements or public interest groups. Social movements, from this point of view, are driven by specific causes such as environmentalism, the women's movement, or an antiwar effort. Public interest groups such as the American Association of Retired People, the National Organization for Women, and the National Association for the Advancement of Colored People focus on constituencies bounded by a unifying identity-defining characteristic such as age, gender, and race. Groups that attempt forms of civic innovation that cross class, gender, racial, and ethnic lines have a more demanding set of challenges, for they must demonstrate to individuals and groups that they can serve their interests even though the identity issues involved are more diffuse. Identity politics based on race, language, class, or gender constitute a continual threat to organizations such as the IAF, which can only build sufficient political power to extract resources from civic leaders if its organizing crosses group lines.

Yet, even in accepting such a rejoinder, one is struck by the limitations of community organizing, reminiscent of Castells's arguments in *The City and the Grassroots* (1983), which assert that community organizing efforts, though they garner sympathy, often lack the resources to challenge the international mobilization of capital, the vagaries of the economic cycle, and the complexities of politics when played out on a national or international scale. This caveat is well taken, and one could add to it an additional concern: Although IAF organizations have displayed great resourcefulness in organizing the poor and the working class, they have failed (with few exceptions) to make common cause with other community-based organizations and political movements. However, if one is serious about developing political power, the ability to negotiate and compromise is critical not only in relationship with civic elites but also in relationship to other community-based organizations, social movements, and public interest groups.

From this perspective, community organizing as practiced by the Texas IAF is one facet of a broader approach to social change that must include alternative traditions that are perhaps more episodic and captive to special interests but also capable of mobilizing groundswells of civic capacity to promote social change. Ganz (2002) has observed that some of the most successful efforts at social change in the United States in the last half century were the civil rights movement, the women's movement, and the rise of Christian fundamentalism, all of which defied the IAF's antipathy toward social movements but have had a much larger impact than the IAF on American political life. Given the legitimacy of this criticism, a more synthetic appreciation of different kinds of strategies for social change is warranted.

Whatever one's point of departure for community organizing, it would seem imperative at this juncture to acknowledge that simply opening up formal procedures for participation—as was done in Chicago, New York, or other cities where various community control strategies have been attempted—will not create desired educational outcomes in and of themselves. Rather, the arts of democratic participation—problem identification, research actions, coalition building, accountability sessions, and a recursive return to grassroots community organizing—must be actively taught and practiced far more systemically. IAF organizing is powerful because it utilizes authentic community bases—inner-city and working-class congregations—to identify grievances, develop potential solutions, and generate political power. Similar community-based organizing skills need to be taught in schools, practiced in community settings, and engendered through a dense array of networks of civic engagement.

The acquisition of such skills is a demanding process, unlikely to generate enthusiasm among politicians and policy makers eager for quick fixes. Yet, as Cuban and Usdan (2003) suggest in the same study referred to by Chou and Tozer in chapter 1 of this volume, the powerful reforms currently being explored in American urban districts are unlikely to succeed because of their shallow roots. Districts hire corporate CEOs to run their school systems with no research evidence to support such innovations, radically transform their governance systems, or align their curricula with their assessment systems in the hopes that teaching to the test will produce better test results. Though Cuban and Usdan are sympathetic to the reforms and the reformers, they nonetheless note that the reformers are on a "fool's errand" (p. 159) if they do not ensure that the reforms are in some way linked to the perspectives and needs of both classroom teachers and the urban communities they are intended to serve. In this way, their research validates Murrell's (1998) insistence upon conjoint practices of educational change and community engagement, as well as Peterman and Sweigard's urban standards related to social justice and community activism (see chapter 2 of this volume). The need for some kind of participatory democracy—however contested and tumultuous—remains a sine qua non of real urban school reform.

Urban educators committed to democratic resolution of school, community, and policy conundrums should carefully study all of the chapters in this volume and develop their own kinds of unified field theories that would unite radical democratic theory and practice. The conceptual initial chapters, combined with the richness of the case studies that follow, indicate that we already have made significant progress in reconceptualizing and enacting a number of critical educational practices that form a coherent intellectual whole, as well as a set of mutually compatible practices that can be played out in a myriad of different urban settings. In addition to these writings by critical educators, urban educators can also benefit by certain advances in political science and sociology, especially innovations in what is now termed *empowered participatory governance* (EPG). As articulated by Fung and Wright (2003), such systems of governance are animated by three design principles. True to the values of the participatory democratic tradition, EPG emphasizes the "devolution of public decision authority to empowered local units" (Fung & Wright, 2003, p. 15). Yet more deliberately than SDS or sympathetic allies in the New Left, EPG also espouses "the creation of formal linkages of responsibility, resource distribution and communication that connect these units to each other and to superordinate, centralized authorities," as well as "the use and generation of new state institutions to support and guide these decentered problem-solving efforts" (p. 16). Hence, rather than the relatively free-floating emphasis on deliberation that SDS enunciated, EPG seeks to transform systems of governance so as to expand civic capacity, especially in regard to historically disenfranchised groups such as the poor, the working class, and people of color.

Much of EPG research thus far can seem remote to urban schools in the United States; case studies of EPG are as far-flung as innovations in participatory budget making in Porto Alegre, Brazil (Baiocchi, 2003); decentralized planning in Kerala, India (Isaac & Heller, 2003); and habitat conservation planning in the United States (Thomas, 2003). Fung's (2002) research, on the other hand, explores increased civic participation of urban African Americans in Chicago both in terms of community policing and the local school councils that were created in two major school reform laws in 1988 and 1995, respectively. Though Fung did find that participation on the local school councils disproportionately favored wealthier and better-educated Chicagoans, he also found that "by far the majority of people of color who are elected officials in Illinois serve on local school councils. This democratic experience," he contended, "favors keeping this institutional design in our repertoire of reform strategies" (Fung, 2003, p. 139). Fung did not address test scores in the Chicago case, and, given the high visibility of the new testing regimes that have swept the United States in the last 20 years, this bracketing out of student learning gains may not be an option for policy makers who have to deal with a public that is in many ways impatient for change. Nonetheless, as Murrell argues (see chapter 3 of this volume), critical educators who have a classroom-based, grounded perspective on urban education recognize that gains in pupil test scores, though most likely indicative of some progress, hardly constitute a satisfactory barometer of real pupil learning gains. Indeed, a growing body of research suggests that school personnel are learning how to "game" high-stakes testing by enacting a macabre form of "educational triage" that selects students whose results are most likely to register short-term gains and providing them with the lion's share of instructional attention (Booher-Jennings, 2005; see also Hargreaves, 2003; Lipman, 2004; McNeil, 2000). The only authentic answer acceptable to radical democratic educators to these kinds of educational distortions is to overcome the growing exclusion of the public from decision-making roles in schools that in so many ways contributes to the "weak roots" referred to by Cuban and Usdan (2003). A disengaged public that transfers control to educational experts is not a model that Americans, given our traditions of democratic public schooling, should find appealing—even if the vision of such schooling has far outpaced the more mundane and troubled reality.

The Chicago case is instructive, not because it is not flawed but because it has indicated that, even in a large urban center in North America, political transformations can be generated that provide ordinary people access to the decisions that influence their day-to-day lives. Mansbridge (2003) and Abers (2003) contend that given the vagaries and indeed the often emotionally upsetting nature of politics, advocates of both participatory democracy in general and EPG in particular must develop an expansive notion of participation that does not idealize deliberation but includes frank expression, negotiation, and compromise around issues of self-interest. Poor and working-class citizens, according to this logic, are not likely to become politically engaged unless they anticipate a realistic chance of winning a palpable outcome of immediate benefit to their families and communities. If advocates of EPG respect the role of self-interest in democratic deliberation, they need not fear such concreteness; rather, they will endorse it, as the IAF teaches in its training institutes.

Much is at stake in these deliberations. The "hot issues" in policy circles today (in particular, the implementation of the No Child Left Behind Act of 2001) are not defined by issues of democratic participation and civic engagement but rather by market-driven solutions that, if realized fully, would amount to a de facto termination of public schools. Such proposals have thus far failed to produce persuasive outcomes of pupil learning gains (Carnoy, Jacobsen, Mishel, & Rothstein, 2005). Although they are alluring in their prospect of delivery from the current cruelties of urban education, these proposals ultimately are barren because of the unintended consequences brought about in schools and communities that have already been served poorly by the unconstrained form of capitalism now so pervasive in the United States.

REFERENCES

Abers, R. N. (2003). Reflections on what makes empowered participatory governance happen. In A. Fung & E. O. Wright (Eds.), *Deepening democracy: Institutional innovations in empowered participatory governance* (pp. 200-207). New York: Verso.

Alinsky, S. (1946). *Reville for radicals*. Chicago: University of Chicago Press.

Alinsky, S. (1971). *Rules for radicals*. New York: Vintage.

Anyon, J. (1997. *Ghetto schooling: A political economy of urban school reform*. New York, NY: Teachers College Press.

Baiocchi, G. (2003). Participation, activism, and politics. The Porto Alegre experiment. In A. Fung & E. O. Wright (Eds.), *Deepening democracy: Institutional innovations in empowered participatory governance* (pp. 45-76). New York: Verso.

Benveniste, L., Carnoy, M., & Rothstein, R. (2002). *All else is equal: Are public and private schools different?* New York: Routledge Press.

Booher-Jennings, J. (2005). Below the bubble: "Educational triage" and the Texas accountability system. *American Educational Research Journal, 42*, 231–268.

Bryk, A. S., Sebring, P. B., Kerbow, D., Rollow, S., & Easton, J. Q. (1998). *Charting Chicago school reform: Democratic localism as a lever for change*. Boulder, CO: Westview.

Carnoy, M., Jacobsen, R., Mishel, L., & Rothstein, R. (2005). *The charter school dust-up: Examining the evidence on enrollment and achievement*. New York: Teachers College Press.

Castells, M. (1983). *The city and the grassroots: A cross-cultural theory of urban social movements*. Berkeley: University of California Press.

Cuban, L., & Usdan, M. (2003). *Powerful reforms with shallow roots: Improving America's urban schools*. New York: Teachers College Press.

Dewey, J. (1966). *Democracy and education*. New York: Free Press.

Fung, A. (2003). Deliberative democracy, Chicago Style: Grass-roots governance in policing and public education. In A. Fung & E. O. Wright (Eds.), *Deepening democracy: Institutional innovations in empowered participatory governance* (pp. 111-143). New York: Verso.

Fung, A. (2004). *Empowered participation; Reinventing urban democracy*. Princeton, NJ: Princeton University Press.

Fung, A., & Wright, E. O. (Eds.). (2003). *Deepening democracy: Institutional innovations in empowered participatory governance*. New York: Verso.

Ganz, M. (2002). Making democracy work? [Review of the book *Dry bones rattling: Community building to revitalize American democracy* by Mark R. Warren]. *Context, 1*(3), 62–63.

Gold, E., Simon, E., & Brown, C. (2002, March). *Strong neighborhoods, strong schools: Successful community organizing for school reform.* Chicago: Cross City Campaign for Urban School Reform.

Goode, J., & Maskovsky, J. (2001). *The new poverty studies: The ethnography of power, politics, and impoverished people in the United States.* New York: New York University Press.

Halpern, R. (1995). *Rebuilding the inner city: A history of neighborhood initiatives to address poverty in the United States.* New York: Columbia University Press.

Hargreaves, A. (2003). *Teaching in the knowledge society: Education in the age of insecurity.* New York: Teachers College Press.

Henig, J. R., Hula, R. C., Orr, M., & Pedescleaux, D. S. (1999). *The color of school reform: Race, politics and the challenge of urban education.* Princeton, NJ: Princeton University Press.

Horwitt, S. D. (1992). *Let them call me rebel: Saul Alinsky—his life and legacy.* New York: Vintage.

Isaac, T. M. T., & Heller, P. (2003). Democracy and development: Decentralized planning in Kerala. In A. Fung & E. O. Wright (Eds.), *Deepening democracy: Institutional innovations in empowered participatory governance* (pp. 77-110). New York: Verso.

Isserman, M. (1987). *If I had a hammer: The death of the old left and the birth of the new left.* New York: Basic Books.

Kaufman, A. (1969). Human nature and participatory democracy. In W. E. Connolly (Ed.), *The bias of pluralism.* New York: Atherton.

Lipman, P. (2004). *Highs stakes education: Inequality, globalization, and urban school reform.* New York: Routledge Falmer.

Mansbridge, J. (2003). Practice—thought—practice. In A. Fung & E. O. Wright (Eds.), *Deepening democracy: Institutional innovations in empowered participatory governance* (pp. 175-199). New York: Verso.

Matusow, A. J. (1984). *The unraveling of America: A history of liberalism in the 1960s.* New York: Harper & Row.

McNeil, L. M. (2000). *Contradictions of school reform: Educational costs of standardized testing.* New York: Routledge.

Mediratta, K., Fruchter, N., & Lewis, A. C. (2002). *Organizing for school reform: How communities are finding their voices and reclaiming their public schools.* New York: Institute for Education and Social Policy, New York University.

Miller, J. (1987). *"Democracy is in the streets": From Port Huron to the siege of Chicago.* New York: Simon & Schuster.

Murnane, R. J., & Levy, R. (1996). *Teaching the new basic skills.* New York: Free Press.

Murrell, P. C. (1998). *Like stone soup: The role of the professional development school in the renewal of urban schools.* Washington, DC: American Association of Colleges for Teacher Education.

Orr, M. (1999). *Black social capital: The politics of school reform in Baltimore.* Lawrence: University Press of Kansas.

Osterman, P. (2002). *Gathering power: The future of progressive politics in America.* Boston: Beacon.

Payne, C. M., & Kaba, M. (2007). So much reform, so little change: Building-level obstacles to urban school reform. *Social Policy, 37*(3-4), pp. 30-37.

Polletta, F. (2002). *Freedom is an endless meeting: Democracy in American social movements.* Chicago: University of Chicago Press.

Putnam, R. (2000). *Bowling alone: The collapse and revival of American community.* New York: Simon and Schuster.

Putnam, R. (2002). Bowling together. *The American Prospect,* Retrieved from http://www.prospect.org/cs/articles?article=bowling_together

Reich, R. B. (1991). *The work of nations: Preparing ourselves for 21st century capitalism.* New York, NY: Knopf.

Sarason, S. B. (2002). *Educational renewal: A self-scrutinizing memoir.* New York: Teachers College Press.

Shirley, D. (1997). *Community organizing for urban school reform.* Austin: University of Texas Press.

Shirley, D. (2002). *Valley interfaith and school reform: Organizing for power in south Texas.* Austin: University of Texas Press.

Sirianni, C., & Friedland, L. (2001). *Civic innovation in America: Community empowerment, public policy, and the movement for civic renewal.* Berkeley: University of California Press.

Stone, C. N., Henig, J. R., Jones, B. D., & Pierannunzi, C. (2001. *Buidling capacity: The politics of reforming urban schools.* Lawrence, KS: University of Kansas Press.

Students for a Democratic Society. (1962). *The Port Huron statement.* In J. Miller (1987). *"Democracy is in the streets:" From Port Huron to the siege of Chicago* (pp. 329-374). New York: Simon & Schuster.

Thomas, C. W. (2003). Habitat conservation planning. In A. Fung & E. O. Wright (Eds.), *Deepening democracy: Institutional innovations in empowered participatory governance* (pp. 144-174). New York: Verso.

Thucydides. (1954). *History of the Peloponnesian war* (R. Warner, Trans.). New York: Penguin.

Traub, J. (2002, October 6). A lesson in unintended consequences. *New York Times Sunday Magazine.*

Verba, S., Schlozman, K. L., & Brady, H. E. (1995). *Voice and equality: Civic voluntarism in American politics.* Cambridge, MA: Harvard University Press.

Warren, M. R. (2001). *Dry bones rattling: Community building to revitalize American democracy.* Princeton, NJ: Princeton University Press.

Williams, K. Y., & O'Reilly, C. A. (1998). Demography and diversity in organizations. In B. M. Straw & R. I. Sutton (Eds.), *Research in organizational behavior* (Vol. 20, pp. 77–140). Stamford, CT: JAI Press.

Wilson, W. J. (1999). *The bridge over the racial divide: Rising inequality and coalition politics.* Berkeley: University of California Press.

CHAPTER FIVE

It's All ABOUT Relationships: Urban Middle School Students Speak Out ON Effective Schooling Practices

MARK G. STORZ

John Carroll University

KAREN R. NESTOR

Institute for Educational Renewal, John Carroll University

> To get a good education, you need teachers that care and students that care. Teachers that care about their students, and the students, they care about themselves.
>
> —TAMEKA, URBAN MIDDLE SCHOOL STUDENT

The current climate in education, fortified by the enactment of the No Child Left Behind Act of 2001, has put great emphasis on the development of rigorous standards and detailed accountability plans for schools, plans that, in many cases, have dampened the activism of teachers in advocating practices that promote students' personal and academic achievement. A similar development has entered the arena of teacher preparation that bases teacher quality on generic competencies determined by various state and national policy makers (see chapter 2 by Peterman with Sweigard in this volume). As the standards movement has gained ever increasing momentum at all levels of education, a singular focus has developed that is based on aligning curricula to state standards and adopting approaches to teaching and learning that are often narrowly directed toward high-stakes testing. This focus on strict accountability has shifted attention away from the interpersonal and contextual factors for which students like Tameka, as indicated in the quote at the beginning of this chapter, are advocating. We suggest that these relational factors are essential to the education of all students and require a new level of activism in the teaching profession.

Recent research asserts that standards-based efforts at school reform have not met expectations (Berends, Bodilly, & Kirby, 2002), and that schools that do not attend to interpersonal factors face an increased risk of weak academic performance and students without the confidence or motivation to achieve (Arhar & Kromrey, 1993; Frymier & Houser, 2000; Ladson-Billings, 1994; MacIver & Plank, 1997). According to Darling-Hammond (1997), the political climate in education forces schools to emphasize technical procedures over regard for people, leading to continued failure. Indeed, what students tell us about their teachers and school experiences confirms that they are acutely aware of the types of teachers that both enhance and hinder their education and of the inequities that exist in urban schools. In their conversations, students identify viable strategies for teaching and developing the relationships necessary for learning, and they call educators to the kind of activism that could liberate urban schools from persistent failure.

As Peterman and Sweigard (see chapter 2 in this volume) suggest in their review of the literature, teacher quality (or lack thereof) has become a distinguishing factor in urban schools. A number of colleges and departments of education have developed teacher preparation programs focused on the preparation of teachers for urban communities (see chapter 3 by Murrell; chapter 11 by Quartz, Olsen, and Duncan-Andrade; chapter 8 by Nordgren and Peterman; chapter 4 by Shirley; and chapter 10 by Yusko in this volume). One of the challenges of such programs is to design experiences and courses of study that respond to the various standards that are externally imposed, while at the same time heeding the call of Peterman and Sweigard, among others, to develop "contextually responsive standards that represent the distinguishing characteristics of urban communities, schools and classrooms, and their students" (see chapter 2 in this volume). In searching to develop such standards, we might turn to effective urban teachers to answer a central question raised by Nieto (2003) and highlighted by Quartz, Olsen, and Duncan-Andrade (see chapter 11 in this volume): What should we know about effective, caring, committed, persevering teachers; and how can we use this knowledge to support all teachers and, in the process, to support the students who most need them? Our work suggests that an untapped resource in this process of developing contextually responsive standards and highly effective urban teachers comes from those who experience urban education on a daily basis: the students themselves. In a sense, this is inviting our urban students into our collaborative efforts—and, indeed, into their own form of activism—to prepare highly qualified urban teachers that will ultimately make a difference in the lives of the students and the communities from which they come.

From our interviews with over 200 urban middle school students, we have found that students can contribute valuable insights into the conditions and practices that can lead to the very results educators and the public seek. When we examined these students' views on their own education, four significant themes emerged: (a) The students describe the characteristics of caring teachers who enhance motivation and learning; (b) the students recognize the need for their own increased responsibility for learning and for the climate of the school and the community; (c) the students offer clear insight into developmentally responsive, learner-centered practices that closely match those outlined in the best-practices literature; and (d) the students are aware of issues of equity and fairness as they describe their educational experiences. All of these themes overlap and affirm the students' understanding that the quality of their relationships and their interactions with teachers affect every aspect of their schooling.

The purpose of this chapter is to make explicit urban students' perceptions and experiences through their own words as we examine the role that relationships play in creating conditions for successful teaching, learning, and achievement in urban environments. Using the students' voices, we support the notion that the quality of interpersonal relationships is a foundational factor in determining how successful middle schools and middle school students will be. Teachers have a clear role in developing such relationships themselves and in advocating for such relationships in schools.

PARTNERING AS THE CATALYST AND OUTCOME OF OUR WORK

The context for the work that we did with urban middle school students emerged from the community-based, action-oriented approach to urban teacher education recommended by Peterman and Sweigard (see chapter 2 in this volume). We were engaged in a university-community-school partnership in which university-based consultants teamed with the faculty of individual schools in an urban district to create professional development activities focused on school improvement. The particular school that led to this research was a middle school with serious academic and climate difficulties that had been reconfigured into a kindergarten-through-eighth-grade school. We were asked to support its teachers' efforts to make this transition and, at the same time, to address the low levels of academic achievement among its student population.

This school presented many challenges that are endemic in urban schools. Teachers were under great pressure to improve performance on high-stakes tests, yet they were still working largely in isolation within the school. The district and the teachers themselves were focused on the behavior of students and felt that discipline was a prerequisite to attempting to address issues of teaching and learning. The school's new principal wanted to support improvement but met with resistance from teachers who were suspicious of new leadership. We were faced with the dilemma that Murrell highlights in chapter 3 of this volume, that of university people entering into partnership with high-need, low-performing urban schools with little or no knowledge about what accomplished practice in such contexts really looks like. To provide us with information and to give teachers and the principal a small window into the possibilities of collaboration, we organized a summer seminar in which participating teachers could air their concerns about the climate of the school while examining adolescent development and practice in an informal setting. As a result of this seminar, teachers made plans for the start of the new school year and agreed to participate in ongoing professional development throughout the year.

At the start of the school year, the teachers presented their work on school climate to the rest of the faculty, creating the beginnings of teacher leadership within the school. A small group of faculty members joined in a graduate course at the school to explore practices that might improve teaching and learning. We also met on a regular basis with grade-level teams and on an occasional basis at faculty meetings to expand the reach of the dialogue. Often, attempts to discuss or implement best practices met with opposition because of teachers' feelings of frustration, anger, and hopelessness about the prospects for improvement. Teachers had come to believe that the contemporary educational theories did not apply to their own students. As we tried to create alternative ways to build dialogue with the teachers, we thought it might be helpful for them to hear what their students had to say about their schooling, so we began interviewing the students. We were stunned by what we learned from them. Their voices have become the basis for our ongoing work in other schools and other settings.

PRIVILEGING STUDENT VOICE

Student voice, often absent in the past from educational research, has emerged as a potential force in educational reform movements. A number of researchers have recognized this absence and have promoted the inclusion of students' perceptions in the discourse on school change (Cook-Sather, 2002; Giroux, 1988; Kruse, 2000; Lincoln, 1995; McLaren, 1994; Nieto, 1994; Waxman, 1989). In heeding this call, a variety of educational research studies have been conducted that privilege students' educational experiences as a means of providing "clear messages about what occurs in classrooms and what is and is not considered effective" (Kruse, 2000, p. 77). Some of this research has been conducted to illuminate at-risk and minority students' insights into how they learn most successfully (Howard, 2001; Muir, 2001), resegregation within desegregated schools (Bush, Burely, & Causey-Bush, 2001), and urban education reform (Wilson & Corbett, 2001) and has served to introduce students' perceptions as a catalyst for change.

Through the use of focus-group interviews, we examined urban middle school students' views on their educational experiences, particularly on the types of teachers and pedagogical practices that they perceived to be most beneficial to their achievement and success in school. Our study took place in four urban middle schools in a large midwestern metropolitan area. Three of the schools were located in an inner-city area and were part of a large urban school district. The fourth school was located in a smaller urban district adjacent to the first. In all, over 200 randomly selected sixth-, seventh-, and eighth-grade students were interviewed. Teachers at the schools reported that the students selected represented a cross section of personalities and ability levels, providing us with what we think is a balanced perspective of these students' experiences, ideas, and beliefs about their education. We jointly conducted the 45- to 60-minute interviews with each group of students. An interview protocol that we developed before the interviews asked students about their perceptions of the quality of education they were receiving and about the types of teachers and instructional practices that both helped and hindered their learning.

WHAT WE HEARD

Listening to the students' voices has been a powerful and enlightening opportunity. Students were thoughtful in responding to our questions, often mulling them over or asking for clarification before responding. At other times, students were immediate, even impulsive, in their responses, particularly to questions they found relevant. Conversations were often animated, with a number of students all trying to talk at the same time. Students' beliefs about best practices and the quality of effective teachers and their awareness and understanding of inequity were substantiated in these conversations time and again. In the following sections, we utilize the students' actual words without substantive editing to illustrate their ideas and beliefs about the types of teachers and practices that help them succeed in school. All of the names are pseudonyms, and the extended dialogue that we include is from actual conversations we had with students. Some of these conversations are fictionalized in that quotes from different interviews have been joined to create a coherent conversation around a particular theme (see Richardson, 1994; Storz, 1998).

Caring Teachers

Barth (1991) has suggested that, among other things, what needs to be improved in schools is the quality of the interpersonal relationships that are at the core of the educational process. The students we interviewed affirmed his assertion, as is noted in the words of one seventh grader who told us, "The better relationship you have with your teacher, the easier it is to learn." The variety of relationships that exist in a school setting reflect the many different dynamics that are based on both function and need. Noddings (1992) uses the concept of caring to describe a particular type of relationship that is integral to the teaching and learning process. Caring was often cited by the students we interviewed as an important component of their schooling experiences. A student named Tameka summed it up this way: "To get a good education, you need teachers that care and students that care. Teachers that care about the students and the students, they care about themselves."

Caring is generally perceived as a prerequisite for establishing an environment that is conducive to children's learning (Collinson, Killeavy, & Stephenson, 1999; Gay, 2000; Knowles & Brown, 2000). The research further asserts that the presence or absence of caring in the teacher-student relationship has a significant impact on student achievement (Gay, 2000; Muller, Katz, & Dance, 1999; Nieto, 1994). Noddings (1992) explains caring as an ethic of relation, a reciprocal relationship that involves the active participation of the persons both providing and receiving the care. In the student-teacher relationship, the teacher, when in the role of caregiver, knows and understands the students well and, as a result, is able to effectively respond to them. The students, for their part, recognize the teacher's efforts, experience the caring, and respond in some appropriate manner. When asked to think about a teacher who cared for them and to describe the teacher's actions that expressed that care, the students we interviewed readily acknowledged the efforts of many of their teachers, while also recognizing the absence of such efforts.

The students distinguished caring in the student-teacher relationship in a variety of ways. As one student noted, "I think all teachers care, all teachers want to see students succeed, it is just their approach. Different teachers give different approaches." Many, if not most, of the students indicated that caring teachers are committed to student learning. One student recalled a fourth-grade teacher who "taught us what we needed to know. She wanted us to learn so bad that she was willing to do whatever it takes, and that's what I call a teacher." "Doing whatever it takes" was often cited by students as they described the characteristics and actions of caring teachers. Muller et al.'s (1999) research supports this aspect of a caring teacher-student relationship. They conclude, in part, that students are more willing to "invest in teachers who care enough to do whatever is necessary to facilitate student learning" (p. 316).

Students recognized the efforts of teachers who provided the support and encouragement necessary for their learning. The following exchange is representative of many of our conversations with the students:

DAVID: Like Mr. L., he always stays on our tail and he never lets us slack up because say we're slacking in doing our homework. He'll get on us and call our house or he'll give us a little tap on the head like, "Come on, you got to do better." He gives us like speeches and he tells us stories from his life. He makes us feel confident because he teaches us what we need to know.

TYRELL: He's encouraging us to get our grades up. ... He puts our confident up saying that we can do it; he doesn't tell us, "Oh, I can fail you."

TAMEKA: That's what's good about him. He's happy when we try. Like some teachers are mad when we get it wrong and they say, "Oh, we already explained this to you." But when we try and we still get it wrong he'll just say, "At least you tried, but let me tell you how to do this." Just like that.

TYRELL: And it makes me feel good when the teacher boosts you up and tells you can be somebody. It makes you feel good. Like one teacher, he always says, "You can be somebody. Don't be nobody at Burger King flipping burgers. Be somebody!" He always boosts our confident up.

TAMEKA: And our teachers tell us that you're going to make it, and they don't just tell you, "Oh no, you're not going to be anything."

Implicit in the conversations with the students are references to high expectations, high standards, and persistence on the part of both the teachers and students. In writing about culturally responsive pedagogy, Gay (2000) suggests that, "Teachers who care hold them [the students] accountable for high quality academic, social, and personal performance and ensure that this happens. They are demanding but facilitative, supportive and accessible" (p. 50). Many students appear to expect high standards and demanding work from their teachers. In talking about a teacher who was not perceived as caring, a student lamented, "Mrs. W. gave out work sheets. We had her for math and science. We did work sheets all day. That's not teaching." Conversely, a student in the same conversation reflecting on a teacher who was considered caring stated that "She's trying to help you out. That's why she's tough. Probably some wouldn't see her as caring, but that's why she's on them all the time, to help them bring in their work right." Another student chimed in, "They make you keep striving. They break it down and explain it, and let you do it over." On this last point, some students indicated that caring teachers were the ones who did not just give students the answers when working to help them understand challenging content, but rather helped them come to their own understanding. "A good teacher," according to one of the seventh graders, "is going to help you figure out why you don't understand it and help you figure it out."

There was also a clear sense of a lack of caring on the part of some teachers and the devastating effect this can have on students. The following conversation serves to highlight this perception:

> TENILLE: You know, the ones that usually don't care are the ones who like quit teaching after awhile. They're not the same as the beginning of year. They'll be really strong, and then they'll just start dropping and quitting and they won't stick with it. The other teachers would stay on us all year and not quit.
>
> CAROL: Some of the teachers they'll tell you like they don't care to hear your problems. "Go to talk to the mediator" or whatever and that would like have the problem grow even more than what it should be.
>
> TENILLE: Most of the teachers, it's like if you don't do your work they don't care. They'd say, "I don't care, it's not my education. This is your education and if you want to fail you can fail on your own."
>
> OMAR: Well, my reaction is that if a teacher doesn't care because I failed one of my classes, then I don't know what to do.

In reflecting on caring teachers, one student suggested that "It's not only about school." Students clearly saw their relationship with their teachers extending beyond the confines of the classroom, suggesting that caring teachers are committed to the social and personal aspects of their students' lives, as well as their academic performance. One student summarized it this way: "If they [caring teachers] see you're in a situation where you're in trouble, they'll try and help you out." Another student spoke of a teacher "who tried to protect me from getting in trouble." Caring teachers were portrayed as those who are willing to listen and get involved in family situations; for example, one student talked about a teacher who "cares about family problems. If I had a parent beating on me, she makes sure that somebody knows about this." Another student affectionately described a teacher who knew that her parents were divorcing: "Everyday, she [the teacher] would ask me how I was doing: 'How's the divorce doing?' And I'd say, 'Oh, it's so nice you asking me.' She didn't have to, but she did anyway."

The students often talked about teachers assuming the role of advocate, particularly as it related to personal and family problems, with trust closely linked to such a caring relationship. One student explained his notion of trust this way:

> Because me and one of my friends, we started having problems, like family issues and stuff. She would help us out because we were too afraid to go to the counselor because we were afraid they would call our parents and tell them what we thought. … She would listen to our problems and she thought it would be better if we went to the counselor, so we went and it all worked out so we knew we could trust her.

Trust was often associated with caring, as noted in this conversation between two seventh-grade students in response to a prompt about caring teachers:

ROCHELLE: I'd say like if you get into something like you didn't want to tell your mother or father, you'll tell the teacher because you need to trust in that teacher.

SHERRY: The reason I think Mr. J. is a good teacher is because he keeps it between you and him, not the office or whatever.

ROCHELLE: He knows everything about me and knows how to help me in my work and what I going through and don't tell my business either.

SHERRY: I agree with both of them. Like what he said: He doesn't go spreading your business.

Active listening, defined by the students as resulting in some action on the part of the teacher on their behalf, was another important attribute of the caring teacher. One story is particularly poignant:

JORDAN: I know Ms. P. cares for us, cares for me, because she listens to what I have to say, and she actually does something about it instead of just saying she will. I see that she does.

DeSHAWN: One of our teachers, she used to be real mean. She took one day to sit down and talk to us and now she's nicer. She looked at our point of view and actually asked us, like, how do we think she teaches?

INTERVIEWER: How did you feel when the teacher asked you what you thought?

DENISE: We were shocked that she would actually ask our input on how to teach.

INTERVIEWER: Now, did you all change your behavior in class after that?

DENISE: We changed a lot. We started acting better and listening to what she had to say, and she started listening to what we had to say.

There was also a sense among the students that caring was associated with respect, which itself was represented by the students as a multidimensional construct. In one particularly animated group, we posed the question, "Do you feel like your teachers respect you?" Without hesitation, the students responded with the following:

EVAN: Not all teachers. Some teachers. They threaten us. And the way they treat you! They want us to treat them with respect, but then we don't get our respect back.

SHARYN: It would help us if the teachers show us respect like they want to get respect. I mean we probably not adults, but we want respect just like they want respect.

JUSTIN: One who cares about me, I give them more respect. I listen to them, and then if I have problems, I come and talk to them, because people that don't show respect, I don't like to talk to them.

SHARYN: Like, I know this one teacher. She kept comparing us to other people. You keep comparing us to other people we won't learn nothing unless YOU [student's emphasis] learn something new. That why we act the way we act. And she compares us to different types of people. Like today, she compared us to Chinese people—how they know how to speak our language better than we do. And comparing us to other classes. We're not like them classes. We're all different people. We think different. Stop comparing us to other classes. It's harder for some kids.

Some students spoke of the tone of the student-teacher relationship when explaining their notion of respect. The following conversation is reflective of much of the dialogue around this theme in other interviews:

INTERVIEWER: How do you know when a teacher is being respectful of you?

TIFFANY: When they don't holler at you. Or like if you're arguing with them and they don't argue back, they show respect to you. Like they're not going to stoop down to your level.

DAVID: Caring teachers don't yell if you don't get it right. … He says "We'll work it out."

TASHARA: She talks to you. She won't scream or yell. She'll take time to listen.

DAVID: Just screaming at the kids, that's not really helping them, because they're going to keep on doing it because maybe at home they get hollered at a lot and so they're used to it and they think that's the right thing that's supposed to happen. They're going to keep on doing the same thing, but if you try to work with them—really, really, really hard—and work out their problems, maybe they won't be the same any more and they'll be a changed person.

Students in our study also made a connection between caring and commitment to the profession. While we may understand that commitment on the teacher's part underlies the type of caring we see reflected in the students' words, the students themselves saw commitment as another discrete quality of the caring teacher. A common theme among many students is summarized in one student's suggestion that a caring teacher "teaches you because she loves it instead of just teaching you to be paid." Striking a similar chord, another student defined caring in this way: "trying to help students instead of just being there to give grades so you can get paid and get out." Yet another student said, "If you really want to teach, then do it. But if you really don't, then don't. It's a job you got to like."

Personal Responsibility

Noddings (1992) described schools as "centers of care—places where they [students] are cared for and will be encouraged to care deeply themselves" (p. 65). The students we interviewed seemed to recognize this aspect of the caring relationship when they linked caring to their own responsibility to participate in relationships within the school in ways that promote effective learning. Many of their comments match the call by Weinberger and McCombs (2001) to give students increased responsibility for their school experiences within a context of strong relationships and to "teach children and youth to avoid negative classroom behaviors, increase personal and social responsibility for school and societal safety, and cultivate empathy and morality" (p. 6).

Both Glickman (1998) and Noddings (1992) describe caring and responsibility in terms of a reciprocal relationship between teachers and students. This reciprocity did emerge in our discussions with the students, as articulated by the student who said, "You can't blame it all on the teachers not teaching. It's part of our fault, too ... in order for them to teach, we have to pay attention." As a result of this emphasis on caring, we began to ask whether the fact that teachers cared had any direct impact on students' behavior or own sense of caring and responsibility. The following exchange illustrates many of our conversations:

THEA: If you know your teacher actually care, you'll try your hardest in there so you like make them feel proud of you. ... But if you know a teacher don't really care, or they seem like they don't care, why would you care? That what it makes me feel like.

KAY: When you get a teacher that cares, you'll try and do your work and stuff real hard. If a teacher's trying to dog you out, some people try to dog them back.

LISA: When they give us respect, we give them respect. We got equal trades. They do their work. We do our work. We do everything for them, and they do everything for us. That's all it about, is respect, that's all.

KAY: It causes me to respect a teacher more and behave more as I should with them because they take their time to help me, and I should take my time to help and respect them.

LISA: Yes. Because if somebody respects you, you should respect them back because you should do unto others as how you want to be done unto.

Students' focus on their responsibility for their own learning extended to working to devise personal learning strategies. One said, "Some people always looking for the teacher to help them, where if you sit down and really pay attention, you will eventually get it. And it helps you to learn better, finding ways to learn on your own." Describing her own role, a seventh grader said, "It takes a teacher AND [student's emphasis] a student to be getting a good education, because it takes participation and being able to listen and understand ... which is the standard of an education." The American Psychological Association (1997) notes that teachers should work with students to develop higher-order metacognitive strategies, because "successful learners are active, goal-directed, self-regulating and assume personal responsibility for contributing to their own education" (p. 1).

Students seem to understand intuitively that learning such strategies will increase their academic efficacy and achievement (Pintrich & Schunk, 1996). One student described a desire for deeper thinking about learning when he said,

> When you give assignments, they tell us to do it, but they don't tell us how to do it and why to do it. ... I said to my teacher, "How would this help us?" and she be like, "Don't be asking so many questions." They teach us but they don't say why or how. ....
> And I think that is a big part of education and teaching itself.

In one school, a number of students talked about a goal-setting process through which teachers worked with them to take responsibility for their own work. They clearly liked the idea of setting goals for their own performance. An eighth grader said, "You have a lot of goals, like personal and educational. And if you meet your goal or you get close, then that's like success because you'll feel better, because you did what you aimed to do." Some, however, did not feel they gained as much as they would from a more complete process:

> I don't know for sure if it really helps ... because if you don't really think about it, then you're not going to do anything. If you just write them [the goals] down just to write it down ... if you don't mean it then it won't make a difference.

Students also told us that teachers rarely returned to these goals to consider if the students had reached them. Middle school teachers who use goal setting with students agree that it can be an important strategy for building student responsibility for their lives (Brown, 2001). Goal setting reinforces that notion that effort leads to success, thus increasing self-efficacy (Pintrich & Schunk, 1996).

Beyond their own learning, students expressed a desire to take more responsibility for the quality of school life by developing strong reciprocal relationships based on caring within the school community. An eighth grader who was elected president of the student council (which rarely met) lamented, "We don't have a voice or say in anything that goes on here. I try, trust me, I try talking to everybody I possibly can." They told us that students want to be of service within the school: "Like people should work in the office and stuff. ... it would be like helping the principal. Teach people about things. Yeah, jobs, at other schools they have jobs." Another said,

> [We should] take time to sit down and talk with [younger kids] and see what they need help in or what's the problem. Like if they can't read, ask the teacher, "Say, Mrs. So-and-so, may I sit down with so-and-so and help him read because he's having trouble."

Expanding this notion further, one student explained,

> Mr. S. is into that whole service learning part, and he told us that he just don't want to teach us, but he wants us to actually get out there and use what we've learned and helping people. ... I think it's made learning easier for me.

Much of the literature on middle schools encourages "integrating community-based opportunities firmly within the curriculum" (Jackson & Davis, 2000, p. 211). There is also an emphasis on meaningful service learning, which, when combined with opportunities for reflection, provides students opportunities to become "more empowered at school because of their sense of having decision-making opportunities and recognition from adults" (Jackson & Davis, 2000, p. 212). The students seem to agree with the literature that suggests that they will feel more respected and perform better when they are held to higher levels of responsibility within the school and beyond.

Learner-Centered Practices

When students told us about teaching practices that are effective, it became clear that the practices they highlighted require strong relationships between students and teachers. Delpit (1994) affirms that educational practices must be rooted in knowledge of students. She says, "You have to know the kids. They teach me how to teach them. They may be from all kinds of backgrounds and cultures, but if you really listen to them, they'll teach you how to teach them" (p. 120). Developing relationships with students and listening to their voices, then, are imperative if educators are to determine which practices will be most effective in producing high levels of student achievement (Glickman, 1998).

Perhaps the most significant aspect of the impact that relationships have on learning is the students' sense of teachers' expectations for them. This is particularly compelling given the literature on urban schools uncovered by Peterman and Sweigard (see chapter 2 in this volume) that underscores the prevalence of low expectations for urban students. In almost every group we interviewed, students referred to the ways in which teachers' expectations affect their school experiences. Students consistently applauded teachers who "push us to do our work," who "expect a lot of me," who "won't let us give up." On the other hand, students were adamant, and at times even angry, about the low level of work they were experiencing. Take, for example, this exchange among seventh-grade students:

RONALD: We just read a book, then do work sheets. Read the next thing, then do a work sheet.

ROBERT: It gets played out. It gets boring doing it over and over and over again.

THOMAS: We need more work to do. Harder work.

ROBERT: We in seventh grade, and they started giving us multiplication.

THOMAS: And they always talking about "you in seventh grade you need to start acting like you all in seventh grade." Well, teach us like we in seventh grade.

The students' comments confirm research which suggests that teachers' attitudes and expectations have a powerful impact on whether students and teachers will have a positive or negative relationship and on the effectiveness of the learning environment (Gay, 2000; Muller et al., 1999).

The need for teachers to know their students well was also apparent as students described the content of the curriculum. The students we interviewed were eager to learn about ideas and things connected to their lived experience and to their views of the so-called real world. They spoke with enthusiasm about learning experiences that focused on topics like the Holocaust, gangs, or the human body. One student summarized this when she said, "We growing up kind of fast, and we need to start learning things more about the real world." Students frequently mentioned their eagerness to learn about their own culture, its history, and its position in society. One asked, "How will I learn without knowing my history?" Another student added,

> Like we said about civil rights. Because when you go back through history books, you see. You know how you watch a movie and you don't understand why they did stuff like that and you want to go to the teacher and ask them, "Why did they hassle like that?" You want to learn about it; that's what you want to learn. Say you want to be a civil rights leader when you're grown up or be in Congress or something like that. You want to know what's politics and you want to know what deals with that. You want to learn what it is about.

After we had interviewed a number of students, we noticed that none had mentioned anything about having a choice of topics or assignments, so we asked one group directly, "Do you get much choice in the work you do?" That entire group responded in unison, "No!" One student complained that he had questions that his teacher was unwilling to explore in class: "When we talked about Black history, I asked him [the teacher], 'What if it was the other way around? What if the Whites were the slaves and the Blacks were rich?'" The student sadly informed us that the teacher did not respond. In one school, a few students mentioned choices, like the one who stressed,

> She [a teacher] lets you talk about yourself. When you tell her the activities you like to do, she lets you make a project, like who invented this, or like back in the days when all White folks did all the stuff—Black folks did a lot of stuff, too.

Another group of students had this exchange around the issue of choice:

> VINCENT: Like in my school, they don't give us choices on what we will learn. Like when Ms. M. taught the book, nobody wanted to read it. So she said, "Take out your books and read." And everybody's like, "no," because they don't want to read it.

STEPHANIE: I want them to do something in school when you learn what you want to be like. Because I want to be an interior designer, but I got to learn graphic design for computer. We don't do that in school.

VINCENT: If we was able to choose something that we like, maybe we'd be more interested in the book and want to read it. They be like, "it's my choice." They just like give us stuff and so that's what we got to do.

The students seemed to agree with Weinberger and McCombs (2001) that "When learners of any age are empowered and feel ownership for their own learning, by virtue of having a voice and a choice, *they are more willing to learn and be invested in their own learning* [italics in text]" (p. 8). The students seemed eager to engage with content that encourages inquiry about important problems and questions, that is culturally relevant, and that uses their own life experiences and values as the foundation for moving beyond their own experiences into a broader understanding of the world (Darling-Hammond, 1997; Gay, 2000; Ladson-Billings, 1994).

The students expressed an interest in exploring important topics and issues, but they also recognized their need for developmentally appropriate practices that scaffold their learning. Once again, they implied that teachers need to know them well enough to recognize their academic needs. According to one seventh grader:

She's [the teacher] give me stuff like ninth grade work and I was in sixth grade. She give me the paper and I didn't know what to do, so I take it home, do research on it, try to learn or whatever. I don't really know it, and she knew that.

Another shared the following comments:,

We were supposed to get up and read our paper and try to persuade her [the teacher], but she didn't teach us how to persuade. She just read out the book and we had to write five paragraphs. But I didn't know how to persuade nobody using that voice.

A third student described a teacher who met her needs:

He would tell you something, and you ask him a question and he give you all this feedback on the thing you asked him, and, he would constantly, constantly give you stuff you can use for it. And if you keep asking him another question, he keep giving you feedback, and he was such a big help.

These students seem to agree with Ladson-Billings (1994), who writes that, "When teachers provide instructional 'scaffolding,' students can move from what they know to what they need to know" (p. 124).

The students were very clear in describing effective teaching strategies that are frequently described in the literature on middle school, developmentally responsive, and learner-centered teaching (Horowitz, et al., 2005; Irvin, 1997; Jackson & Davis, 2000; Knowles & Brown, 2000; National Middle School Association, 2003). The students with whom we spoke embraced active, engaged learning. They expected and desired challenge. They did not reflect the complacency that is often associated with young urban adolescents. They in effect contradicted the notion of "good teaching," as it is often defined in urban contexts, as "merely a matter of teachers getting the students to do their work under an uncomfortable détente with the students" (see chapter 3 by Murrell, in this volume). For example, one student, when asked about the type of teaching that helped her learn, blurted out,

> Experiment. Cause I always believe that we make learning fun, we learn more. You want to get energized. I couldn't stand science, but last year we did a lot of experiments and it got me active and got me to like it.

A classmate added,

> I just want to do it. I don't want to be just hearing it. I want to be actually feeling what she [the teacher] saying. It doesn't have to be this really big thing. Anything will help. Cause even the littlest thing matter. Cause if you see, if you have a visual scene of something, then you really understand it more than just hearing it from someone. You can actually see what you doing and see how it was done and see the outcome. You dying to jump in.

Students had varied opinions of cooperative learning or other forms of group work as effective strategies. Most of them agreed with the student who said the following:

> I like group work. But sometimes people be wigging on the group. Then you don't learn as much. But you learn a lot better if everyone's working. Yeah, especially with a couple of student in my homeroom. I like to work with them because they real smart. I like working with those kind of people.

Another added, "Group work helps us to learn better because we can discuss our answers and questions within the group." When we probed further, we found that students often worked in groups without first receiving from their teachers the "time and effort dedicated to preparing students for the cooperative experience and for their roles as peer tutors to the other members of their teams" (MacIver & Plank, 1997, p. 245). Again, the quality of the relationships, this time among the students themselves, seems to have a direct impact on the outcomes. Students might agree with Gay (2000) that they want to engage in caring relationships and work closely with competent peers to achieve learning outcomes.

Equitable Relationships

In our discussions thus far, we have focused on the students' beliefs and understandings about how the teacher-student relationship influences their school experiences. This focus on the teacher and student is an obvious one, and one that is typically associated with the public debate on accountability as well. Some of the students we interviewed had a more broad understanding of shared responsibility, which suggested the role the larger community plays in their success in school. What we heard suggests that some students are keenly aware of the literature's assertion that urban schools are "politically inequitable, too complex, and resource poor to address the concerns of all constituencies" (see chapter 2 by Peterman with Sweigard in this volume). It is interesting and, we think, important to note that students' discussions about the relationship between the individual and the community emerged from them and their thinking about the quality of their schooling experiences, not from a specific prompt in our interview protocol that would lead them to discuss the issue.

Some of the urban middle school students in our study seemed to understand that they have a relationship with society that is flawed, and, as a result, the quality of their education is compromised. The inequities identified by the students were most often associated with curricular issues and lack of resources—human, financial, and physical. Researchers in the area of educational equity have highlighted similar issues. Murphy (1988), for example, has suggested an emerging conception of educational equity that is "concerned more with the distribution of alterable educational resources and school practices (i.e., time, quality of teaching, course content covered, and homework) than with the allocation of aggregated resources per se" (p. 146). Similar criteria for judging educational equity have been suggested by Davidman and Davidman (1998), with attention also focused on the quality of pedagogical practices and on student morale in the classroom.

The comments made about issues related to inequities associated with curriculum often came from students who previously had gone to schools in other districts or from students who had contact with students from other districts, particularly in suburban areas. What we heard confirmed the students' awareness of the reality that, as Fuhrman suggests, urban students suffer from "low achievement—generally significantly lower than suburban districts" (as cited in chapter 2, by Peterman with Sweigard, in this volume). Two students reflected on this situation when they commented:

> TENILLE: They're teaching stuff in the eighth grade that I learned like probably in third or fourth grade because at [this more affluent district] they teach you stuff that's real hard so you really, really know something. Now here, they teach you stuff that's real easy.

> ANSON: My cousins go to Lakeview and we call each other every day on the phone and they ask me "what did you learn?" I really can't tell them nothing because, every time it's the same thing, and they tell me different stuff every day. When they ask me, I'm telling the same thing over and over again and they say, "Do you learn anything new?" and I'm saying, "No not really."

Another eighth-grade student, in discussing his experiences taking an entrance exam for a private high school in the area, shared at length a conversation he had with a friend and the friend's father, who was a principal from a local suburban district. Here, he was trying to explain why he didn't do as well as expected on the test or as well as his friend:

> I thought that I did a bad job. I thought I was sleepy. ... I wasn't focused enough but as we talked I showed him [the principal] our math book and our language book, and their books are way more advanced than ours. They only in the seventh grade and have more advanced books than us. They start off with multiplication like we do, but then they go straight to algebra and stuff. We take the basics. They jump into what they need to learn.

In analyzing the students' thoughts and ideas about issues related to equity, it is evident that, in their own way, they see inequity as being closely intertwined in the teaching and learning process and in the various levels of relationships that exist in the school environment. In the following conversation, which resulted from a question about achieving success, curriculum content, pedagogical practices, and resources all intersect to help explain the students' lack of confidence about passing the state's proficiency examination:

> PAUL: We got to take the ninth-grade proficiency test. In certain sections, like math, I don't think we going to pass, and in science, too.
>
> INTERVIEWER: You don't feel like you are being prepared in science?
>
> PAUL: He just puts the words on the board and we copy them down.
>
> VALERIE: He'll explain some of it, but ...
>
> INTERVIEWER: How would you learn better in science?
>
> PAUL: If he stand in front of the class and would explain it and just go step by step.
>
> JOSEPH: Do experiments, like science book experiments.
>
> PAUL: Like if they got more teachers, like [another school district] do. Then everybody would pass.

This issue of a lack of human resources was on the minds of a number of students at a building where having permanent teachers during a given year was a challenge. Students recognized teacher turnover as having a direct impact on their not receiving a quality education:

INTERVIEWER: Do you feel you are getting a good education?

PAUL: We ain't getting it here.

INTERVIEWER: Why do you say that?

LISA: We ain't got no teachers.

PAUL: And we still ain't got no teacher. She been gone since last marking period and no principal, nobody never made an effort to get a teacher in that class. They want to keep getting a substitute. We don't need to keep on changing teachers. We need a permanent teacher that's going to sit there and teach. How we going to be so smart when we don't have nobody to teach us?

As Noddings (2002) notes, "One of the essential elements in learning to be cared for is continuity" (p. 26). Some students were clearly frustrated by the lack of permanent teachers during this particular academic year, yet another indication of students' awareness of the contextual factors that distinguish urban schools. The following exchange is particularly interesting:

DANIELLE: First we had Ms. P. She said she couldn't teach because the class was all talking. So then after her we had Ms. W. Ms. W. gave out work sheets all day. That's not teaching though. Then we had Mr. M. He only stayed for what, three days?

DONALD: Then we had that guy that looked like Austin Powers, and then that old man.

REGGIE: Now we got Mr. P., but we don't know if he gonna stay because our school is just off the hood.

Students also recognized the impact on their learning experiences of what they perceived to be a lack of financial and physical resources. One eighth-grade student raised the issue of money and suggested that "They [students in suburbs] progress more faster than us, probably cause of the money situations or probably because we don't have that many teachers that know all the material without getting it out of a book." In the following excerpt from a conversation in which students were talking about creative instructional practices, the issue of resources was raised again:

TAMEKA: Everyone wants to have a science lab but this school don't have money to do stuff like that. We don't have a lot of materials to do stuff like that.

JASMINE: It is a big problem. Like in art, we don't do nothing. We just sit there and do homework for other classes. Cause we got broke up crayons and broke up chalk and stuff.

TAMEKA: We have no money, we are just like so broke.

CAROL: We could do our own fund-raiser …

JASMINE: Or a grant or something …

TAMEKA: They could get us to write a grant. That way when they teach us, higher percentage of the people pass the test, and that way the school could raise more money and buy whatever they wanted, the materials that they need.

CAROL: Ain't nobody trying to do nothing. That's the problem.

In this exchange, the students suggested that they were willing to share in the responsibility for addressing the lack of resources in the school. In another of our interview groups, the president of the student council lamented about the obstacles he faced in that position. He shared with us the following:

Students come to me and say, "Man, you supposed to change things." Well I mean, I try. Trust me, I try talking to everybody I possibly can. I went downtown [to the school district central office] and try to talk. They told me I couldn't do it, cause it was already written up. Went to the principal try to get her to talk to them. Couldn't do it. Education, everyday in class we ask the teachers for more materials. We can't learn like this.

For the students who recognized the various sources of inequity in their education, there was a passion in their voices that underscored the significance of this issue for them. This final quote from a seventh-grade girl demonstrates her acute awareness of inequity, the complexity of the issue, and the depth at which it can affect urban middle school students:

Why we got a new stadium when no books. ... Don't nobody want to talk about that ... they always want to write about what's wrong with our school, but they don't know. Some of these kids in here got a 4.0 average ... when they come here these teachers don't want to teach. They would just give up. If something don't go their way, they will get up, walk out of class, put on their coat, go jump in their new car, and then just leave. Then they expect everything to be just handy dandy gravy. Then you go out to the suburb ... that's what they always comparing us to. Well, when you hear this is this and that is that because it's teachers that care there. I mean probably they get paid more than these teachers here. ... I don't understand.

CONCLUSIONS

Insights gained from this research provide policy makers, teacher educators, in-service teachers, and preservice teachers a glimpse into how urban middle school students at four particular schools perceive their daily life experiences in school. More specifically, this study illuminates the way in which the quality of relationships provides the foundation for environmental conditions and instructional practices that students see as both enhancing and inhibiting their overall achievement and success in school. Such insights may provide teachers at all levels an opportunity to reflect critically on their own practice and the practices within their schools, particularly as such practices serve to promote or obstruct meaningful learning experiences for their current or future students. More specifically, we believe that the students' insights call educators to action and provide them with material for discussion and further research in each of the thematic areas we have explored.

Caring Teachers

The students to whom we talked clearly affirm the connection between the care teachers show toward their students and the quality of the learning environment that results. These urban middle school students recognize teachers' efforts to care in both the academic and personal realms, and they identify specific qualities that a caring teacher demonstrates. As noted by one of the students we interviewed, "all teachers care," a sentiment with which most of us would agree when reflecting on ourselves. However, the care described by the students to whom we talked was more than a feeling or a sentiment. It involves action, persistence, and involvement—"doing whatever it takes," as one student reminded us. Listening to the voices of these students provides insights into how they perceive their relationships with their teachers and challenges us to reflect and reconsider the relationships and interactions we have with our students on a daily basis. The lack of care identified by the students requires teachers to exercise leadership among their colleagues in order to develop and nurture caring behavior throughout the school environment. Further research examining students' responses to their teachers' efforts to care for them may serve to illuminate connections between teacher care and students' personal responsibility. In addition, research that seeks to uncover the obstacles to teachers caring in meaningful ways for their students might highlight ways of enhancing student-teacher relationships.

Personal Responsibility

Students recognize their own need to take greater responsibility for their personal and academic growth. This is an important aspect of our work with students, since there is a common misconception about young adolescents as being unmotivated, apathetic, and unwilling to take personal responsibility for their learning, as well as with other aspects of their lives. The students we interviewed seem to see that responsibility, rooted in an environment of trust, respect, and high expectations, builds their capacity for contributing within the school and community. Teachers can explore the extent to which school practices that involve students in curriculum decisions, team planning, goal setting, and regular follow-up on goals, self-evaluation, and service within the school and the community might enhance the students' academic and personal success. While some research indicates a positive connection between service and a reduction in risk factors for youth (Schine, 1997), further research needs to explore the ways in which service supports academic achievement. After listening to students, it appears that teachers should look for ways to involve the students themselves (in partnership with teachers) in forms of activism that will lead them to "actually participate in a pluralistic community, talking together, making decisions, and coming to understand multiple views" (Darling-Hammond, 1997, p. 30).

Learner-Centered Practices

Students' perspectives confirm various theories and strategies in the literature that affirm developmentally appropriate, constructivist practices and that contribute to a science of teaching. Teachers in urban settings sometimes believe that the theories they have learned do not apply to their own students, yet the students' voices call for high expectations and positive encouragement for achievement. They assert that they learn best when they are engaged in active learning within an inviting, supportive, and safe environment. Listening to students helps teachers to discover what students value and need as learners. It is clear from this research that the students we interviewed challenge the notion of détente between urban teachers and their students. In fact, many of the students with whom we talked refused to play that game, as noted by their demand for high expectations, challenging work, and, in one case, even the refusal by some to read a book because of its irrelevance. Students taking on activist roles in their education alert us to the need for activism on the part of teachers. Students describe their desire to pose questions and find answers to those questions, like the boy who wants to be a civil rights leader or a congressman who asked, "What if it was the other way around? What if the Whites were the slaves and the Blacks were rich?" Teachers need to respond by "teaching against the grain" in order to meet the learning and relational needs of their students. The students' insights remind us that all of these practices depend on teachers knowing their students well. Only when teachers have established trusting relationships with students do they gain the insight to identify and respond to students' readiness, interests, and learning profiles (Tomlinson, 1999) in culturally responsive (Gay, 2000; Irvine & Armento, 2001) ways that are essential for successful outcomes.

Issues of Equity

The passion with which some of the students spoke about issues related to educational equity highlights the importance of the issue, not only for the students, but also for teachers and the larger community. We see here, in the experiences of these students, that there is awareness and understanding of how inequity affects their education and, in some cases, a sense of shared responsibility for action. What is not clear is the extent to which they understand the source of the inequity and its long-term implications for their success in life. Here is an area that the research community might pursue. Listening to the voices of urban students enables us to understand the political nature of schooling from their perspective, providing educators an opportunity to revisit curriculum and instructional practices, school policies, and personal attitudes and beliefs in a way that may help teachers empower students to address and interrupt the inequities that exist.

Smith (as cited in Brooker & MacDonald, 1999) cautions those of us who seek to privilege students' experiences, beliefs, and critiques in educational research not to relegate the students' voices to "an end in itself—a celebration after which we return to the everyday" (p. 86). We agree that using students' voices in that latter way undermines the spirit and intent of this line of inquiry and serves only to continue to marginalize students. If we are to privilege students' experiences and involve them in educational reform efforts, we need to find ways to bring these voices to the fore. Teacher education for both teacher candidates and practicing teachers provides one such venue. This line of research provides the potential for engaging teachers in listening to their own students' voices in systematic ways in an effort to enhance the learning experiences for all students. It is possible. As we have provided teachers the opportunity to listen to their students' voices through professional development activities with urban teachers, we have observed an eighth-grade team decide to invite students to their weekly team meetings. At another school, teachers used their students' comments as data sources for action research projects they were undertaking as part of our work with them. We have also used the students' voices with preservice teachers to help them prepare for entering urban field placements and for understanding best practices in middle child education. The possibilities are endless. Inviting students into our various levels and forms of university-school-community partnerships adds a new dimension to our important work of preparing activist teachers who have the knowledge, skills, and dispositions to be successful in our urban schools.

REFERENCES

American Psychological Association. (1997). *Learner-centered psychological principles: A framework for school redesign and reform.* Retrieved September 15, 2005, from http://www.apa.org

Arhar, J. M., & Kromrey, J. D. (1993). *Interdisciplinary teaming in the middle level schools: Creating a sense of belonging for at-risk middle level students.* Paper presented at the Annual Meeting of the American Educational Research Association, Atlanta, GA.

Barth, R. (1991). Restructuring schools: Some questions for teachers and principals. *Phi Delta Kappan*, *73*(2), 123–128.

Berends M., Bodilly, S., & Kirby, S. N. (2002). Looking back over a decade of whole-school reform: The experience of new American schools. *Phi Delta Kappan*, *84*(2), 168–175.

Brooker, R., & MacDonald, D. (1999). Did we hear you?: Issues of student voice in a curriculum innovation. *Journal of Curriculum Studies*, *31*, 83–97.

Brown, D. F. (2001). The value of advisory sessions for urban young adolescents. *Middle School Journal*, *32*(4), 14–22.

Bush, L. V., Burly, H., & Causey-Bush, T. (2001). Magnet schools: Desegregation or resegregation? Students voices from inside the walls. *American Secondary Education*, *29*(3), 33–50.

Collinson, V., Killeavy, M., & Stephenson, H. J. (1999). Exemplary teachers: Practicing an ethic of care in England, Ireland, and the United States. *Journal for a Just and Caring Education*, *5*, 349–366.

Cook-Sather, A. (2002). Authorizing students' perspectives: Toward trust, dialogue, and change in education. *Educational Researcher*, *31*(4), 3–14.

Darling-Hammond, L. (1997). *The right to learn: A blueprint for creating schools that work*. San Francisco: Jossey-Bass.

Davidman, P. T., & Davidman, L. (1998). On the teaching and personal construction of educational equity. *Multicultural Education*, *5*(3), 18–22.

Delpit, L. (1994). *Other people's children: Cultural conflict in the classroom*. New York: New Press.

Frymier, A. B., & Houser, M. L. (2000). The teacher-student relationship as an interpersonal relationship. *Communication Education*, *49*, 207–219.

Gay, G. (2000). *Culturally responsive teaching: Theory, research, and practice*. New York: Teachers College Press.

Giroux, H. (1988). Literacy and the pedagogy of voice and political empowerment. *Educational Theory*, *38*, 61–75.

Glickman, C. D. (1998). *Revolutionizing America's schools*. San Francisco: Jossey-Bass.

Horowitz, F. D., Darling-Hammond, L., & Bransford, J., with Comer, J., Rosebrock, K., Austin, K., & Rust, F. (2005). Educating teachers for developmentally appropriate practice. In L. Darling-Hammond & J. Bransford (Eds.), *Preparing teachers for a changing world: What teachers should learn and be able to do* (pp. 88–125). San Francisco: Jossey-Bass.

Howard, T. C. (2001). Telling their side of the story: African-American students' perceptions of culturally relevant teaching. *The Urban Review*, *33*, 131–140.

Irvine, J. J., & Armento, B. J. (2001). *Culturally responsive teaching*. New York: McGraw Hill.

Irvin, J. L. (1997). *Reading instruction for the social studies classroom*. Austin, TX: Holt, Rinehart & Winston.

Jackson, A. W., & Davis, G. A. (2000). *Turning points 2000: Educating adolescents in the 21st century*. Westerville, OH: National Middle School Association.

Knowles, T., & Brown, D. F. (2000). *What every middle school teacher should know*. Portsmouth, NH: Heinemann.

Kruse, S. (2000). Student voices: A report from focus group data. *NASSP Bulletin*, *84*(617), 77–85.

Ladson-Billings, G. (1994). *Dreamkeepers*. San Francisco: Jossey Bass.

Lincoln, Y. (1995). In search of student voice. *Theory Into Practice*, *34*, 88–93.

MacIver, D. J., & Plank, S. B. (1997). Improving urban schools: Developing the talents of students placed at risk. In J. L. Irvin (Ed.), *What current research says to the middle level practitioner* (pp. 257–264). Westerville, OH: National Middle School Association.

McLaren, P. (1994). *Life in schools*. White Plains, NY: Longman.

Muir, M. (2001). What engages underachieving middle school students in learning. *Middle School Journal, 33*(2), 37–43.

Muller, C., Katz, S. R., & Dance, L. J. (1999). Investing in teaching and learning: Dynamics of the teacher-student relationship for each actor's perspective. *Urban Education, 34,* 292–337.

Murphy, J. (1988). Equity as student opportunity to learn. *Theory Into Practice, 27,* 145–151.

National Middle School Association. (2003). *This we believe: Successful schools for young adolescence.* Westerville, OH: Author.

Nieto, S. (1994). Lessons from students creating a chance to dream. *Harvard Educational Review, 64,* 392–426.

Nieto, S. (2003). *What keeps teachers going?* New York: Teachers College Press.

Noddings, N. (1992). *The challenge to care in schools.* New York: Teachers College Press.

Noddings, N. (2002). *Educating moral people: A caring alternative to character education.* New York: Teachers College Press.

Pintrich, P. R., & Schunk, D. H. (1996). *Motivation in education.* Columbus, OH: Merrill.

Richardson, L. (1994). Writing: A method of inquiry. In N. Denzin & Y. Lincoln (Eds.), *Handbook of qualitative research* (pp. 516–529). Thousands Oak, CA: Sage.

Schine, J. (1997). Service learning and young adolescent development: A good fit. In J. L. Irvin (Ed.), *What current research says to the middle level practitioner* (pp. 257–264). Westerville, OH: National Middle School Association.

Storz, M. (1998). *Constructing understandings of race: Tales from an urban professional development school's foundations course.* Unpublished doctoral dissertation, Cleveland State University, Cleveland.

Tomlinson, C. A. (1999). *The differentiated classroom: Responding to the needs of all learners.* Alexandria, VA: Association for Supervision & Curriculum Development.

Waxman, H. C. (1989). Urban Black and Hispanic elementary students perceptions of classroom instruction. *Journal of Research and Development in Education, 22*(2), 57–61.

Weinberger, E., & McCombs, B. L. (2001). *The impact of learner-centered practices on the academic and non-academic outcomes of upper elementary and middle school students,* Paper presented at the Annual Meeting of American Educational Research Association, Seattle, WA.

Wilson, B. L., & Corbett, H. D. (2001). *Listening to urban kids: School reform and the teachers they want.* Albany, NY: SUNY Press.

CHAPTER SIX

Families AND Schools Apart: University Experience TO Assist Latino/a Parents' Activism

CRIS MAYO

University of Illinois at Urbana-Champaign

MARIA ALBURQUERQUE CANDELA

EUGENE MATUSOV

MARK SMITH

University of Delaware

In this chapter, we share the findings and dilemmas raised by our work helping Latino/a parents engage with their children's schools. For over a year, we worked closely with three Puerto Rican families and one Mexican family who asked us to help them negotiate with their children's schools (these included elementary, middle, and high schools in northern Delaware). All parents were concerned that their children were experiencing different sorts of troubles in school: educational, relational, behavioral, racial, attitudinal, and so on. All families were active participants in their children's education. All of them felt that they exhausted their own means and resources to find a solution to the problems their children were having at school.

PARENTAL ACTIVISM VERSUS PARENTAL INVOLVEMENT

We will argue that the parents we observed and worked with were involved in parental activism and that that style of interaction with the schools was out of step with school expectations for parental involvement. Following a sociocultural approach (Lave & Wenger, 1991), we reject the binary notion of parental involvement, with its two main possibilities being either parents who are involved in their children's school education or parents who are not. We think that this notion of parental involvement is hegemonic, essentialist, and manipulative, because it implies that there is one authority (usually the school) that defines what counts as involvement. In the discourse of parent involvement, parents seem to be placed in a double bind in regard to the schools. On the one hand, they can become involved on the school's terms in their child's education or else be viewed as a problem; on the other hand, they are expected to protect their children's interests but, by doing so (or not doing so), may be viewed by the school as overinvolved (or underinvolved) and recognized as a problem (Nakagawa, 2000). As Fine (1993) argues, parents "are usually not welcomed, by schools, to the critical and serious work of rethinking educational structures and practices" (p. 682). By controlling the definition of *involvement*, the authority frames the ways in which the parents must participate in their children's education and manipulates the parents by inducing a sense of guilt when the parents fail to fit the tacitly imposed image of "involved parents" (cf. "management by guilt" in Hargreaves, 1994).

In our view, the discourse of parent involvement is in part responsible for a sad phenomenon of parent bashing that is common among teachers—teachers' negative predisposition to parents (negative prejudice). Parent bashing, or what we term *parentism* (H. Pleasants, personal communication, March 31, 2003), often takes two distinguishable forms: bashing against low-income parents for their "underinvolvement" in school and against middle-class parents for their "overinvolvement" (Nakagawa, 2000). In the first type, lower-income parents are described, as "neglectful", "uninvolved", and "disinterested" in their children's education and even well-being. Working for many years with preservice teachers, we have been faced with these forms of parentism on a regular basis. This is how one of our preservice teacher education students described low-income parents in general on the class electronic forum after spending just one day in her first teaching practicum:

> The demographics in this classroom affect the learning in there because many of the children come from low-income areas and have large families. Their parents don't have time like they should to care about their children's schoolwork. Since they do not get much support at home, most of them do not do as well in school as they probably could.

Other students responded, "There are parents out there that just don't think it is important to get involved in their children's education." "It is the teachers' job to get the child involved ... and to inspire them to continue their learning at home no matter how uninvolved their parents are." Like low-income children, low-income parents are often viewed as a deficit by schools (Delgado-Gaitan, 1991). Delgado-Gaitan writes, "Deficit perspectives depict inactive parents in the schools as incompetent and unable to help their children because they have a different language, work long hours away from home, belong to different ethnic groups, or are just not interested" (p. 22). Parent participation has the potential to exacerbate rather than alleviate educational inequity by further marginalizing families who define their roles with respect to family-school interactions differently than what schools demand (Crozier, 2000; De Carvalho, 2001).

The second type of parentism is set against primarily middle-class parents who are considered to be involved too much in their children's education by vocally and forcefully expressing their disapproval and disagreement with the teacher or school practices. This is how another student, a preservice teacher, put it:

> I'm really nervous about many things that I might encounter [when becoming a teacher], but when I think about it, most of these worries stem from parents. I'm worried about parents. I know that I'm going to dread conferences because parents are going to tell me that I'm wrong about things and that I'm not doing a good enough job with some aspect(s) of teaching. I'm scared to death to hear those hurtful words because I know that I'm going to be trying my hardest, but that still won't be good enough for some people.

It is interesting that our preservice teachers have rarely mentioned school administrators as their concern, although it is the school administration that will closely monitor, supervise, and judge their teaching. Although rarely labeled as middle class, the preservice teachers seem to imply that those vocal parents have societal power.

In our observations, fear of and prejudice against parents have developed before preservice teachers go to their first teaching practicum, although, often, their parentism becomes stronger through interactions with in-service teachers who support the prejudice themselves and validate those prejudices with their own experiences with so-called bad parents. Our preservice teachers often portray teachers as experts on children, while viewing parents as ignorant people who must listen to the teachers. When we asked our preservice teachers to describe an ideal parent, many of them described a so-called teacher slave, a parent who does exactly what the teacher told him or her to do. Similarly, Minke and Anderson (2003), in reviewing parent-teacher conference literature for teachers, note that an emphasis is placed on teachers delivering information to parents (rather than listening to parents' concerns), all the while expecting conflict with the parent to emerge. Time for parents to express their concerns is thought to be best given at the end of the conference time. The overall impression that the literature gives, Minke and Anderson point out, is to regard the parent as an "enemy" whose input must be "managed."

In other words, ideal parent involvement demands parental acquiescence to school authority. In schools, we often experienced the expectation that parental contact with the school was simply to attend teacher-parent conferences. Furthermore, school personnel expected that the institutional purpose of the conference remained the same, whether the parent called and scheduled the conference or the parent wanted to change the format. One of the parents with whom we worked insisted that she had arranged to meet with her twin daughters' teachers because she was concerned about their grades. She called us and said, "I made an appointment with the principal." But, when we arrived to assist her, we were told that she had been called by the school and, according to the secretary, had chosen among a few options of times to meet. Even though the mother had called the principal for an appointment, she was given a time to meet with her daughters' teachers, and no one explained to her that the meeting was on their terms, not hers. In another situation when a student told her parents about her difficulties in school and the parents contacted us to make an appointment, we found that the same institutional expectations and patterns of interaction. In this particular case, the student had been to school for only three days, had her grades being transferred from another institution, and was experiencing harassment because of her nontraditional gender orientation. When we began the conference and before they knew who had called the meeting and why, the student's teachers took turns reciting their evaluation of her academic achievement.

In contrast to the traditional monological notion of parent involvement, we argue that all parents participate in their children's education—the issue is what form this participation takes and who is able to shape the conditions and practices of that participation (cf. "participatory notion of learning," as defined by Lave, 1992). All parents have to deal with their children's schools in one way or another. Paraphrasing Heidegger (Heidegger & Stambaugh, 1996), by the simple fact that their children are in school most of the day, parents are thrown into their children's schools whether they want to be there or not and are forced to relate and deal with their children's education and schools. The parents of schooled children cannot avoid positioning themselves in relation to the school. They have to participate in school. This participation can be positive or negative, depending on the type of participation, their and our perspectives on that participation, and their and our values. For example, Delgado-Gaitan (1991) found in her research that Latino parents were supportive of their children's education, though not in ways usually recognized by the school. As Latino parents noted, the range of their participation varies broadly: volunteering in school, helping with homework, advocating for the child's well-being and education, resisting oppressive school practices, providing the child with food and housing, crossing the national border to give the child a better education, and even neglecting the child's educational needs. The parents' notion of participation in their children's education is democratic, dialogic, interpretive, and relational, inviting different parties to define it. In this chapter, we want to discuss Latino/a parental activism as a form of parent participation in schools, as well as our university-based role in that process.

We witnessed the parents of the Families and Schools Together (FAST) program as they planned meetings to help everyone involved in their children's education to see the problems the school was having with their kids and the schools' inadequacies in educating their kids. School personnel would almost uniformly reply that the problems were either intractable or imply that the parents were not adequately attending to their children's education. In our study, by their lack of attention to the needs of Latino/a students, schools reinforced monologic parental involvemment. In cases where kids improved dramatically in schools, the most apparent casue of the improvement was what we call "the teacher-child divorce:" The parents removed their children from a bad school or the teacher was changed. In one case, a student who had not done well in a conventional high school excelled at her studies while in juvenile detention. Children's problems at school often disrupted their lives in other spheres: at home, at the local community center, and with friends. We found that when parents provided strong support for their children and took their children's side in the conflicts with schools, they not only secured their relationship with the children but also contributed to the children's well-being and prevented them from experiencing dangers of alienation, such as running away from home, using drugs, distrusting parents, and other unsafe behaviors. While not all parents were able to ensure their children's academic success and their well-being, they believed they benefited from the experience of challenging the authority of the schools and insisting on better educational practices. In so doing, parents positioned themselves as political advocates for their own families and their communities. More than anything else, through their visits to the schools, they found they were not isolated; their problems were not theirs alone.

WHY DID WE SEEK COLLABORATION WITH LATINO/A PARENTS?

We were actively looking to work with Latino/a parents for several reasons. First, for the last nine years, we have involved our preservice teachers at the Latin American Community Center (LACC) of Wilmington, Delaware, as a part of teaching practicum that we organized for our cultural diversity course. Our students were engaged with Latino/a children (mainly Puerto Rican) in an afterschool program called La Red Mágica, helping the children with their activities—games, computers, arts and crafts projects—and learning from the experiences (and the children) how to provide culturally sensitive guidance (Matusov & Hayes, 2002). The preservice teachers learned that although the children may be very successful at the LACC, they may fail in school and have problems there. A few years ago, together with the LACC officers and our students, we developed a short questionnaire for the teachers of the LACC children. We asked the teachers about the LACC children's strengths and ways that we can help the children at LACC with their education. By doing that, we hoped to build relations with the teachers. However, many of them commented that the children "do not have any strengths" and only listed long complaints about their students. Our university students and we knew the LACC children differently: We saw strength, potential, and community- and family-based educational resources. We thought that, by working together with the LACC children, their parents, LACC staff, and teachers, we could solve educational problems that the children face in their schools.

The second reason that we wanted to work with Latino/a parents was our concern with teachers' tendency toward parentism, as described previously. Our La Red Mágica model of teaching our preservice teachers how to provide culturally sensitive guidance through their engagement with Latino/a children in a safe and nonthreatening informal learning environment worked really well for them (Matusov & Hayes, 2002). We thought that we could expand the model by engaging the LACC parents with preservice teachers who would see the strengths, potentials, and resources in low-income parents and not deficits and uninvolvement. We wanted to give a human face to the "low-income parents" as we have done rather successfully with the "minority students" in our La Red Mágica project. To achieve this goal, we sought opportunities to develop relations with the LACC parents. Finally, we heard from the LACC staff that many parents were desperate in their struggle with their children's schools and would appreciate help from us, as university educators. Thus, we found that the interest was mutual. We were happy to help.

We started our work with parents through informal interactions with parents coming to pick up their children during the work of the La Red Mágica project. Those informal contacts led us to LACC parents' meetings of FAST, a nationwide and international organization involving "a collaborative team of parents, trained professionals and school personnel" in "a multifamily group intervention designed to build protective factors for children (4 to 12 years old) and empower parents to be the primary prevention agents for their own children," focusing mainly on serving "teacher-identified, at-risk 5- to 12-year-old elementary school youth and their families; however, universal recruitment is now the recommended strategy" (Wisconsin Center for Education Research, 2006).

The LACC chapter of the FAST organization met once a month at the LACC. Initially, we had a peripheral role, attending the FAST meetings and talking informally with parents during the breaks after formally introducing ourselves at the beginning of the year. In the middle of May 2002, we were formally invited by FAST to discuss the Delaware Student Testing Program (DSTP), new high stakes standardized tests, and their consequences for the LACC children. At this point, we realized that collaboration with the LACC parents had begun. We started writing field notes on each encounter with the parents to learn and reflect on our experiences. We often checked our notes with parents, confirming our understandings of the events and parents' perceptions and ideas through phone calls or in discussions during meetings. Details of our colloborating with and supporting three families follow.

FAST MEETING: "IT IS THE LAW"

When FAST and LACC organized a meeting for parents and school district personnel to talk about their mutual concerns, parents came with many different concerns to which the two attending district representatives provided monotonous responses. One parent was deeply concerned that her child had not done well on the DSTP and was scheduled to be retained the next year. She wanted to know why the school didn't educate her child and why the child was not given more help and brought up to grade-level work. She wanted to find out if there was a way to keep her child in the age-appropriate grade level and access additional help. When this parent challenged the district's retention of her child, the school district representative only repeated, in Spanish, "It is the law; it is the law." When parents expressed worries that their English was not good enough for them to help with their kids' homework, the district representative said that teachers were not solely responsible for their children's education and told the parents that they were the children's primary educators.

While this was a relatively short meeting, it was characteristic of every parental interaction with schools in which we participated. In our presentations to the FAST parents, we validated their concerns with research findings, encouraged them to share more concerns, and discussed possible solutions. We also described in detail the La Red Mágica project and our work with their children at the LACC. We told the parents that one of our goals was to see their children as students at the University of Delaware. We offered our help, and the parents were eager to take our contact information that we gave them. Out of about 20 families present at the meeting, seven contacted us by phone and/or by meeting at the LACC. Some contacts were facilitated and initially mediated by the LACC staff, many of whom actively supported our collaboration with parents. From the beginning, our involvement with the parents centered around their children's problems with schools: discussing the problems with parents, validating their concerns, planning together the next steps, talking with their children, contacting schools on their behalf, and going to schools with them.

University Memorandum About Our Expected Work with LACC Children, Parents, and Teachers, the End of May, 2002

Developing productive family-school relationships with families of diverse backgrounds is acknowledged as particularly problematic (Hanafin & Lynch, 2002; Lareau & Shumar, 1996; Minke & Anderson, 2003).One of the most frequently encountered problems faced by many Latino/a children is that they do well in after-school, community-based programs but not as well in school. Many Latino/a families do not know how and what their children are do at school. Most teachers do not know how and what their Latino/a students are doing at home or in the after-school programs. Thus, problems and misunderstanding arise among the families, the children, and the school.We wondered: Should we connect the home, school and community contexts and their different voices to help parents and teachers better understand every child's learning? Should we connect these everyday contexts for learning to build a community of practice in which every participant, including the children, will have the possibility to work together? Should we create spaces in which future teachers will have the opportunity to be conscious about multiculturalism? Some educators see the last two approaches as the most favorable, not only because they may help parents, educators, and the children better comprehend and be more consciously aware of children's situations and experiences to prevent their becoming oppressors and victims of bureaucracy and allow children to grow towards learning of freedom.

To build relationships among the schools, the families, the children, and the afterschool programs, we went to the LACC with the intent to know the families of the LACC children. The families were organized in one big group and held monthly meetings where parents and people who work at the center shared their concerns, ideas, and problems. In addition, every month, they invited a speaker who addressed topics such as how to rent an apartment for the first time, what to do if your teenager becomes pregnant and how to prevent the situation, what the standards exams are and what their consequences are, and what rights families have when they go to the school and talk to teachers. Families learned and resolved their concerns but also found that other families shared many of the same problems. Most importantly, the parents had the space to discuss and organize their points of view related to any issue of concern.

After some months of being there not only as observers but also as participants in these events, we realized we could provide parents with an orientation towards the problems they explained, which, overall, were related to how the teachers said that the children were not doing well at school.

We expected that building relationships between the school and the community would help motivate children, parents, and teachers to believe in themselves, and in their potential and, therefore, encourage them to learn. We decided to help parents and families go to their children's schools and talk to the teachers, thereby building relationships between the teachers and the children that would help them have a better time at school and become full participants in the classroom community, which would hopefully begin to embrace local communities. To accomplish these relationships we enacted the La Red Mágica's Principles of Working with Parents, Teachers, and Children which included:

1. Create "crossroads," a physical possibility for conferences among the teachers, parents, children, and the University of Delaware faculty and researchers (Austin, 1994).
2. Make sure that everyone can talk and see others as genuinely interested in what one says. Avoid fake or rhetorical questions and talking over or on behalf of the present parties (Cormier & Hackney, 1999; Hanhan, 1998; Sarason, 1995).
3. Help the child to be an active agent for his/her own learning (Austin, 1994; Matusov & Rogoff, 2002; Rogoff, Matusov, & White, 1996; Sarason, 1995).
4. Avoid blaming the parties involved in the dialogue (Epstein, 1993).
5. Focus our narrative and discourse on the child's strengths, interests, and problems (as stated by the child) and on interpersonal problem solving (Minke & Anderson, 2003).
6. Make specific proposals (Fine, 1991; Robinson & Fine, 1994).
7. Set future meetings to implement and test consequences of the proposed actions (Robinson & Fine, 1994).

THREE CASES

As we worked to build relatiopnships, we documented the following case studies.

"They Have Too Many Friends"

Middle school Latino children often sensed racism and bias in their interactions with schools. The first parent with whom we went to school—a mother of two twin girls in the seventh grade—said to us before the meeting with the principal that she was not sure if her twins' troubles at schools were motivated by teachers' bias as her daughter insisted. We were told that we were meeting with the principal; but, like every other time visited a school, we were told that our appointment was with the principal, the principal was unavailable and we were directed to a classroom where three of the twins' teachers were sitting in a semicircle. The empty chairs in the classroom were stacked against a wall. The seated teachers asked us to bring the chairs for other teachers and ourselves. (They apologized for this command as soon as we gave our university business cards). Eugene introduced us to the three teachers and explained why we were there, that we were from the University of Delaware, that we worked with LACC parents, and that Maria would be the translator. We handed out our business cards and said that we would be glad to provide any help that we could and that they should not hesitate to contact us. We said that we were interested in finding positive ways to help the girls have a good education.

The first teacher omitted the subject in all his sentences. He stated, as if reading a prepared bulleted list: "has no strengths," "doesn't even try," and "doesn't do any good work." We didn't understand whether he was apologizing for not knowing how to deal with the girls or if this was an odd way of criticizing them. It turned out that he was assessing one of the twins. As soon as we caught a pause in the teacher's monologue, we told the teachers that we thought that we came to help to solve problems and that the children's participation in the conversation was crucial. The teachers were openly surprised by this idea, but they called for the twins. The girls came and joined the circle. We explained to them what the meeting was about, who we were (the twins recognized some of us from seeing us at LACC), and what we were trying to accomplish—to help them and their mother resolve some issues with the teachers.

As the twins explained that their mother had not yet arrived because she was involved in an auto accident the day before and her minivan was not out of the shop in time, several teachers rolled their eyes and opined that parents did not always care enough to come. The teachers stated that maybe their mother had just expected that the university representatives would be there and indicated that we should just start. Another teacher chimed in that he thought the twins were mentally disabled. We asked what led him to think this, and he said that they weren't good in class but that maybe they had too many friends and relatives in school to pay attention to classes. We asked what he meant by "too many friends and relatives," and he said, "*They*'re always late because *they*'re always running into some cousin or another on their way to class." By his intonation the teacher meant "they" were not just the twins but Latino children in general. We told the teacher that we also noticed in our work at LACC that Latino children have many relatives and friends, and, because of this, children help each other and take care of each other. The twins nodded and validated that. We told the teachers how we encourage the kids at LACC to provide guidance and support to each other. We asked teachers if it would be possible to use the strong social milieu of Latino children in a positive way. However, the teachers did not respond to this question. Two other teachers came in and sat outside the circle and began to quietly converse between each other. Suddenly, one teacher asked the girls, "And, are you coming to the classroom? Are you aware that you are here to come to class and not to be in the hall all day with your friends?" The girls did not answer at all. There was a silent pause in which the teachers turned to us as if saying, "You can see it now yourself—further comments are unnecessary!"

Again, we took initiative and directed questions to the girls instead of supporting a conversation with the teachers in the presence of the girls. We asked the girls if they have any space at home to study and read books, if they sleep well and eat well. The girls answered "Yes". We then asked them who helped them with their homework if they had difficulties. The girls told us that tutors at LACC helped a lot, but, unfortunately, they could not come to the LACC every day because they live far away, and their mother could only bring them to the LACC twice a week. They said that their uncle sometimes helped, but he also lived far away. We asked if they could ask for help from the teachers the next day in school. The twins were surprised with this idea and firmly said "No," explaining that the teachers would yell at them. We asked the twins, "Why? Your teachers are here to help you, and they want to know why you could not do the homework." One twin said, "Because our teachers are mean and will not help us." We turned to the teachers expecting them to deny the twins' negative remark and to invite the girls to ask for help. The teachers denied that they would yell at the children, but one also validated the girls' expectations. A reading teacher responded that she had too many students in her class to give the girls her "individualized attention." The other teachers remained silent.

We followed the conversation with the children, asking them about their interests, strengths, things they like to do in their free time, and their aspirations for their future. The twins answered that they liked to clean the house and to go out and play on the street with their friends. As for the academic subjects, they said that they both liked English a lot but disliked reading, writing, and math because these subjects were "boring" to them. One of the twins said she liked science a lot, while the other said science was "so, so."

When asked about their aspirations, one of the twins said that, after finishing school, she wanted to be *a teacher*. We expressed our excitement about the possibility for us to be her university professors. We invited her to come to the university next fall and explained that if she came to visit, she might have a better idea of what she would do to become a teacher. The girl seemed to like the idea of visiting the university. We also emphasized that her current teachers would be her future colleagues and that she could start learning from them how to become a good teacher.

The other twin said that she wanted to be a teacher in the past but that she had now become "too mean" for this profession. The teachers did not say anything in reply. We told the girl that, in our observation of her at the LACC, her perception of herself as being mean was wrong, because she willingly helped so many children there with computers and art drawings. The girl nodded in agreement with us. One teacher suddenly said, "Well, you know when you do bad things, don't you? And you are big enough now to know that what you do is not good, right?" (The teachers seemed to attack instead of to guide and to support the girls).

When the twins' mother arrived, she immediately apologized for being late because of her problems with her car. The teachers did not apologize for their inaccurate suspicions regarding the mother's absence. The mother began explaining how she organized her children's homework time and her expectations for her children's hard work and honesty. Sra. Allende[1] spoke in Spanish, and we translated what she said to English. Also, we translated what the teachers and we said to Spanish. Sra. Allende chided the teachers for not giving enough homework, saying that she asked the girls "What is your homework?" and then made them sit down at their desks until it was done. The teachers looked shocked. They had already expressed that Sra. Allende was a noncaring parent; yet, the mother came into the meeting with clear expectations and specific references to her attempts to help the children at home. One teacher then introduced all the other teachers present in the room, even the two in back who briefly stopped talking to each other to introduce themselves. When one teacher explained that one of the twins was not giving her mother an accurate story about homework, Sra. Allende apologized, clearly angry at the twins, and said that if she had known that her daughters really had homework, it would have been done. She made it clear to all present that this was unacceptable and that her standards for her daughters were higher than that. The teachers probably expected "yet another" situation where a parent did not care, but may have realized that these were supervised kids in an interested family.

Sra. Allende articulated to the teachers that she was ready to help her daughters but that it would be better if they would have some texts that were also in Spanish, so that she could help the girls, because she didn't read English. The language arts teacher suggested that she get a Spanish-English dictionary, halted as if she thought that didn't sound quite right, and revised her idea to say that the twins could use it to practice. The language arts teacher, Jennifer, then explained how she had tried to help the girls by providing work sheets in Spanish, but, with so many children in her class, it was hard for her to give individualized attention to the twins. It seemed to us that the teacher was fairly nice and certainly eager to try to use her Spanish, but we were surprised at the suggestion of a dictionary, since it is not really the easiest thing to use when you have to deal with tenses and try to figure out a sentence word by word. Another chimed in with stories of the girls doing very well in classes that had small projects. Two other teachers remained outside the circle, still talking to each other, and Maria said, "Excuse me, do you want to say anything that I can translate for Sra. Allende?" They didn't and kept talking.

The language arts teacher was also willing to do more individualized work. The other teachers did not add anything to the discussion. We asked the teachers what would help the girls to improve. One teacher said that they need to get more help if they do not understand things.

Also, Sra. Allende insisted that the twins should be given homework to do if the twins are suspended from school again for wrongdoing. The teachers promised to do that and showed us and the mother where they would leave the homework assignments in the future. But, to our knowledge, they never made any attempts to do this.

Sra. Allende also wanted to let the teachers know that she did not agree with the idea of suspensions as punishments to get the kids to understand the rules of the school. She explained to the teachers that she wanted her daughters to be respectful girls with a bright future. She wanted her daughters to go to the university, and she wanted them to learn how to speak English in order to be able and ready to be independent women. She also offered alternatives to the suspensions: She suggested that, instead of putting the kids on the street for two or three days, they could better explain to the kids what the rules of the school are and put them in a room with texts, books, or some task to do. She argued that, if the teachers do not do this, then every time her daughters or other kids miss school, they are missing lessons and possibilities to learn.

In response, the English teacher showed a book with the rules of the school to the mother and, looking toward the kids, said,

> *They* perfectly know the rules because we read to *them* from this book at the beginning of the year. *They* know exactly which things are forbidden and the reason why we suspend them is always because *they* are fighting with other kids and *they* know that this is forbidden.

The teacher continued saying that she and some other teachers in the room did not agree with some of the rules, especially with the rules that require leaving the children without instruction during the suspension and with the rules giving suspensions for minor infractions. But this teacher felt pretty powerless about the suspensions. "In any case," the teacher said, "you should talk with the principal because all we do as teachers is write a referral, and it is the principal, who decides to suspend them." She also said that she disagreed with suspensions as well, but it was not her policy. The teachers agreed to give homework to the girls during future suspensions (but they never did). We asked where the mother could pick up the homework, and the teachers replied that they would leave it in the main office. We also gave our phone numbers to the teachers, so that they could call us in case they need to send Sra. Allende a message—we could then translate their message to Sra. Allende (they never called us).

The mother said again that she thought that suspending the kids is not a solution and told the teachers that her daughters often lied and did not share with her why they were suspended from school and why they were fighting. She turned to the girls and told them to ignore the kids who want to fight and, if it is so difficult to do so, to ask the teacher for help with the situation. At this point, we asked the kids, "Why do you fight?" The girls replied, "We fight for two reasons. One is because some kids are calling our names and insulting us; the other is because if we are not fighting the offender, another kid older than us will fight against us." The teachers said nothing, and the mother told them that they will have to ignore the other kids or to talk to the principal and teachers.

At this point, we explained to the teachers that, when we started to work at the LACC five years before, the LACC also had a problem with many kids fighting with each other. The adults at the LACC started to think about how they might help the children. They decided to all sit down together, kids and adults, and asked the kids to create the rules that would help them avoid fighting. After that, the number of fights started coming down, and now there are not very many fights at the LACC. The mother listened intently to us while the teachers remained silent.

The science teacher and the reading teacher told the mother, nearly at the same time, that another reason why the girls were suspended was that they were skipping a lot of classes. At this point, one of the twins asked us not to translate this point to her mother, because the mother knew already, or maybe she could say this to her mother by herself later. We told the girl that we were there because her mother wanted to help them, and because she also trusted us translating everything correctly and that was why we must do that. It was apparent that the girl did not agree with us. She laughed a bit in apparent embarrassment. Upon hearing the news about her girls' skipping science classes, Sra. Allende was openly angry that the girls were lying to her. She yelled at the girls. Sra. Allende apparently wanted to make her anger known to the teachers while projecting that she deeply cared about her daughters' education and wanted to work together with the teachers in disciplining her daughters.

We said that we were surprised that the girls were skipping subject classes that they liked. One of the twins replied that she enjoyed the science experiment "with the light," mentioning a particular experiment. Then the second science teacher said somewhat apologetically, "We don't have enough money to do a lot of experiments because we don't have a lot of funds for equipment." We asked the science teacher what kind of science equipment kit would be good to buy for the kids to use in the LACC after school, but the science teacher did not know because the school does not have many science kits. Two teachers, both the woman who did work sheets in Spanish and the science teacher, agreed that the girls did better in settings involving activity and variety. The science teacher said he would try to have whichever twin he had do more of that, but that there were also other parts to his class on which they would have to work. The science teacher also explained that, while the girls may enjoy experiments, a lot of his class requires reading comprehension and math skills, and, even if they're interested in the experiment part, they don't do well enough on the main part of the class. (Both of these were teachers at whom the girls looked when they said they could not ask for help because their teachers were mean.)

At this point, we introduced the idea of enrolling the girls into the LACC summer camp. The mother liked the idea, although she had a problem with tuition and transportation, and so did the girls. We explained the different opportunities and facilities available for the kids if they attend the LACC summer camp (e.g., poetry club, math tutoring, computer lab, Internet chat, and opportunities to draw and to learn dance, among others). A twin said that she made a dolphin picture when a guest art instructor from Colombia was present the previous summer at the LACC. We congratulated her because we saw this picture and explained that children at the LACC wanted to make postcards out of pictures and sell them.

We walked out with Sra. Allende, asking the girls how they felt and telling them that we thought they were quite brave to be in a room full of adults talking about them. They said, "It was okay" and they weren't really scared because they recognized Eugene from the LACC. Sra. Allende thought that the teachers were less racially biased than she expected based on the daughters' reports, but she was very disappointed that the girls had been lying to her about homework. Sra. Allende asked us if we agreed with her daughters that the teachers were racists, and we brought up the example of the teacher's open prejudice about Latino children having too many relatives and friends, a sentiment apparently shared by the other teachers. She did not witness that, as she came to the meeting later). Sra. Allende expressed concern that the girls were not getting enough of the kind of instruction with which they seemed to do well. She had expected overt racism but found instead that teachers were mostly "nice," even while they were saying very disrespectful things. She said that she had begun to doubt that the schools were racially biased, because everyone was smiling and being encouraging, but she also realized that their form of disrespect was harder to pin down, because it was so seemingly polite.

Months later, the girls continued to do poorly in school, often not attending classes and school all together. When Sra. Allende noticed that they came home without homework, she contacted the school. She was informed that the girls were often not in class and that they may be getting of the bus before getting to school. She began driving the girls to school, but they still failed in all their subjects. She said, "I am very worr[ied] because although there is one teacher who knows how to talk our language, normally I do not have anybody who is helping me to understand what is wrong with my daughters." While she continued to have problems with her girls and the school, she thought that going to school to talk to teachers was important, because it helps the teachers realize "that schools need translators to help families like us to understand the problems that our kids have, and also that it is very important to know and to be in contact with teachers and principals from the beginning." She also wished that we could all go to school together again to "make teachers and parents understand each other."

In a later conversation with Sra. Allende, it became apparent to us that Sra. Allende was siding more and more with the school as her daughters' conflicts grew there. She saw that

> the [main] problem here is the attitude of my daughters. Normally they are not listening to me at all or to the teachers. So, what I have been thinking is to make them scared, to make them understand the importance of studying and to become somebody. If not, they will finish at the court and in the prison.

She was apparently scared about her daughters' future, but she saw the solution as changing her daughters' attitudes and making them more compliant to the teachers' demands. However, from our interaction with the teachers described previously and their lack of any follow-up actions based on suggestions that emerged in our meeting, we found the teachers' demands unrealistic, unsupportive, and unprofessional. The parent thought that the solution was her daughters' listening to the teachers and to her, ignoring what she learned *by listening to the children* about the teachers' racism and what was going on in school. As Sra. Allende told us, she could not move the children to another school or enroll them into the LACC that year because of financial, transportation, and institutional policies. The only viable solution she saw was to become a conduit for the school's impossible demands—to become a school policewoman for her daughters. She reported one of the girls to the police when she did not come home to sleep at night. By "scaring" the children and being tough with them. while also advocating for them at school, she created a "schizophrenic double bind" (Bateson, 1987) that often tears a child apart psychologically (leading to a situation where no one wins). When we tried to discuss alternative approaches, Sra. Allende became frustrated with us.

We worried about the twins and their mother, Sra. Allende. Another LACC Puerto Rican high school girl who recently surrendered herself to police, asked the court to interrupt her probation because her life in school and at home became unbearable. Juvenile detention was the only place where she experienced unambivalent success and even support from adults. The case is very complex, but like Sra. Allende, the girl's parents' double-bind approach of being child advocates and school policemen (school conduit) prevented their listening to their children.

Divorcing School

Another LACC parent named Cindy, who was also faced with her children being retained, was interested in knowing what her rights were. She knew that there was some provision for parental refusal of retention but had been unable to stop her son's retention from fifth grade. Her daughter, Felicia, had been retained the previous year, and the mother, despite her weekly attempts to get a response from her teacher, had been unable to have the teacher tell her the kind of extra work Felicia needed to do. Cindy arranged for the LACC education director to give Felicia extra tutorials at the LACC, but, without any teacher response to a single request, Felicia continued to do poorly. When Cindy received a letter from the school about her son, Fernando, she decided it was time to go further up and talk to the principal. A form letter arrived a few weeks before the end of the school year. It indicated that a district-level decision had been made to retain her "son/daughter," since he had "failed one or more of the following courses" (followed by a list of all possible academic subjects that one could fail and thus be retained). The letter also mentioned that Cindy could dispute a decision to retain her "son/daughter," and she called the phone number on the letter. The person who answered at the district office said that she was not the person to call for disputes and told her to contact the school principal (who had signed the letter).

Cindy made an appointment, and we all drove down to a brand new school at the edge of the district's boundaries, several miles from the family's home. We walked into the office and said that we had an appointment with the principal. The secretary said that the principal was out sick that day and that she would contact the assistant principal. We waited about 10 minutes until he arrived and introduced himself to Cindy, and we went into a conference room. He told us all that he was the assistant principal and started to ask Cindy why she was there. She said, "Aren't you going to ask who these other people are?" and then she introduced us, as we handed out our business cards. He said, "Oh, you're from

University of Delaware? I got a degree in engineering from Delaware. I was nominated to go to West Point, but I wound up going into engineering instead." Cindy showed him the letter she had gotten from the district, and he said that he would get Fernando's file and his teacher. His teacher came in very briefly, but Cindy wanted to talk with the assistant principal, not the teacher, since it was already too late to do something, and the teacher had misled her in past. Cindy had her son's report card, and his grades for math were passing (one was even a B) until the last quarter, when he failed. Cindy said that the teacher had said that since Fernando had done so badly the last quarter, he doubted that the other quarters reflected his ability accurately, and he decided to fail him. The vice principal seemed to find this an adequate explanation, but we did not.

Cindy also showed the vice principal Felicia's homework notebook in which she had requested additional help and homework every week yet the teacher ignored her requests. Cindy told the vice principal that she called the teacher every week to ask if Felicia could do more and what could her tutor do to help her. Every week, the teacher said, "She's doing fine, but her grades continue to be marginal." She kept a written record of these attempts, which she showed the principal. The assistant principal asked Cindy why she didn't call him instead, since the teacher wasn't responding. She said she didn't know she was supposed to call him, and since she had tried to call the central office person about Fernando's retention and been told she had to start further down the hierarchy, why should she be expected to jump over the teacher? He said that if she had called him earlier, they wouldn't be having this problem. She said that if he'd supervised his teachers better, we wouldn't be having this problem. She asked, "Don't you watch what these teachers do?" He said Felicia's teacher was new. She said, "Then you should be more careful with her and make sure she knows how to teach. What kind of teacher doesn't give any homework at all?" Cindy said that Felicia had been retained last year, and she knew that Felicia was supposed to have an individualized educational plan (IEP) to help her do better this year but that one hadn't been prepared. The assistant principal said that wasn't his fault, because this school wasn't even open then, so it must have happened at another school. Cindy pointed out that he wasn't responsible for Felicia's retention but that his school should have provided an IEP *this year* and had not. The assistant principal replied that developing an IEP for Felicia would be unfair for other kids who do not have IEPs. Cindy also said that she was not going to let them retain Fernando, since they didn't know how to educate Felicia and weren't helping this year. The assistant principal said, "but we won't retain Felicia because we can't retain a student twice." Cindy said, "I know, but you are still not educating her. I ask for homework, and I don't get homework. What good does it do to retain her and then do nothing?"

We talked with Cindy after the meeting, and all largely agreed with her idea to get her kids out of this elementary school. A few months later, after having seen Cindy, Fernando, and Felicia a few times a week at the LACC, we found them very eager to talk about their new school, and they brought in report cards, exams, and papers to show. Fernando got straight As, and Felicia had an A and a mixture of Bs and Cs and was very proud of an exam on which she got a 92 and an essay on which she earned an A. By then, our preservice teachers at the LACC had begun to get to know these kids and talked about them as examples of two students who were very enthusiastic about their school. Cindy was empowered by her ability to effect change in her children's educational outcomes and was eager to help other parents work their way through difficulties with schools. She started by being well organized and strongly committed, and she managed, through the frustrating negotiations with the school hierarchy, to remain confident that there was a better solution. Cindy wasn't able to change that school's practices Making sure that all students in the school are provided with adequate education remained the responsibility of the vice principal.

Cindy's strong voice of advocacy was amazing. Our numerous informal conversations with Cindy at the LACC, where she worked, indicated that she stayed in close touch with her children, listening to them. She did not accept unrealistic, unsupportive, and unprofessional demands from the teachers and did not hesitate to express her opinions. She constantly monitored the children's homework to figure out if they can do it and if the homework makes sense. If not, she contacted the school. Although Cindy insisted that, without us, she would not have made the decision of transferring the children to another school, we think that our contribution was minimal—we only provided moral support and validation of her decision and her advocacy. Due to her success and position at the LACC, Cindy became influential for other LACC parents in providing advice to other parents in need. Also, it is important to mention that to make a school transfer across two school districts required Cindy to have access to an informal network of friends and relatives to make the change possible.

Mario and the Eggs (and the Pencil and the Notebook...)

On October 1, 2002, Sr. Hector and Sra. Amelia Guillet had just finished moving. Hector told us he was up until 2:30 a.m. still moving things to their new house and then had to go to work early, so he only got about three hours of sleep. Very concerned about Mario, their 12-year-old son, Hector took some time off work in the middle of the day and gave up his lunch hour, so that he could go with Amelia and us to the middle school. We also brought their two-year-old Lesley who was very good the whole time, coloring and having fun. We asked if Hector liked their new place, and he said that they had to move, it was a better apartment, but it was a worse neighborhood, because there were drugs all over. In Spanish—she spoke Spanish the whole time, except at the end, and, near the end, she started to answer questions I asked Hector in English, Sra. Amelia explained that Mario had been suspended because he didn't have a pencil in one class and he talked to friends in another class. None of us understood how that could be true.

On the drive to school, Sr. Hector said that he thought Mario must be sitting in the principal's office because the letter from the principal said that Mario would not be allowed back into classes after his suspension until the parents had a conference with the teacher. The principal was expected to be present at the meeting. When we got close to the school, we were looked around, because the buildings were very grand and impressive, and we weren't sure we were really at the right place. Sr. Hector and Sra. Amelia said they hadn't been to the school before, and Hector said, "I don't think this is right [that is, the right place]. It looks like a castle." It did turn out to be the school (which, by the way, had almost no parking, as if the school didn't expect visitors).

We went in the office, and the secretary was very nice, suggested we have a seat, while she found the principal, Mrs. Homer, and he came to meet us. (It turns out that Mrs. Homer is not the principal, but no one ever explained that the principal would not meet us or who Mrs. Homer was, so we just assumed she was the principal). We also asked that she get Mario and a translator. The translator never arrived, but his social studies teacher spoke Spanish. Mario brought his lunch to the office.

His social studies teacher, Britney came to the office, because she wanted to talk in detail to the Guillets before they met the principal. She was surprised that Mario was in class, because she knew that the Guillets were here because he was suspended. She explained that Mario had been suspended because the policy is that if a student is sent to the time-out room twice in one day, he gets a one-day suspension. She assured us that the teachers were just following policy. Sra. Amelia asked if it was for lacking a pencil and talking in class, and Britney said that she didn't think those were all the reasons for the suspension. She explained that teachers were concerned that Mario wasn't attending class, didn't hand in his homework, and was disorganized. Officially, Mario was suspended for not having a pencil in one class and not having his notebook in another.

We then walked down to what we thought was the principal's office (and continued to think was the principal's office, until we found out on the third visit that Mrs. Homer wasn't the principal), where we met Mario's reading teacher, Mrs. Sicilia. Before anyone had a chance to say anything, she started talking very quickly, saying that Mario was disruptive and he "owed" her seven homework assignments and two tests. She said that he was very disorganized. Maria said, "Let's try to do this a little differently" and asked Mario what he liked best about school and if there was something about his favorite subjects that he thought was most fun. He said that he liked gym and social studies. He liked gym because he got to play, and he liked social studies because they were always doing projects.

We explained that he was very good at the LACC, that he helped other students, and that he was very respectful and organized there. We asked him if there was anything about school that made it less fun, and he said it could be boring sometimes. The reading teacher didn't seem to like this and said she was going to get his transcripts to show that the suspension didn't just come out of nowhere. When she went out, Britney, the social studies teacher, explained to the Guillets that her class does lots of little projects and that Mario gets to move around the room and work with others. She said that not all teachers teach like that, so we would need to help Mario to also do well in other kinds of classes, too.

Sra. Amelia said that Mario did do his homework at the LACC, and she signed off on it. Britney said that maybe he didn't hand in his homework and needed to work on organizational skills. She also said that, in her class, when he needed to get out a sheet of paper, he lay down on the ground and spread out his things while he tried to find paper in his notebook. She said that, because kids are always moving in her class, it doesn't bother them, but other teachers find it a problem and may consider this disruptive.

The reading teacher came back in with Mario's transcripts and said that he was failing every class and had failed every class last year. The teachers then started to try to figure out if he had been retained the year before. Sr. Hector explained that, about two years ago, his family had gone back to Mexico for four months, and Mario's schooling got interrupted. It sounded to us like they weren't all sure that he was in the right grade, but they were particularly concerned because he was in the fifth grade when the consequential, state-administrated DSTP is given. Britney explained that Mario was getting an extra class in math to help prepare for the test. The reading teacher started to complain about Mario, and the social studies teacher said, "I think we should do what [was suggested] and be more positive about Mario."

We asked Mario if he liked to read, and he said that he liked to read about wrestlers but that reading class was boring. He said this was so because they read boring books. He said that he likes to read to his brother, but the books are for little kids, so sometimes he gets bored with that. We asked if he would read with our university students and pick books that he liked, and he said he would. The reading teacher had to leave at that point.

Mario's social studies teacher suggested that she would help him reorganize his notebooks and that he find someone to take him to the bus stop. He said there was an older kid in his neighborhood, maybe an eighth grader who could help. One of his parents reminded him that they had just moved, so he would need to find someone else to help him get to the bus on time.

That reminded Sra. Amelia that they needed to get information about buses (that was part of what we were going to do at the school anyway), and the social studies teacher and the principal's secretary identified which bus Mario rode and provided a form he needed to give to the bus driver. However, Mario was assigned a detention that day, had to stay late, and had to ride another bus, so the teacher explained. (We never learned why Mario was given a detention, because no one could find the form that explained the reason.)

The social studies teacher asked Mario if there were other problems, and he said that there were some kids who were giving him problems. She said you should go to a teacher to help you with that, so that you don't get in trouble. He said that the teacher doesn't care. She said that not all teachers are the same; you may have to go to a few teachers before you find one that will help you. She said that she would take her lunch hour to help Mario straighten out his notebook and meet him before he went home on the bus to make sure that he was staying organized. She went out to get the principal.

While she was gone, we asked Mario if he was nervous. He said no, but he did look deflated (he is usually so active at the LACC!). We asked him if reorganizing things would help or if there was something fun we could do at the LACC with our preservice teachers. He said he thought maybe reading with them would be good.

The social studies teacher came back and said that the principal would be right there. The social studies teacher said that there were parent-teacher conferences in two weeks when they would see if things had improved and talk with other teachers. She asked if the Guillets could come at 2:30 or 4:30 p.m., but Hector explained three times that he worked until 5:00 p.m. The teacher replied, "Then can you come at 3:00 p.m.," and they went back and forth. Hector said over and again "No, I work until 5:00," until the teacher said, "Okay, come at 5:00."" Hector said that he would leave work at 5:00 and so would be there a little after that. She asked if he could come earlier, and he gave up and said he'd work through his lunch hour, so that he could leave to be there at 5:00. Britney then gave Sra. Amelia her home phone number and said that, if she couldn't reach her at school, please call her at home, that her husband speaks Spanish, and that she could call anytime, because they stay up late. She repeated this several times, expressing concern that the Guillets to feel comfortable calling her.

The principal then came in and asked if we'd covered everything because she didn't want to repeat the policy. She seemed nice but spoke in a very loud voice. She said she wanted her school to be a place where all kids were welcomed and did their best. She called in the teacher who supervised the kids in time out and suspension, and he came in. He was young Latino man, maybe in his late 20s. He said, "Mario's problem is he's lazy. And, disruptive." The principal told Mario that she wanted him to do well and feel like this was his school and that we all wanted him to do his best.

We all thanked everyone and started to leave, and the social studies teacher came out to walk with us. There was much hand shaking and exchanging of cards and phone numbers. Mario waved good-bye and went back to class. The Guillets didn't look satisfied, but the social studies teacher said, "Call me in a week. We'll see how Mario is doing, and then we'll all meet at the parent teacher conference." She repeated that they should feel that they could call her at home. She added that we would all keep close watch on Mario. We asked Hector on the way home if he felt that he understood why Mario had been suspended, because we were still confused. He didn't understand but hoped things would get better, but he wasn't confident that they would. Amelia remained frustrated that little things that Mario did could be taken so seriously and that the school would demand that the parents come to school just to find out that Mario hadn't brought a pencil to school, a fact they already knew. (The social studies teacher later told us, in a phone call, that her solution to such things was to have extra pencils.)

Within a month, we got another call from Sr. Hector. Mario was suspended again, this time because he brought eggs to school. Because we had Britney's phone number, we called her and asked for a fuller explanation. She said that Mario had written in his notebook that he needed eggs for science class, so that his mother would get him eggs. That was not true. Mario brought the eggs to school to throw them at the school buses. He did not do this but was nonetheless suspended. Now, at half a dozen suspensions, Hector once again gave up lunch hour to visit school, but Amelia was too frustrated to come again. We picked Hector up at his new apartment, further up the hill. He said that this was a worse area for drugs than the old place. This time Hector was very irritated at the school, saying "If you find eggs, why don't you just call me, and I'll take care of it? Why do you have to suspend him for three days and have him get more behind?" His main source of frustration was that Mario had intended to throw the eggs but in fact had not done anything. Hector reasoned that the school could save a lot of time and effort if they would just contact him instead of taking him away from work every few weeks, so Mario could go back to school. He was also even more frustrated at how minimal the infraction was, but one of Mario's teachers said repeatedly, "Los huevos son muy peligroso" (in Spanish, "The eggs are very dangerous"[2]). We all paused, likely in respect for the fact that none of us will ever hear that particular phrase again. In the school meeting, Mrs. Homer opined that Mario could have done a lot of damage if he had hit a bus with an egg and distracted the driver. She also said that, if he continued to get suspended, Mario may be put in an alternative setting. In the car on the way home, Hector said, "First they suspend him for not having a pencil, and then they suspend him for eggs; education is more important." We asked him if he would mind if Mario was put in a different setting, and he said that as long as he gets an education, it would be all right, but he didn't want Mario put somewhere where he wouldn't learn as much as other kids.

Within two weeks, Hector called again because Mario was suspended. We had another parent-teacher meeting that day, so we could not join him at the school as he requested. We saw Mario at the LACC and asked what had happened at school. He said that a kid was picking on one of his friends, and he stepped in. The teacher only saw him doing anything wrong, and he was the one who got in trouble. He said that he thought he had done the right thing by trying to stop someone from bullying his friend, and he did not think it was right that he was the one in trouble. Mario seemed, each succeeding time we saw him, to be less and less interactive. We saw them once more at the LACC, and Hector was not hopeful about how things were going.

However, Mario began doing better at school and extremely well at the LACC. We ran into Mario several times in February and March of the following year, and Mario told us that he liked the school and liked not being suspended this year. Mario's father also told us that Mario was doing much better in school. Scott, the computer coordinator at the LACC, told us that Mario got much more relaxed at the LACC and was extremely cooperative and helpful.

At the same time, Amelia, Mario's mother, credited a new teacher for the change:

> I wanted to tell you about Mario. The most important thing for my husband and for me is that Mario now is happy, and he is doing very, very well at school and at the LACC. At the school, he is passing all the exams and subject[s], since he has a new teacher. He is right now in sixth grade, and he is very happy talking only when he has problems to understand the teacher and not talking all the time as he use[d] to do before. And Mr. Scott, at the LACC, often gives him he responsibility to be the only one who is taking care of the group in the computer room, and Mario feels great with that, because Mr. Scott believes in him, as you, Cris, and Eugene, Sra. Maria. My husband and me are feeling and noticing month after month how much Mario is learning and how much he likes to go at the school and the LACC.

However, the apparent victory for Mario's education had taken its toll on the family. Because the parents had to go to school, their employment as well as the family's financial well-being suffered. As Amelia described,

> The reason why we started to have so many problems with our jobs was because every time that we use[d] to go to the school because our Mario was excluded or suspended from the school, we had to ask for a permission to leave the job and talk with his teachers. Unfortunately, and Cris knows a lot about that, we had a time in which our Mario used to be suspended nearly once or twice a week and for terribly simple reasons like to forget a pencil one day or to misunderstand a schedule one afternoon.

Amelia's analysis of the situation points to the importance of schools understanding that their strength comes from the strong involvement of their communities:

> Mario is doing very, very well, and my husband and I are not feeling lonely, because we can feel how the people at the LACC and also you, Cris, and Eugene are always there for our son and for us. The problem is that, in this country, the schools did not understand how important the Latinos and the Latinas are, and it is unthinkable to me and to my husband not to have help from the school in terms of [a] translator. For example, at Mario's school, the science teacher, who is Latina, from time to time, helps me at the meetings, but it very often happens that, when I am having the meeting with the teachers, she is teaching. Well, the good news is that there are people like you, Cris, and Eugene who are taking seriously the voices, the work, and the needs of us Latinos, and I am very sure that very soon this country will realize that, without Latinos and other cultures who are living here, this country is nothing.

She also explained that

> … it is very important to be in contact with other families. Time to time, Sr. Nicholson holds [FAST] meetings. Normally, my husband and I always attend, because it is very important for us to be together with other Latino families and to listen to problems others have with other schools. … It was very important to us, and we believe that it is very important to make the school understand that Latinos and Latinas are not alone, and it is easier, at least I understand it is, to make my voice visible when we have support. My dream is that teachers will understand our cultures and at least, if not all of them, at least some of them will also speak our language. … Because I still cannot understand how it is possible to suspend a kid because he forgot a pencil. … But now it is not like that, now Mario is happy, and he is doing very, very well at the school and at the LACC. We need [people] to make our voices more visible and to make pressure to the schools to let them understand that our kids are as important as the kids from other cultures, like American.

FACING OBSTACLES WITH OTHERS

While not all of our experiences with schools were immediately successful, there were some positive results. First, and most importantly, parents realized that they had significant and powerful issues to raise with schools. That the schools did not always respond with respect, and their contacts were typically "crisis-driven" (Epstein, 1986), in the end, made the parents more aware of the importance of their critique. All of the parents with whom we went to schools felt that having someone else go with them and witness their struggles was useful. It gave them confidence to realize that their experiences of racism, which appeared less overt, were still very bad. Rather than making direct racist statements, teachers and

administrators appeared to care deeply and sincerely about the kids' trivial infractions. Furthermore, they "cared" so much that they were willing to damage the
kids' educational experiences in order to express that "care" (Rolon-Dow, 2002).
The teachers' care was imaginary care for imaginary children, while real children
got hurt. After leaving a school, we most often shook our heads in disbelief and
anger (but we would also remark, "Everyone was so nice").

We suspect that some teachers may sometimes use rigid school policies to get
rid of, even temporarily, children with whom they cannot work. We wonder if it is
time for educators to reconsider the idea that every teacher must be able to work
with every child in the classroom and acknowledge that not every teacher can work
effectively with every child, and, as a result, schools must develop appropriate policies and possibilities for legitimate *teacher–child divorce* (e.g., by transferring the
child to another classroom or school without stigma attached either to the child
or to the teacher). We found that divorcing from schools or teachers was the main
factor of educational success for the children with whom we worked for the year.

While institutionalizing teacher-student divorce can be helpful in many cases, it
does not help to improve the situation for all children and families. Another lesson
we have learned from our work with parents, children, and schools is that, for the sake
of children's educational success and general well-being, teachers and parents have to
listen to the children. They have to attend to and authentically care about children's
voices, concerns, interests, and needs (cf. Rolon-Dow, 2002). Genuine teaching and
parenting occur not when children have to listen to the teachers and parents but
when everyone listens to everyone and when there is a dialogue (Robinson & Fine,
1994). If parents choose to please the school and become school conduits pushing
their children to achieve unrealistic and harmful school demands, the parents may
push the children toward self-destructive behavior and may lose their children.

Parents found that they wanted to share their experiences at school with others and preferably have other people go to school with them. In part, this enabled
parents to hear about other situations and to understand that their experiences
were not isolated. Sharing with others also enabled parents to use the skills they
had developed to help other parents with similar issues. All of the parents, especially Cindy, seemed interested in attending parental meetings and using their
experience to empower other parents to also make demands of schools.

Just as the kids who went to the LACC did better at interacting with others and
learning with others when they were at the community center, the parents also recognized the social importance of their interactions with schools. The issues they faced
were not simply the result of isolated kids having individualized problems—though
certainly all kids need to be treated as the distinct individuals they are—but were also
problems facing Latino/a families as a community. Thus, the parents understood
themselves to be part of a community interacting with schools in the name of that

community. They pointed out that they were not isolated, both because advocates went with them and because they were, in fact, representatives of other Latino/a families who also struggled with the local schools. Furthermore, the LACC gave the parents a chance to see their children's strengths by watching them in the computer room, the homework room, the art room, and the other activity areas. The LACC also gave the kids a context in which they received positive feedback from adults. So, when things started going wrong with schools, it was easier for all involved to see where the problem was: Largely, the schools were making the problem.

Finally, we want to reflect on our participation. We have been faced with several dilemmas. First, the project took a big toll on our time. Between the end of May 2002 and March 2003 (excluding the summer of 2002), we had 12 meetings with parents, 8 meetings with schools, more than 30 phone conversations with parents (and children), and a dozen phone calls to schools and other child-related agencies (including the court). Clearly, we became another social agency subsidized by the university and our own commitment (by donation of our personal time and energy). This cannot continue for long. We see solutions for this in (a) the LACC getting funds for this type of work, a very unlikely possibility in the budgetary deficit atmosphere and current political meanness in the country, and (b) developing informal parent networks at the LACC where parents help each other. The latter sounds more realistic, although many LACC parents do not have time resources for helping each other (e.g., going to schools with each other during the day).

Our second dilemma is about our position regarding the parents' double bind of mixing advocacy for their children with a willingness to be a school conduit for the school's unrealistic, unreasonable, unsupportive, and unprofessional demands. So far, it is clear to us that we should elevate and amplify the voices of the children, who do not have much power in the adult world. But what about parents when they are in the role of school conduit? Should we keep silent about our discomfort? Should we support the parents no matter what? Should we provide alternative points of views? Should we take the children's side? Should we criticize the parents? The issue is complicated by the fact that we are not the parents' friends, equal to them, but representatives of a powerful institution (i.e., the university has a power of knowledge that is recognized by society). Although our loyalty seems to gravitate to the children, we are uneasy to criticize the parents in a role of school conduit, because we also know what they are going through.

We feel also a bit irresponsible in that we have not investigated situations in the schools our LACC children attend nor have we specifically looked into the labor and practice conditions of the children's teachers. For instance, Rolon-Dow (2002) found that a "lack of a culture of institutional caring limited the effects of individual [teachers'] acts of caring on students' engagement in school" and "trickled down to affect classrooms and individual students" (p. 187). This lack of a caring culture limits teachers', parents', and students' interactions with one another, focusing interactions toward purely technical concerns and away from the genuine engagement and concern with personal lives that are crucial to students being understood by the teacher in a way that allows engagement in school to be meaningful to the children. Rolon-Dow points out that a "critical care" perspective, an institutional (on the part of the school) and personal (on the part of the teacher) commitment to creating the conditions that allow teachers to understand students and their families' unique needs and perspectives, is crucial to allow teachers to see how families and the children themselves already do care about education and learning (and what they care about).

Our parent-teacher-child-university conferences focusing on elevating children's strengths, voices, interests, and needs were unsuccessful. Our failure supports the findings of others that changes in school conferencing involves a long and guided process for teachers to learn any new type of teacher-parent-child relations (Minke & Anderson, 2003 in press). It is too easy to blame teachers that they are not caring. It is more challenging to examine and reveal what institutional practices and conditions make uncaring the norm, and, while genuine caring seems near impossible in the schools that many of LACC children attend, how can such practices can be disrupted and what can be an alternative (Hargreaves, 1989, 1994).

Finally, we did not achieve one of our goals of addressing parentism in our preservice teachers. We should probably work further on organizing regular parent meetings at the LACC that involve our students. We hope, however, that this chapter will help us dissolve the myth of so-called uninvolved, low-income parents that we see in our work with preservice and in-service teachers.

NOTES

1. All names in this chapter, except ours, are pseudonyms.
2. In Spanish, the word *los huevos* (eggs) has a double meaning, like the English word *balls*, which also means *testicles*. It is doubtful that the teacher meant this double meaning, but it has strong a connotation in Spanish, and it transforms the sentence into "Balls are dangerous" for the Spanish ear.

REFERENCES

Austin, T. (1994). *Changing the view: Student-led parent conferences.* Portsmouth, NH: Heinemann.

Bateson, G. (1987). *Steps to an ecology of mind: Collected essays in anthropology, psychiatry, evolution, and epistemology.* Northvale, NJ: Aronson.

Cormier, L. S., & Hackney, H. (1999). *Counseling strategies and interventions* (5th ed.). Boston: Allyn and Bacon.

Crozier, G. (2000). *Parents and schools: Partners or protagonists?* Sterling, VA: Trentham.

De Carvalho, M. E. P. (2001). *Rethinking family-school relations: A critique of parental involvement in schooling.* Mahwah, NJ: L. Erlbaum Associates.

Delgado-Gaitan, C. (1991). Involving parents in the schools: A process of empowerment. *American Journal of Education, 100,* 20–46.

Epstein, J. L. (1986). Parent reactions to teacher practices of parent involvement. *The Elementary School Journal, 86,* 277–293.

Epstein, J. L. (1993). A response to [ap]parent involvement. *Teachers College Record, 94,* 710–717.

Fine, M. (1991). *Framing dropouts: Notes on the politics of an urban public high school.* Albany, NY: State University of New York Press.

Fine, M. (1993). [Ap]parent involvement: Reflections on parents, power, and urban public schools. *Teachers College Record, 94,* 682–710.

Hanafin, J., & Lynch, A. (2002). Peripheral voices: Parental involvement, social class and educational disadvantage. *British Journal of Sociology in Education, 23,* 35–49.

Hanhan, S. F. (1998). Parent-teacher communication: Who's talking? In M. L. Fuller & G. W. Olsen (Eds.), *Home-school relations: Working successfully with parents and families* (pp. 106–126). Boston: Allyn and Bacon.

Hargreaves, A. (1989). *Curriculum and assessment reform.* Toronto: OISE Press.

Hargreaves, A. (1994). *Changing teachers, changing times: Teachers' work and culture in the postmodern age.* London: Cassell.

Heidegger, M., & Stambaugh, J. (1996). *Being and time.* Albany, NY: State University of New York Press.

Lareau, A., & Shumar, W. (1996). The problem of individualism in family-school policies. *Sociology of Education, 69*(Extra Issue), 24–39.

Lave, J. (1992). *Learning as participation in communities of practice.* Paper presented at the meeting of the American Educational Research Association, San Francisco, CA.

Lave, J., & Wenger, E. (1991). *Situated learning: Legitimate peripheral participation.* Cambridge, UK: Cambridge University Press.

Matusov, E., & Hayes, R. (2002). Building a community of educators versus effecting conceptual change in individual students: Multicultural education for preservice teachers. In G. Wells & G. Claxton (Eds.), *Learning for life in the 21st century: Sociocultural perspectives on the future of education* (pp. 239–251). Cambridge, UK: Cambridge University Press.

Matusov, E., & Rogoff, B. (2002). Newcomers and old timers: Educational philosophy-in-actions of parent volunteers in a community of learners school. *Anthropology & Education Quarterly, 33*(4), 1–26.

Minke, K. M., & Anderson, K. J. (2003). Restructuring routine parent-teacher conferences: The family-school conference model. *Elementary School Journal, 104,* 49-69.

Nakagawa, K. (2000). Unthreading the ties that bind: Questioning the discourse of parent involvement. *Educational Policy, 14,* 443–472.

Robinson, E. L., & Fine, M. J. (1994). Developing collaborative home-school relationships. *Preventing School Failure, 39*(1), 9–15.

Rogoff, B., Matusov, E., & White, C. (1996). Models of teaching and learning: Participation in a community of learners. In D. R. Olson & N. Torrance (Eds.), *The handbook of education and human development: New models of learning, teaching and schooling* (pp. 388–414). Malden, MA: Blackwell Publishers.

Rolon-Dow, R. (2002). *School matters: A contextual exploration of engagement, identity, and ideology in the educational journeys of Puerto Rican girls*. Unpublished doctoral dissertation, Temple University, Philadelphia, PA.

Sarason, S. B. (1995). *Parental involvement and the political principle: Why the existing governance structure of schools should be abolished* (1st ed.). San Francisco: Jossey-Bass Publishers.

Wisconsin Center for Education Research. (2006). *FAST*. Retrieved May 2003, from http://www.wcer.wisc.edu/fast

From Radical Visions TO Messy Realities: Complexities IN THE Preparation OF Urban Teacher Educators

AFRA HERSI

Loyola College in Maryland

DENNIS SHIRLEY

Boston College

Most teacher educators began their careers as elementary or secondary school teachers. For experienced teachers entering doctoral programs, the transition from the world of kindergarten through 12thgrade (K–12) education to university- based teacher education can be surprisingly abrupt and disorienting (Labaree, 2003). Teachers move from being professionals in charge of their classrooms (with all of the pleasures and challenges that implies) into the relatively more passive role of the university student who receives knowledge and needs to prove mastery of it. Although there has been valuable discussion recently about the transition teachers make when their careers shift from teaching to educational research (Pallas, 2001), comparatively little attention has been devoted to how beginning teacher educators negotiate this transition (Russell & Korthagen, 1995; Zeichner, 1995).

We would like to suggest that, although not exactly part of a hidden curriculum, the experiences of new doctoral students in the culture of the university outside of their formal course work rarely receive much concerted attention. Yet even as we advance this suggestion, it is important to note that the culture of the university is hardly uniform. In fact, scholars of higher education disagree as to whether there is a common culture and have been more apt in recent years to consider the university "an environment full of contradictions" (Slaughter & Leslie, 1997, p. 210), in which the traditional esteem for teaching has largely (but not entirely) lost ground to scholarly productivity and grant-funded research. The growing ambiguity in the purpose of the university has not been lost on students, who, like faculty, struggle to discern their roles in an environment of not only intellectual ferment but also institutional unclarity.

In the case of teacher education, external grants, typically funded by the United States Department of Education and large philanthropies, provide a double-edged sword in terms of teaching and research. In 1999, the largest federal grants dedicated to teacher education in the history of American education were approved under the auspices of the reauthorization of the Higher Education Act. These Title II grants were broad in scope and purpose but were especially significant insofar as they entailed partnership grants to support collaborative activities between schools and universities dedicated to improving teacher quality. As this volume goes to press, another reauthorization of Title II partnership grants appears imminent, thus building an apparently long-term economic support system for collaborations between high-need local education agencies and colleges and universities.

As teacher education gains increasing attention from educational reformers, and as large federal and private grants continue to transform the profession, it appears that the traditional roles of our graduate and doctoral students as research and teaching assistants also become modulated and take on new dimensions. This development is noteworthy, because the emergence of new roles, as shaped by policy initiatives, entails not only the acquisition of new skill sets but also, to a certain extent, the development of new identities (Ball, 1994). Policies are more than random guidelines or aberrant cultural epiphenomena; rather, for those affected directly by the policies, they entail the emergence of new subjectivities as well as a certain sense of loss that accompanies all change processes (Hargreaves, 1994).

As Huberman (1999) observed, albeit in a highly attenuated and largely suggestive form, graduate students in education programs can take on roles as "boundary spanners" that link universities, K–12 schools, and broader school communities. In this chapter, we wish to extend Huberman's insight and submit that large federal grants, such as the Title II grants, provide entirely new venues for graduate students to engage with educational change and that those venues in and of themselves deserve scholarly investigation and analysis. This is especially the case because while professors of education acquire large research and training grants with school intervention components, in many cases, it is the graduate student who is the on-the-ground boundary spanner who keeps communication flowing and really develops civic capacity between schools and their higher education partners over time.

These considerations are especially salient in light of the complex interface between urban schools, teacher preparation programs that aim to prepare teachers for urban environments, and urban communities. Peterman and Sweigard (see chapter 2 of this volume) have indicated that it is not sufficient simply to adapt state standards for pupils in urban schools; rather, one should identify specific features of urban education and develop ensembles of standards that meet the social and educational needs of the largely low-income pupils of color who are concentrated in urban schools. Likewise, Shirley (see chapter 4 of this volume) has sought to elaborate the need for participatory democracy in the revitalization of American education and cities, while recognizing the daunting nature of such undertakings in the current context. Urban teacher education, it would appear, will never be a smooth technocratic operation; rather, it will always be a culturally contextualized project, requiring a special sensibility and a broad repertoire of skills to educate the diverse learners in our cities' schools (Cochran-Smith, 2004).

Given these complicated phenomena, our goals in this chapter are as follows. First, we will describe Afra Hersi's evolution as an educator, with particular attention given to her very different experiences as an urban and suburban teacher. Second, we will discuss Dennis Shirley's development as a teacher educator who sought to integrate principles of community organizing into his teaching practices based upon his experiences working with Alinsky organizers in the urban Southwest. Third, we will then describe, in a very abbreviated fashion, how Afra and Dennis used Title II support to collaborate over three years in a community organizing project based in an urban high school in Boston. Finally, we will review some of the most salient points of this collaboration for Afra's evolution as a teacher educator and will suggest some future directions for research in the preparation of urban teacher educators.

AFRA HERSI'S TEACHING TRAJECTORY AND QUEST FOR SOCIAL JUSTICE

Afra Hersi is of Somali background and immigrated to the United States when she was 10 years old. She attended public schools in northern Virginia and began her career as a world history teacher in Fairfax County, a resource-rich suburban school district in northern Virginia. Afra's entrance into the profession was supported and guided by a robust induction program that assigned a highly accomplished mentor to each beginning teacher. Afra's mentor, a 25-year veteran, helped to her to navigate the myriad of demands placed on teachers.

Afra found tremendous satisfaction in her new profession by helping students understand and appreciate world history, a subject she loved. Encouraged by her mentor, she used a mélange of primary and secondary sources in her classroom, engaged students in a variety of student-centered activities that provoked critical inquiry into the history curriculum, and developed collaborative relationships with her colleagues in history and English. With growing confidence in her abilities as a teacher, she quickly began to take on leadership roles in her school. Given her international and immigrant background, she was especially interested in supporting student clubs, such as the Model United Nations and Amnesty International, that exposed pupils to world issues. In addition to leadership at her school, Afra served on a number of district-wide committees, including a committee to revise the history curriculum at the 10th grade.

In her fourth year of teaching, Afra began to look for further challenges and opportunities for growth. She transferred to Robinson High, a nearby secondary school in the same district. This was an especially fulfilling time because Afra and an English teacher at Robinson were able to co-teach a new interdisciplinary ninth-grade humanities course. They shared students, planned lessons, and delivered instruction together. Although there was an accordion wall dividing their classrooms, it was not uncommon to find the two classes working together. Rather than the "cellular" forms of organizing instruction that Dan Lortie described many years ago (1975, pp. 13–19) and that persist in many schools, Afra experienced teaching as a collaborative venture with abundant resources and excellent professional collegiality.

With five years of successful teaching under her belt, Afra wanted to experience another side of teaching and decided that she would like to expand her repertoire of practices by relocating to an urban school in New England. Although initially excited by this prospect, this experience was to test her confidence, her understanding of her role as an educator, and her perspective on American society at large. The urban high school became a kind of critical catalyst that provoked and unsettled Afra's political and social consciousness.

The school Afra now worked in served approximately 930 students, 58% of whom qualified for free and reduced-price lunch. Located in a former middle school, the physical plant was dilapidated and unwelcoming. Pupils struggled with overcrowded classrooms, outdated textbooks, little or no school supplies, and no computers. Afra had always had racially and culturally diverse colleagues at her schools in northern Virginia, but she found herself to be the only Black faculty member at her new school. Due to a shortage of custodial staff, the school was locked down by 3:00 p.m. This was in sharp contrast to Afra's experience at both Lake Braddock and Robinson, which were open until 11:00 p.m. and provided a wealth of extracurricular activities and adult education classes.

Unfortunately for students in the urban high school, the locking up of the building in the middle of the afternoon meant that many of them could not stay after school to make up work or to receive tutoring support. Working with a ninth-grade team, Afra proposed to the principal a plan to open a Homework Support Center three days a week. A key aspect of this plan was the need to keep the building open for students who want to stay after school, while maintaining its safety and security. Members of the ninth-grade team agreed to staff the center and oversee its operation.

To Afra's delight, the principal agreed to support the creation of the Homework Support Center. It proved to be a popular innovation that was heavily utilized by students and appreciated by their parents. Yet, while the implementation of the Homework Support Center was a success, other problems remained.

Perhaps the biggest challenge Afra faced in the urban high school was the politically charged and adversarial nature of the culture. Part of this polarized culture had arisen in response to the principal's efforts to reorganize the school day in the form of block scheduling. All teachers were required to receive professional development training to support the new 90-minute long classes. In response to the reorganization, teachers divided themselves into three camps: those who supported the principal, those who were in open opposition, and those who observed cautiously from the sidelines. Afra experienced tremendous lack of trust and respect among the teachers, with only a few daring to cross firmly established party lines to try to build a common culture of inquiry and collaboration.

In addition to this tension, there were rampant discipline problems in the urban high school. Each classroom was equipped with a phone that was used primarily to alert administrators about fights and other disruptions in classrooms. Some teachers used behavioral management strategies based on intimidation and fear; others could be heard yelling at their pupils as one walked through the corridors of the building.

Perhaps Afra's most demoralizing experience at the school occurred when there was a major drug bust in her classroom. The incident, which occurred during a ninth-grade study skills period she was supervising, involved a quiet, well-mannered student who had struggled academically but was making steady progress in his studies. Afra confiscated marijuana and bags of money from the student, which suggested that he had been selling drugs in the school or its environs. The student was completely cooperative with the administration and the police, and Afra learned soon afterward that drugs were used openly by many pupils and the adults in their community.

As the year unfolded, Afra's anger at the disparity between wealthy suburban school districts and resource-strapped urban schools sharpened. In addition to an ever-widening economic gap, there was an immense "expectations gap" at her new school. Teachers at the school, discouraged by its many problems, had adapted by holding low expectations for their students. Afra found that it was not unusual for some pupils to sleep through entire class periods, with the teachers never responding by either reprimanding the students or asking what it was that led them to be so tired every day. Although the primary motivation behind block scheduling was to allow teachers to develop more creative lesson plans, in reality instruction still consisted of teacher talk, and students still spent most of their time listening to their teachers and filling out work sheets.

Afra and other colleagues on the ninth-grade team—who by and large wanted to give block scheduling a chance to improve pupil achievement—found themselves criticized by veteran teachers who were opposed to the principal and the new reforms. Most of the instruction at the school appeared to consist of what Haberman (1991) calls a "pedagogy of poverty," in which the predominant goal is simply to maintain control in an environment dominated by mistrust and adversarial relationships. In such settings, academic achievement and sociocultural supports for students generally give way to an emphasis on surveillance and regimentation, which, once in place, is extremely difficult to overcome (Anyon, 1997; Lipman, 2004).

Although there were many seemingly obdurate problems at the high school, Afra encountered teachers and parents who were committed to its improvement. Although parent involvement at the school was extremely low—for example, less than 20 parents came to Parents' Night at the school in the fall—there was a small group of very active parents determined to change the situation. Nonetheless, Afra felt overwhelmed by the many problems and the overall environment of high pressure and few resources. After just one year, she decided to leave the school to assume a teaching position at the History Department at Lexington High School, in one of Boston's affluent suburbs.

Afra's two-year tenure at Lexington High School was happy and, in many ways, brought her back to the familiar setting of a high-achieving secondary school with broad parental and community support. Yet her nerve-wracking experience in the urban environment continued to gnaw at her. Why had her students there been treated so shabbily, in terms of the physical infrastructure, the locked-down nature of the building after hours, and the low teacher expectations? Why had she, who had been so successful in Fairfax County and was once again successful at Lexington, felt so helpless in the urban environment? In pursuit of answers to these questions, Afra decided to take a leave of absence from teaching, to enter the master's program in curriculum and instruction at the Lynch School of Education in Boston College.

DENNIS SHIRLEY'S EDUCATION IN COMMUNITY ORGANIZING

Dennis's early years as a teacher educator in the 1980s and 1990s at Rice University in Houston, Texas, were fraught with discouragement, as the urban settings in which his student teachers were placed seemed inhospitable not only to intellectual inquiry but also, in many ways, to respectful environments for both teachers and students. A professional development school venture explored by his colleagues and him in the Houston public schools provoked not only conceptual disagreement, but also a destructive enmity among multiple stakeholders. Alas, familiar patterns of mistrust in school and university partnerships surfaced quickly and were difficult to overcome over time. Faculty in the university, unfamiliar with the complicated political landscape of urban education, inferred a higher degree of organizational coherence and effectiveness to school administrators than turned out to be the case. Most of the administrators with whom we worked found themselves to be subject to a dizzying array of political factions that were difficult, if not impossible, to bring to consensus. Our understanding about the challenges of leadership in large multiracial districts only emerged in retrospect, after much time had been lost in planning and implementing core features of the new school.

Faculty in the schools, on the other hand, though respectful of the disciplinary expertise of higher-education colleagues, came, over time, to consider their university partners as inexperienced in regard to the many conflicting demands placed upon teachers and administrators. Higher-education faculty knew little, if anything, for example, about the Texas Assessment of Academic Skills (TAAS) that was introduced in 1990 and that played a major role in ranking schools in the state's rapidly expanding accountability system. Nor did higher education faculty seem to know much about the needs of students with learning disabilities or issues related to learning English as a second language. Though many valuable exchanges of information occurred, the gap between the discursive communities of the elite private research university and the urban public school system was so large that any common meeting ground in terms of instructional approaches or curriculum reforms seemed elusive.

At the same time that he was working on the new school venture, Dennis began collaborating with community organizers struggling to improve urban education in Texas and working out of the tradition of Alinsky organizing (Alinsky, 1946, 1971). Though community organizing has its own complexities and difficulties (Polletta, 2002), Dennis was taken with the ability of Alinsky organizers to identify latent political capacities in working-class populations and to target community grievances in a focused and deliberate way. In particular, Alinsky organizations seemed to be successful at producing broad-based community engagement on public issues, such as affordable housing, health care, environmental safety, and the condition of the public schools.

The story behind the development of a network of Alliance Schools in the metropolitan Southwest by Alinsky organizers in the 1990s is insufficiently known by teacher educators, although this work has been well documented (Murnane & Levy, 1996; Osterman, 2002; Sarason, 2002; Shirley, 1997, 2002; Sirianni & Friedland, 2001; Warren, 2001). Community organizers work with neighborhood leaders through a series of strategies that start with one-on-one conversations, evolve into house meetings, develop capacity through home visits and research actions, and culminate in large public accountability sessions in which elected officials, civil servants (such as police, health, or school officials), and business leaders commit themselves to a given community organization's agenda. In the following discussion, we describe briefly three facets of this organizing approach and its relevance to education.

The first facet is the "iron rule" of this kind of community organizing: "Never do anything for others what they can do for themselves" (Shirley, 2002, p. 11). The iron rule often strikes against the grain of teacher educators and school reformers, who can be caught up in "the culturally mainstream perspectives of faculty and students and their tendencies toward 'helperism' in relationships with school and community partners" (Murrell, 2001, p. 35). This helperism is endemic in the literature of professional development schools and urban schools; the impulse to help often is used to acquire external grants for colleges and universities and transforms higher education institutions into perpetual grant-seeking machines, as well as auxiliary social service agencies.

The well-intentioned argument that urban schools are underresourced and that urban populations are disenfranchised can, if uncontested, unintentionally lead to an assertion of professional expertise that reduces citizens to clients and transforms political problems into issues of technical inefficiency. Unless checked, the tendency of professionals, such as professors, teachers, social workers, and school counselors, can be to reinforce a sense of dependency upon external actors, not only among urban parents, but also among teachers in urban public schools.

The iron rule is intended to mitigate the tendency to helperism, but it must be understood correctly. It is not intended to convey indifference to social injustices or to legitimize the withdrawal of civic engagement from the body politic. Community organizers practicing out of the Alinsky tradition acknowledge that the working poor in many American cities attended schools that de facto practiced racial and class-based segregation and emphasized order and discipline over content knowledge and participatory democracy (Texas Interfaith Education Fund, 1990). Learning to translate vague grievances into political problems, developing social capital through networks of broad-based civic engagement, and acquiring the public speaking and organizing skills to confront and persuade power holders are skills that require careful mentoring and support for adult learners. In a sense, citizens may not know that they *can* act efficaciously on behalf of their communities because of a complicated blend of political, cultural, and educative factors. These obstacles to change require agitation, a deliberately disruptive intervention, and careful scaffolding of political skills.

A second facet of Alinsky organizing concerns the Industrial Areas Foundation's (IAF's) focus on winnable issues. Essentially, the line of interpretation here is that community organizations based in poor and working-class neighborhoods can only afford a small number of defeats and hence must carefully select the issues for which they wish to battle. Alinsky organizations are sometimes faulted for focusing on topics that can seem relatively trivial to political radicals who desire sweeping social changes. For example, the IAF often begins organizing projects with undertakings that can seem trivial to some who are more interested in sweeping social changes. These projects can be as mundane as installing a traffic light at a dangerous intersection, shutting down a crack house, or improving neighborhood drainage systems. The essential point here, from the IAF's perspective, is not so much the significance of these changes, but rather the development of a measure of confidence in a community that, if mobilized, changes can be brought about at all. For the working poor and the working class, a crack house across the street from an elementary school is generally not viewed as a symptom of the failures of capitalism (although it is that) but is much more likely to be perceived as an insult to the community and a danger to small children who have to find their way to and from school each day without an adult escort. In such situations, organizers need to identify and work with indigenous community leaders to develop confidence that political engagement can produce visible results.

The third strategy used continually by IAF organizers is a relatively simple one: that of actively listening to community concerns and using those concerns—and not the organizer's assumptions of what the community might most need—as the point of departure for organizing. "If we have a fixed idea in our heads of what our agenda is," one Alinsky organizer remarked, "then there's no point to doing house meetings." (quoted in Shirley, 1997, p. 62) In Alliance School culture, house meetings in which community residents and stakeholders meet to identify core grievances and develop political strategies are the core forum for developing civic capacity.

These insights into community organizing—the iron rule, the selection of winnable issues, and the importance of active listening—shaped Dennis's education as a teacher educator influenced by many years of study and collaboration with Alinsky organizations in the 1990s. Lured by an offer by Boston College in 1998, he relocated to New England and sought to develop a new network of educators, students, and community activists to improve urban education.

THE MASSACHUSETTS COALITION FOR TEACHER QUALITY
AND STUDENT ACHIEVEMENT

Dennis's move to Boston was fortuitous, for at roughly the same time that he moved the U.S. Congress was reauthorizing the Higher Education Act and providing new funding for school and university partnerships. Dean Mary Brabeck of the Lynch School of Education played an invaluable role in mobilizing higher education institutions and urban school systems in Massachusetts to apply for the Title II funding contained in the reauthorization. With remarkable coherence and discipline, 7 colleges and universities (Boston College, Clark University, the University of Massachusetts at Boston, the University of Massachusetts at Amherst, Northeastern University, Lesley University, and Wheelock College), 18 urban schools (in Boston, Springfield, and Worcester), and 12 businesses, community-based organizations, and nonprofits all came together in several months of breakneck organizing in the spring of 1999 to compile a grant proposal. The new network, known as the Massachusetts Coalition for Teacher Quality and Student Achievement, received $7 million in grant funding in September 1999 to redesign teacher education programs and practices. Linked with formal educational institutions but also autonomous from them, networks such as the coalition can use their funding lines and social capital to leverage progressive changes in school, university, and urban policies (Lieberman, 2000; Murrell, 2001).

In the original grant proposal to the U.S. Department of Education, the proposal writing team of the Massachusetts Coalition established six goals (Massachusetts Coalition for Teacher Quality and Student Achievement, 1999). These were worked out through a lengthy process of deliberation, debate, and compromise and represented our best effort to address what we viewed as the critical issues in contemporary urban education. Our objectives were to (a) increase the participation of arts and sciences faculty in teacher education to ensure strong content knowledge; (b) expand the school and community-based nature of teacher education; (c) organize broad-based "communities of inquiry and practice" among school, university, business, and community stakeholders to inform teacher education; (d) improve instruction in literacy across the content areas both in teacher education and in our partnering public schools; (e) recruit, train, and retain cohorts of ethnically diverse beginning teachers; and (f) promote the coalition's capacity to conduct research and inform public policy on issues of teacher quality.

Especially noteworthy for our current consideration is the emphasis on the school and community-based nature of teacher education linked with the inclusion of community stakeholders in the communities of inquiry and practice. For although it was clear to the writing team that collaboration with arts and sciences faculty and K-12 faculty was nonnegotiable, the teachers, professors, and activists in the coalition insisted on developing a theme that we considered radical in nature. We all knew that American society is stratified by race and class and that those broad social dynamics have tremendous impacts on the challenges facing urban education and teacher education (Ladson-Billings, 1994). Following up on a critique of professional development schools developed by one of our writing team members (Murrell, 1998), but also shaped by a larger sense that teacher education programs are in many ways culturally disconnected from the communities they are ostensibly created to serve (Shirley, 1997), the coalition decided to organize to give teacher education a community base, both physically (by teaching classes on-site in urban schools and community-based organizations) and pedagogically (by integrating community members into our communities of inquiry and practice as key stakeholders and decision makers).

After a series of long meetings in fall 1999 to establish our organizational structure and set priorities for launching the coalition, activists in the coalition initiated a series of strategies for working with communities to promote culturally responsive critical pedagogies and to promote student achievement. Faculty members at Northeastern University broke with the teacher education tradition of school-based placements and placed students in their Introduction to Education class in community settings such as churches, sports facilities, and libraries, to teach reading and writing (see chapter 3, by Murrell, in this volume). The teacher education faculty at the University of Massachusetts at Boston held department meetings at the Dudley Street Neighborhood Initiative in Roxbury; hired the Chair of the Education Committee at Dudley Street to serve as a liaison between the schools, the university, and the community; and developed a substitute teacher induction program in collaboration with activities from the Boston chapter of Association of Communities Organized for Reform Now (ACORN). A professor-in-residence from Lesley University hired a parent activist to coordinate communication between teachers and parents in her urban elementary school. Urban schools and universities in Boston, Springfield, and Worcester used coalition resources to promote stronger ties to Spanish-speaking immigrant parents. Coalition conferences and newsletters emphasized the parent engagement thrust of this work, seeking to reanimate a spirit of participatory democracy and to enhance community accountability for urban schools (Liston & Zeichner, 1991; Oakes, Quartz, Ryan, & Lipton, 2000; Shirley, chapter 4 in this volume).

The preceding provides a schematic overview of the Coalition's activities in terms of community engagement. As Murrell (2001) maintains, the Massachusetts Coalition operates at a "macro-level system of practice" (p. 174), connecting urban communities and schools with one another and providing political opportunities for improving education that cannot occur if institutional boundaries are rigid, bureaucratic, and impermeable. Murrell further suggests that macro-level changes, though important, must be integrated with "meso" and "micro" levels of practice at the school and classroom level to develop truly effective activity settings. In an effort to instantiate joint productive activity in such settings, we will describe one attempt to confront the community engagement challenge, based on a course taught on-site at an urban high school from 2001 to 2003.

COMMUNITY ORGANIZING AT BRIGHTON HIGH SCHOOL

For many years, Boston College has collaborated with schools in what is now called Cluster V of the Boston Public Schools. These schools are concentrated in the northwest segment of the city known as Allston-Brighton (although, in 2001, several schools were added in Mission Hill and Roxbury), which is the largest of nine major neighborhoods in Boston and is home to roughly 70,000 people (*Boston Redevelopment Authority*, 2000). One urban high school, Brighton High, serves roughly 1,200 students. Of these, approximately 27% come from Allston-Brighton, with the other 73% bused in from the other clustered neighborhoods and with many of the pupils traveling for more than an hour each way on public transportation. Sixty-five percent of the students qualify for free or reduced-price lunches; because of the high poverty level, the entire school receives Title I funding.

As part of Dennis's work with the Massachusetts Coalition, he began teaching his classes on-site at Brighton High in fall 2001. From September through May, the school served as a site for master's degree–level teacher candidates and doctoral students to study instruction, curriculum, and assessment issues. Afra Hersi was a student in the Social Contexts of Education class that Dennis taught at Brighton High in 2001, and she heard leaders from community-based organizations speak to the class about their efforts to strengthen school and community relationships. This initial period of relationship building consisted of a relatively quiet and circumspect effort simply to learn about the culture of the school and its many strengths and challenges; in terms of community organizing, it corresponds to the initial phase of one-on-one meetings and research actions deployed by Alinsky organizers.

For Afra, the Social Contexts of Education class represented her first return to an urban high school in years. As she drove the short distance from Boston College to Brighton High School for the first class meeting, Afra felt both anxiety and excitement, as she wondered what it would be like to walk into an urban high school again. Finding the school in and of itself was not hard—Brighton High School looks like either a penitentiary or a cathedral, depending on one's point of view—yet actually finding the driveway was a challenge. After a wrong turn into the hospital next door, Afra was able to find the narrow driveway along the side of the building. To get to the library, one had to drive around to the back to a small parking lot and walk past an overflowing dumpster. The passageway was often propped open by a brick. As she learned later in the semester, without that brick, she would be locked out of the building unless a janitor responded to the bell one could press to the left of the door.

Mindful of the difficulties of simply accessing the school building, Dennis sought to design the class so that, once the Boston College students found their way to the library, they would have multiple opportunities to interact with Brighton High School teachers, students, and local community activists. It is extremely important to note that the class was planned in such a way that students would not simply be thrown into those encounters, but rather were prepared through sets of readings to engage in critical inquiry about urban education today. From Dennis's vantage point, Afra stood out in the class because when a complicated topic—such as race relations, the situation of gay and lesbian students in the urban school setting, or the acquisition of critical thinking skills in an age of high-stakes testing—was being probed, Afra often would turn directly to a high school student guest in the class and solicit his or her ideas to contribute to the class discussion. There was a natural ease in Afra's queries and a sense of genuine curiosity about the students' experiences that both brought the class conversations down to earth and exposed new facets of change as experienced by students that are often overlooked when one has a single-minded focus on learning outcomes. On Afra's part, she found the small and dialogical nature of class interactions to be supportive of her own reflections on her experiences in urban education.

Impressed by Afra's encounters with the diverse array of those who were teaching and learning in Brighton High School, Dennis encouraged her to apply to the doctoral program in curriculum and instruction at Boston College. By doing so, he was simply extending a key principle of community organizing as practiced by Alinsky organizers, which entails the identification and recruitment of talented individuals who can bring their commitment to social justice to the development of powerful new social change networks like the Massachusetts Coalition for Teacher Quality and Student Achievement. At the end of the fall semester, the class evaluated its activities and determined that, while it was valuable in and of itself to convene the class in the urban high school setting, Dennis indicated that in the next iteration of the course he might try to link the class activities with the real needs of Brighton High in a more overt and sustainable way.

Afra applied to the doctoral program in curriculum and instruction in winter 2001 and was accepted into the program the following February. Dennis immediately offered her a graduate assistantship, funded by the resources of the Massachusetts Coalition, anticipating that she could play a critical role in building the partnership between Brighton High and Boston College. Meanwhile, the Brighton High School headmaster, seeking to capitalize on the school's growing partnership with Boston College, invited Lynch School of Education faculty to attend a whole-school professional development day in April 2002.

At the school, Dennis heard teachers express their frustration about many facets of life in their school. Though they did not manifest the hardened kind of "parentism" identified by Mayo, Candela, Matusov, and Smith (in chapter 6 of this volume), they were concerned that it was so difficult to establish contact with parents, especially with parents of failing pupils. Rather than blame the teachers, Dennis was able to use his background in Alinsky organizing to recognize an organizing opportunity. He proposed to his Brighton High School colleagues that his Social Contexts of Education class explore with the school ways in which parent participation could be increased. The proposal was accepted, and, over the summer 2002 months, Dennis and Afra worked with the headmaster, teachers, parents, and community-based organizations at the school to develop an action plan for increasing parent engagement. Together, they decided to see if the Social Contexts of Education class could play a role in promoting greater parent engagement at a Parents' Night event held in the school each fall.

In September, the headmaster and a teacher from the school visited the opening Social Contexts class and requested that the teacher candidates work with the school to increase parent engagement. Subsequently, the Social Contexts class convened weekly in the Career Services Library of Brighton High and interviewed teachers, students, and parents to learn about multiple facets of the Brighton High pupils' lives relevant to education. Simultaneously, teacher candidates studied research on community organizing, parent involvement, urban education, and multicultural education and brought questions generated by the readings to the class's engagement with the organizing process. Grant funds from the Massachusetts Coalition provided tuition remission for four teachers from the school to take the class, and those teachers educated the entire Social Context class, including the professor, on the very real challenges (as well as their significant victories) that they experienced on a day-to-day basis in the school.

At the same time, a Boston College–based team, led by Afra, began meeting with teachers, parents, and representatives of community-based organizations to plan the Parents' Night activities in November. Simply targeting the Parents' Night as a priority months in advance was in many ways a first for the school, which had previously waited until November to set the date of the Parents' Night. Throughout the fall, Afra and Dennis brought a broader base of teachers and community activists into the circle to coordinate strategies for the Parents' Night and to lay the groundwork for a long-term parent engagement component of the school's whole-school improvement plan.

Much of this work was tenuous and difficult. A drug bust, a fight between students, and heating problems could easily deflect attention away from a theme like parent organizing. Nonetheless, throughout the fall, a small cadre of teachers, led by those taking the class, nurtured relationships with parents, primarily through extensive telephone calls, as well as mailings and notifications sent home with pupils. Those notifications were primarily in English, but Spanish and Portuguese translations were also made for the school's numerous Hispanic families. A parent liaison working with Gaining Early Awareness and Readiness for Undergraduate Programs (GEAR UP), a federally funded college preparatory program, made phone calls to the Spanish-speaking parents to keep them abreast of developments. Afra's organizing efforts throughout the fall so impressed Dennis that he joked that she "made Saul Alinsky look like a slacker."

Simultaneous with these efforts, planning was underway to consult the parents at the Parents' Night about their own opinions about Brighton High and to solicit their ideas about work that could be accomplished to improve school and community ties. Much of this planning was informed by the deliberations of the Community Engagement Task Force of Urban Network to Improve Teacher Education (UNITE), which Dennis chairs and on which Afra serves. The task force consists of higher-education faculty, teachers, administrators, parents, and community activists and is affiliated with the Holmes Partnership. As part of its study of the community engagement problematic, the task force read Dennis's book, *Community Organizing for Urban School Reform* (1997), as well as a synopsis of an 11-city National Science Foundation study by Clarence Stone, Jeffrey Henig, Bryan Jones, and Carol Pierannunzi entitled *Building Civic Capacity: The Politics of Reforming Urban Schools* (2001). In each case, those works emphasized the finding that successful school reform depended upon strong parent engagement components, not as the only facet of school improvement but as one critical strand of it.

Given the themes of parent engagement and civic capacity that emerged during the planning process, it became critical for our planning group to include a broad array of community-based organizations in the Parents' Night activities themselves. Hence, a wide variety of such organizations were contacted and became part of the planning team. We then determined that the Parents' Night should evolve to be more in the nature of a community fair, in which different organizations could inform parents about their activities and solicit their participation in work related to youth development, health services, and community organization. We agreed that part of the school's cafeteria, where parents would be receiving their children's fall semester report cards, should be turned over to the community groups whose services would be intermingled with food and drinks set out for the parents.

When Parents' Night finally arrived on November 20, 2002, the number of parents in attendance rose 59%, from 145 parents in 2001 to 231 parents in 2002.

On the one hand, the increase could seem small, given the effort that went into recruitment and the size of student enrollment in the school. Nonetheless, the faculty, parents, and teacher candidates who put the effort into Parents' Night were pleased, and teachers who had worked in the school for years affirmed that the turnout was the highest they had ever seen. Some teachers had lines of parents waiting outside of their classrooms to meet with them, a sight that none of the teachers in the school had ever experienced. Perhaps best of all, the real diversity of the school was present: Brazilian, Dominican, and Haitian parents were at the school in abundance. Dennis had a chance to roll out his (frankly atrocious) Spanish, and Afra had the pleasure of chatting in Somali with a Somali family.

Where did the iron rule fit into this organizing effort? The significance of the work at Brighton High School is not really that parent participation went up at the Parents' Night, although that is an important first step. What is more significant is that school faculty working with parents and Boston College teacher candidates learned that they could change the culture of their school and collaborate to raise parent participation. This is the critical contribution of the iron rule—the development of leadership capacity (in this case) in the school itself.

In addition to the iron rule as an organizing principle, the selection of the fall Parent Night as a target for raising parent participation also proved to be a winnable issue. The critical point to acknowledge here concerns the specific definition of a *winnable issue*, which refers not so much to a spectacular triumph but more to a cultural shift. After the fall Parents' Night, the collective sensibility that years of low parent participation were a naturalized part of the school culture was disrupted. Teachers saw that parents could and would come to the Parents' Night, given sufficient prior notification, phone calls home, and handouts to students. The theory behind Alinsky organizing is that the sense that things *can* be different is tremendously important to leadership development—and that this acknowledgment is far more important than mere parent turnout, programmatic changes, or other similarly static kinds of outcomes.

Finally, the listening process of this work should also be underlined. The activities with Brighton High differed from IAF organizing insofar as the professional development day that spawned the organizing effort surfaced tremendous frustration among Brighton High teachers about the lack of community involvement in the school. Most IAF organizing has started with parents' grievances and worked toward the school, rather than from the school to the community. Despite this reversal of direction, the same principle of active listening to disappointed stakeholders was employed, with positive results.

For Afra, the organizing work at Brighton High served to overcome her previous sense of frustration and to solidify her commitment to urban schools and urban teacher education. Reforming urban schools requires addressing systemic problems. A key reform strategy that stands out is the attempt by teachers and administrators to develop a more collaborative culture in the urban school (Fullan, 2001). At Brighton High, a major step was taken to change school culture through the Parents' Night—and Afra saw that she could play a key role in bringing that change about. It is critical to note that the Social Contexts of Education class did not operate in isolation from other changes that were occurring in the school; for example, the school had a new headmaster, and numerous faculty from Boston College were working with support from the Massachusetts Coalition, as well as independently, to create a new culture of inquiry and action. As part of this new culture, teachers began engaging in professional dialogue with colleagues; shared ideas, knowledge, and techniques; and participated in collaborative problem solving.

At the microlevel of the class in the Social Contexts of Education, the experimental design of the class—organized around a Brighton High faculty-identified priority—appeared to have generated the results that Afra and Dennis had intended. The student evaluations of the class were positive, although some students clearly found the unpredictability entailed in working with a large urban school around community engagement to be disconcerting. In a final survey of students in the class, all 29 students agreed that the class should continue to be taught on-site at Brighton High, and 28 students agreed that the class should "continue to link Brighton High School goals with Social Contexts curricula" (with only one student disagreeing).

Following up on the 2002 iteration of the class, Dennis and Afra were determined to take the class to yet another level in fall 2003. Hoping that we could expand the class activities beyond parent participation into genuine parent leadership, we assembled an instructional team consisting of two classroom teachers and another Lynch School doctoral student. Because we cared about diversity, and because we were friends and colleagues, we wanted to assemble a team that we felt would be most efficacious in advancing our commitments to social justice. Our final team consisted of Afra, Dennis, Liz MacDonald, Patrick Tutwiler, and Maria Teresa Sanchez. Liz is a White, fourth-grade teacher who was active in the Massachusetts Coalition, Pat is an African American doctoral student at Boston College and also a ninth-grade teacher at Brighton High. Maria Teresa is a Peruvian doctoral student at Boston College who had worked with the Massachusetts Coalition. We carefully planned the class throughout the summer and believed that we got everything off to a smooth start in the fall.

The 2003 class was very different than its two previous incarnations. Student enrollment had increased from 14 students in 2001 to 28 students in 2002 to 42 students in 2003. The collaborative instructional model was far more deliberate and labor intensive in the course preparation stage than either of the two previous classes. Additionally, as the collaborating instructors pushed the organizing component of the work more aggressively, we sought to go directly to the community, not only holding many classes with Brighton High school pupils and teachers but also convening one of the classes in the community center of a housing project adjacent to Brighton High.

To our surprise, what we hoped would be one of our students' most exciting and fulfilling academic experiences turned into something fractious and complicated. Although many students liked the site-based part of the course, others complained about difficulties in making the trip to Brighton High School from Boston College. Some students were curious about meeting with Boston Public School students and parents in the community center of a housing project, while others expressed discomfort and seemed to consider such activities to be of peripheral importance for their preparation as teachers. Others simply found the theme of community engagement overstated and resented the urban focus of the course, desiring instead a broader array of activities that would include themes directed toward those of them who would be working in suburban public or private schools. The larger course enrollment made it easier for students (who may have experienced similar feelings in earlier versions of the course but did not express them) to find and support one another.

On the other hand, a number of students liked the course design and activities and became resentful of the critics. Students who had experienced family tragedies or had to finance their own higher education found that they could identify easily with some of the challenges of Brighton High School pupils and distanced themselves from their peers when they found little of value in listening to urban high school students presenting their hopes and dreams as part of class activities. The instructors began receiving papers in which our students took sharp issue with one another on a number of topics, and some of the papers became almost personal in tone. Without perhaps intending it, it appeared that the instructors had created a setting in which a certain kind of refracted, educationally mediated, and eventually visceral class conflict surfaced in the Social Contexts class.

For most of the course, however, normal class activities related to course readings, and short writing assignments took place. The one part of the class that was distinctive related to our efforts to connect Social Contexts class readings about urban education and community engagement to practices that would assist the high school (albeit in a very modest way) with its ongoing school improvement strategies. Although it was complicated in the first two years to place a university class in an urban high school setting and to dovetail it with activities in the school, in the third class it became even more challenging. Following up on student-teacher feedback from the second iteration of the class, we wanted to continue to work on the fall Parents' Night as a core theme for the Social Contexts class. During our attendance that fall with the school's instructional leadership team, we learned that Brighton High School was endeavoring to promote college and university attendance for all of its pupils. To make the Parents' Night congruent with this theme, the instructional leadership team decided to use the Social Contexts class to promote college attendance as part of the school and university collaborative. We subsequently asked our students to contact the admissions offices of their undergraduate colleges or universities and to solicit materials that would especially be targeted at diverse urban public school pupils on the evening of the fall Parents' Night. Our student teachers appeared to be receptive to this idea, which formed part of a menu of suggested activities that they could take to contribute to the partnership between Brighton High and Boston College.

To our delight, Brighton High School teachers and parents became far more active in the third year of the course in mobilizing parent participation in the fall Parents' Night. The instructional team had originally planned for our Social Contexts student teachers to make phone calls to parents to invite them to the Parents' Night; instead, this activity was taken over completely by the school itself, in a perfectly choreographed instantiation of the iron rule. Our students still had plenty to do in terms of preparing for the Parents' Night, however, and some of them were quite inventive, preparing materials sent by their alma maters in appealing ways and exploring ways that pupils from low-income households can finance their higher education expenses with the right combination of scholarships and work-study jobs.

When the evening of the fall Parents' Night arrived, we began our class by attending a brief awards ceremony for Brighton High School pupils and then fanned out into the building to welcome parents, promote college and university attendance, and chat directly with the pupils. Although we had collaboratively planned this activity for many months, our plan for the evening did not work out so easily. Some of our pupils immediately began talking with parents and pupils and enjoying a relaxing evening. Others, however, felt completely out of place and fell into small groups, chatting amongst themselves and just waiting for the evening to end. When the Parents' Night was mostly over, the instructional team reconvened the class in the school's library and got an earful on how much these latter groups resented the evening and how they considered it to be a waste of their time.

Afra and Dennis, along with the other three members of the instructional team, were stunned by this reaction. We were forced to acknowledge that student teachers, who we thought would be energized by a site-based course in an urban high school, could protest quite assertively about their opposition to the placement of a course in such a setting and the auxiliary activities that required students to spend some time in the school and community interacting with pupils, teachers, and parents. This was especially striking to us because several members of the Brighton

High School community came to the class and expressed their gratitude to the class for the work they had done in preparation for the night. Unfortunately, our oppositional students were not able to acknowledge that, even if they experienced discomfort with the Parents' Night, the participation of the Social Contexts class in it was viewed as a real contribution to a struggling urban high school by the school community itself. As instructors, we were compelled to grapple with the possibility that we could have positive outcomes in terms of sheer numbers of parents coming to Parents' Night but alienated student teachers who were not receptive to the appreciative reaction of members of the urban school and its community.

These complicated outcomes indicate that our radical visions for the Social Contexts course, informed by Afra's previous teaching positions in urban and suburban schools and Dennis's prior experiences with Alinsky organizing, could have quite messy outcomes. It is important not to overstate the case, for, as had been the case in the past, the majority of the students viewed the course favorably. Yet, we view the message of our oppositional students as an important learning opportunity. In interviews conducted with Social Contexts students after the course, we learned that most of our oppositional students were not so much opposed to the principle of placing the Social Contexts class in the urban school as they were simply unfamiliar with the urban environment and, to a certain extent, uncomfortable at coming to terms with their own sense of privilege. The following quote from one of our students captures well this sentiment:

> The class overall was like a big bucket of cold water over my head ... [it made me realize] things from my background I hadn't thought about ... like parents without cars who can't get to the school ... or parents who work at night. It's crazy, but in my high school everybody worked nine to five, so if you wanted to have a parents' night, they would show up. In my high school everybody spoke English. ... It blew my mind ... all the things [the staff at this high school] has to think about before they even try to have a parents' night.

Another student stated that the course evoked feelings of guilt and shame:

> I was always uncomfortable because when I was growing up I would have things and I just had access to money and I would be able to do things that these kids just wouldn't be able to do, just on account of the fact that they don't have the money or the resources that I do. And just the whole life background is so different with that situation that I guess I just feel some liberal guilt about the situation and I guess I just feel very ashamed about it. I am uncomfortable and I don't want to think about it. So I just avoid the situation and I'm very nervous when I'm in those situations.

Reflecting upon these students' perspectives after the course ended, it became clear to us that the instructional team's planning of the collaborative activities at

Brighton High School had been a powerful experience, even (and perhaps especially) for those students who were most vocal in opposing parts of it. In retrospect, the instructors most likely underestimated the affective dimension of the site-based Social Contexts class, and one important learning outcome for us for future classes will be to ensure that students have opportunities to process their emotional reactions in class discussions and writing assignments in an iterative fashion throughout the course.

Throughout our collaborating experiences on the instructional team, through reactions to our presentations at academic conferences, and from our general impression of the field, Afra and Dennis have come to suspect that a large amount of research about outcomes from school, community, and university partnerships is systematically distorted in favor of positive outcomes. The reasons for this have little to do with individuals' desires to be disingenuous. Finding ways to deal with the messy realities of urban school and university partnerships is labor intensive and emotionally demanding work. Furthermore, grant-funding agencies rarely inquire after the quality of cultural interactions between teacher education students and school and university-based partners; as part of the current emphasis on quantitative research, most annual reports simply focus on issues such as the number of student teachers placed in urban schools or the number of teacher preparatory courses modified to meet grant objectives.

From our vantage point, no one has articulated this latter point about distortions entailed in grant funding and reporting better than Howell Baum (2000), a professor of urban studies at the University of Maryland. In a provocative article entitled "Fantasies and Realities in University-Community Partnerships," Baum writes about a partnership in which he played a leadership role over several years. He notes a host of complicating realities in the urban educational field that complicate change processes. For example, he points out that faculty members with federal grants commonly are asked to report grant outcomes on an annual basis in a bureaucratic, checklist manner that portrays nothing of the depth or complexities of the changes. As faculty career ladders and funding lines become more and more dependent upon a perpetual process of grant applications, the push to inflate positive outcomes and to avoid the disappointments or messiness of change can lead to a shift in the culture of higher education that promotes "academic capitalism" (Slaughter & Leslie, 1997, p. 8), rather than the disinterested search for the truth in a given situation. Unintended outcomes from grant-funded activities, and those that fall afoul of funders' expectations, are easily pushed off to the side or conveniently forgotten about as one emphasizes positive outcomes that can build a foundation for acquiring new grants in the future.

For Afra and Dennis, then, perhaps the major outcome of the work at Brighton High was not the increase in parent participation at the fall Parents'

Night nor even the boost in morale experienced by teachers and parents linked with the school. Rather, their and our primary learning from the three years of the Social Contexts class is that such work is rife with complexities and that the positive gains experienced in a school as a result of collaborations can evince a range of responses from different constituencies. Real change, we learned, is likely to meet with opposition—especially if one is attempting to link students in affluent universities like Boston College with underresourced and struggling urban schools.

In addition to the unintended outcome of student opposition, a major component of teaching the Social Contexts course at Brighton High School involved a staggering amount of additional responsibilities and tasks. Afra's workload at Brighton High School in the second and third years of the course required hundreds of hours spent coordinating the parent and community engagement activities, bringing in guest speakers, conducting one-on-one or small group meetings with teachers and students, and making sure that both Brighton High students and Boston College student teachers were receiving sufficient individual attention, so that our projects cohered not just intellectually but also in a more emotional sense of community development. This was an exceptionally demanding undertaking for a doctoral student, especially when one considers the conflicting and busy schedules of all the participants.

Given these messy realities, we return now to the major question posed at the beginning of this chapter: What was the impact of this school, community, and university partnership on Afra's socialization as a teacher educator? On the one hand, her experiences serve as a kind of cautionary tale, for although the collaborative activities in which she engaged were beneficial for the urban school and its community, they entailed a demanding intensification of Afra's workload that pushed her to the limits of what can reasonably be expected from a doctoral student. She was, after all, taking classes of her own with their own academic demands. In all honesty, though it is wonderful to receive funding for change activities such as those entailed in the Title II grants, educational reformers (and Dennis includes himself in this group) may need to reconsider just how much can be accomplished through partnerships, especially given the real divisions between urban schools and universities and the real social class divisions that riddle American society that become visible for all parties once the collaboration begins in earnest.

On the other hand, one can also draw a more radical lesson from these experiences. Partnerships exist in a broader social context that, in many ways, has worked to isolate urban schools and to intensify class stratification in recent decades (Anyon, 1997). Though partnership grants are able to raise valuable additional resources to improve teacher quality and student achievement, and they can indeed catalyze important transformations (such as the rise in parent participation at Brighton High), educators are fighting an uphill battle against larger social forces that the nation as a whole has not been willing to engage over many decades. During the last decades, the United States has more and more turned to marketplace models of reform rather than the state-sponsored and professionalizing agendas that have worked well for other nations, such as Finland, South Korea, and Singapore, in terms of raising student achievement. Although those models should not be emulated uncritically—because they tend to involve either homogeneous populations or curtailments on civil liberties that most Americans should not find acceptable—they highlight the manner in which experimental tinkering at the margins, rather than a broad-based strategy to reduce poverty and improve urban education systemically, appears to be normative in the United States. Indeed, one irony that Dennis experienced while leading the Massachusetts Coalition was a kind of grant-funded game of musical chairs, as follows. Given the recession that the nation faced in the first years of the Bush administration, the state or an urban district would cut core services in urban schools, and the Massachusetts Coalition, responding to pleas from our struggling urban school partners, would step in to plug the gap with its own resources. In many instances, the coalition was not adding new resources to urban districts, it was just replacing resources that had been cut. Yet, how does one write this up on an annual report? And how does one document the value added by such interventions?

Partnership work, alas, proves to be far messier in practice than policy makers typically imagine. Though it is true that the federal role in education has increased dramatically with the No Child Left Behind Act of 2001, most of that role has played itself out in assessment rather than in additional resources for instruction and curriculum improvement. Testing alone does not a cohesive and serious national policy make, and partnership work cannot be expected to make major transformations in urban education in the absence of a broader and deeper national reform effort.

Precisely because partnership work is so extraordinarily complicated and because the path from planning to outcomes is mediated on so many levels by culture, class, race, and gender, it is extremely important that graduate students who find themselves in the midst of these change processes are able to participate in national networks that will help them make sense of their experiences and gather new ideas to improve the quality of their collaborations. In this regard, Afra's service with the Community Engagement Task Force of UNITE and its many Leadership Development Institutes was especially helpful. She was also one of three doctoral students from Boston College inducted into the Holmes Scholars Program of the Holmes Partnership, one of the few national programs devoted to the development of faculty of color in education. In addition to the annual meetings of the Holmes Partnership, Afra participated in summer 2004

Leadership Institute for Holmes Scholars sponsored by the Holmes Partnership, George Washington University Graduate School of Education, and the American Association of Colleges for Teacher Education (AACTE). Focused on the theme of Public Engagement in an Increasingly Diverse World, institute participants had the opportunity to meet with individuals and organizations that shaped national educational policy. The institute and the annual meetings offered Afra rich professional experiences and opportunities to reflect upon the myriad of experiences she had undergone through her work at Brighton High School, in particular, and with the Massachusetts Coalition, in general.

A final component of the Social Contexts collaborative at Brighton High School should be mentioned here because it is especially important for the future prospects of doctoral students such as Afra in teacher education. We submit that, if one is to sustain these kinds of initiatives, it is paramount that the teacher education professoriate dedicate time to coauthor research with their doctoral students on educational change processes. From our vantage point, it is of great importance that volumes, such as this one, that are dedicated to the creation of a culture of critical inquiry in teacher education appear and that they have the imprimatur of the AACTE. Without such scholarly self-reflection and analysis, teacher education can easily become a nonreflective implementation of whatever a given presidential administration or private foundation chooses to emphasize as its agenda. Important as they are, from one point of view, there are more outcomes to educational change in our era than pupil test scores (Cochran-Smith, 2005). We cannot ignore those other outcomes, and the processes that shape them, without capitulating to an unacceptably truncated vision of what it means to be a critical teacher educator working in solidarity with urban pupils, teachers, schools, and their communities.

REFERENCES

Alinsky, S. (1946). *Reville for radicals*. Chicago: University of Chicago Press.

Alinsky, S. (1971). *Rules for radicals*. New York: Vintage.

Anyon, J. (1997). *Ghetto schooling: A political economy of urban educational reform*. New York: Teachers College Press.

Ball, S. (1994). *Education reform: A critical and post-structural approach*. Buckingham, UK: Open University Press.

Baum, H. (2000). Fantasies and realities in university-community partnerships. *Journal of Planning Education and Research, 20*(1), 234–246.

Boston Redevelopment Authority. (2000). Retrieved June 2003, from http://www.cityofboston.gov/bra/

Cochran-Smith, M. (2004). *Walking the road: Race, diversity, and social justice in teacher education*. New York: Teachers College Press.

Cochran-Smith, M. (2005). Teacher education and the outcomes trap. *Journal of Teacher Education, 56*, 411–417.

Fullan, M. (2001). *The new meaning of educational change.* New York: Teachers College Press.

Haberman, M. (1991). The pedagogy of poverty versus good teaching. *Phi Delta Kappan, 73*(4), 290–294.

Hargreaves, A. (1994). *Changing teachers, changing times: Teachers' work and culture in the postmodern age.* New York: Teachers College Press.

Huberman, M. (1999). The mind is its own place: The influence of sustained interactivity with practitioners on educational researchers. *Harvard Educational Review, 69*, 289–319.

Labaree, D. (2003). The peculiar problem of preparing educational researchers. *Educational Researcher, 32*(4), 13–22.

Ladson-Billings, G. (1994). *The dreamkeepers: Successful teachers of African-American children.* San Francisco: Jossey-Bass.

Ladson-Billings, G. (2001). *Crossing over to Canaan: The journey of new teachers in diverse classrooms.* San Francisco: Jossey-Bass.

Lieberman, A. (2000). Networks as learning communities: Shaping the future of teacher development. *Journal of Teacher Education, 51*, 221–233.

Lipman, P. (2004). *High stakes education: Inequality, globalization, and urban school reform.* New York: Routledge Falmer.

Liston, D., & Zeichner, K. (1991). *Teacher education and the social conditions of schooling.* New York: Routledge.

Lortie, D. C. (1975). *Schoolteacher: A sociological study.* Chicago: University of Chicago Press.

Massachusetts Coalition for Teacher Quality and Student Achievement. (1999). *Grant proposal to the Office of Postsecondary Education, United States Department of Education, Washington, DC* (Grant #P336B9900015). Chestnut Hill, MA: Author.

Murnane, R. J., & Levy, R. (1996). *Teaching the new basic skills.* New York: Free Press.

Murrell, P. C., Jr. (1998). *Like stone soup: The role of the professional development school in the renewal of urban schools.* Washington, DC: American Association of Colleges for Teacher Education.

Murrell, P. C., Jr. (2001). *The community teacher: A new framework for effective urban teaching.* New York: Teachers College Press.

Oakes, J., Quartz, K. H., Ryan, S., & Lipton, M. (2000). *Becoming good American high schools: The struggle for civic virtue in educational reform.* New York: Free Press.

Osterman, P. (2002). *Gathering power: The future of progressive politics in America.* Boston, MA: Beacon Press.

Pallas, A. (2001). Preparing education doctoral students for epistemological diversity. *Educational Researcher, 30*(5), 6–11.

Polletta, F. (2002). *Freedom is an endless meeting: Democracy in American social movements.* Chicago: University of Chicago Press.

Russell, T., & Korthagen, F. (Eds.). (1995). *Teachers who teach teachers: Reflections on teacher education.* London: Falmer Press.

Sarason, S. B. (2002). *Educational reform: A self-scrutinizing memoir.* New York: Teachers College Press.

Shirley, D. (1997). *Community organizing for urban school reform.* Austin: University of Texas Press.

Shirley, D. (2002). *Valley interfaith and school reform: Organizing for power in south Texas.* Austin: University of Texas Press.

Sirianni, C., & Friedland, L. (2001). *Civic innovation in America: Community empowerment, public policy, and the movement for civic renewal.* Berkeley: University of California Press.

Slaughter, S., & Leslie, L. L. (1997). *Academic capitalism: Politics, policies, and the entrepreneurial university.* Baltimore: Johns Hopkins University Press.

Stone, C. N., Henig, J. R., Jones, B. D., & Pierannunzi, C. (2001). *Building civic capacity: The politics of reforming urban schools.* Lawrence, KS: University Press of Kansas.

Texas Interfaith Education Fund. (1990). *The Texas IAF vision for public schools: Communities of learners.* Unpublished manuscript.

Warren, M. R. (2001). *Dry bones rattling: Community building to revitalize American democracy.* Princeton, NJ: Princeton University Press.

Zeichner, K. M. (1995). Reflections of a teacher educator working for social change. In T. Russell & F. Korthagen (Eds.), Teachers who teach teacher educators: Reflections on teacher education (p. 11–24). London: Falmer Press.

CHAPTER EIGHT

Facing THE Dilemmas WITHIN Creating AND Supporting Urban Teacher Education WITH A Social Justice Agenda

FRANCINE P. PETERMAN

R. D. NORDGREN

CLEVELAND STATE UNIVERSITY

Preparing and retaining highly qualified urban teachers has been a longstanding, though frequently unstated, goal of Cleveland State University (CSU), which has a more than 30-year history of partnering with local urban districts to do just that. Many CSU projects have been initiated to recruit and prepare teachers to meet local needs for more minority teachers, especially those prepared to teach in mathematics, science, and special education classrooms. These projects partnered CSU with urban districts and included scholarships, support systems, and licensure programs to ensure graduates' success in local classrooms. As part of one initiative, classroom teachers were invited to serve as participants in the Visiting Instructor Program—becoming university faculty members for up to three years to teach courses, supervise interns in the field, and assist with the redesign of programs. Other programs involved faculty members as mentors to new teachers and as collaborative professional development providers at school sites or provided alternative licensure coursework to change-of-career professionals. In any event, the programs may have been based upon partnerships among schools, districts, and the university, but they were not intended as professional development schools.

In fall 1999, however, CSU launched its first academic program focusing solely on the preparation of urban teachers through a professional development model—its Master of Urban Secondary Teaching (MUST) Program. According to historical documents, initially two assistant professors were hired to teach courses in a school-based masters program, work closely with supervising teachers and their administrators, and manage school partnerships that supported the program, which was based upon a social justice agenda that focused on preparing local teachers to engage in critical activities geared toward addressing inequities and urban school and community renewal. This chapter is an account of the development and implementation of an urban teacher education program that faced the challenges of enacting a social justice agenda through partnership by a department chair and an assistant professor, who assumed the position after having served as an assistant principal and a teacher in a professional development school in Florida. Suggestions for facing the challenges of this work emanate from R. D. Nordgren's four years of experience in the program and through his discussions with Fran Peterman, who founded the program eight years ago. (Note: To delineate the voice of each writer, Fran's story is presented in *italics*.) The chapter reflects the ongoing deliberations that Fran and R. D. have had about the program and the position that R. D. holds.

INTRODUCTION

As a new assistant professor at CSU in 1996, I believed I had found a new home—someplace quite different from the rural state teacher's college where I had previously been employed and Dade County, Florida, where I had grown up and learned to be an urban teacher and administrator. In many ways, I had come home because, upon my arrival, I slowly began to explore and renew my interest in urban teacher preparation through the indoctrination of my faculty mentor, who coordinated a partnership with an urban middle/high school. With support from the Joyce Foundation, three women—my mentor and another faculty member, along with the school's principal—created a school partnership to support a social justice agenda for teacher development at both the university and the school. As a result, preservice teachers were able to take their social foundations and educational psychology classes and participate in a 30-hour field experience. These women spearheaded a social justice curriculum—specifically focused on antiracist teaching practices—that engaged faculty in both institutions and the interns enrolled in their program in dialogue and activity to change how they taught and engaged with interns and colleagues at partnering institutions. The partnership was not long-lived, however, as each of these women made career changes that moved them to different roles and institutions. My mentor moved closer to home in a small, liberal arts college with a commitment to social justice; her colleague moved to other administrative roles, and the principal took a position in a teacher preparation program at a private midwestern college.

Before leaving, the principal joined the staff at CSU and served along with me on a committee to envision the latest brainstorm of the dean of CSU's College of Education and Human Services (COEHS): a master of arts degree program. (After all, the dean's previous institution and other institutions had one—so it seemed only appropriate for CSU to have one.) Chaired by a former dean, the committee consisted of representatives of every teacher education program and course in the college (general methods, educational psychology, literacy, special education, secondary education, middle childhood education, and elementary education) and the principal, who represented the community. The dean's directive at the first meeting was succinct: "Create it, create it quickly, and don't say it can't be done." Despite the committee chair's valiant and skillful attempts to move the dialogue forward (and the dean's scowl, "Fran, I've given my directive, there is no more time. Get to work!" when I raised issue with the mere 18 months he had allowed for the program's planning and implementation), the first two meetings of our committee moved slowly, as each constituency seemingly stalled any movement toward accomplishing our goals by raising concerns rather than proposing actions. But I had been mentored well: "If you want your idea to fly, simply be the first one to put it in writing and present it," my mentor had told me about how committees worked at CSU and, no doubt, elsewhere, "Your proposal will then become the text from which things emerge." After the third woefully painful meeting (I must admit that I am no good at participatory democracy, despite my best efforts to support it), I asked the principal to join me in my office. "Look," I told her, "let's simply put together a proposal for a secondary teacher education program like the one you all started at [another high school]. We'll align the curriculum with the existing postbaccalaureate program and build in more requirements than we want so that we can bargain away that which is not important to us and end up with what we desire." (With this strategy in mind, the principal and I met several times before the next meeting, laying out the nonnegotiables, adding some negotiables, satisfying what we thought would be desirable to each constituency— notably, special education, diversity, and literacy coursework and full practicum and student teaching experiences).

We came to the next meeting with a proposal including a program rationale, admission requirements, a course of study aligned with the current postbaccalaureate secondary licensure program (neatly detailed in the alignment chart we distributed), and a timeline for coursework to be completed in 14 months. (See Appendix A for the original proposal, which remained relatively intact through committee actions and its seven-year history.) As my mentor had predicted, our text became the design thereafter negotiated and promoted by the committee, with only one attempt by the literacy faculty to submit, too late in the process to forestall the idea moving forward, a counterproposal for another program. Through numerous bureaucratic machinations, the MUST program was established as the first—and currently only—master of teaching (MAT) program at CSU. The principal and I created the acronym MUST, as in the "We MUST focus on preparing teachers for urban schools" declaration we proclaimed in my office one afternoon as were crafting the name. It was interesting to see how the program title changed to Master of Arts in Teaching when it was presented in official documents issued from the dean's office and then back again to MUST as it passed through the committees on which I served and then through the Department of Curriculum and Foundations, which I began to chair in 1998. The dean decided to house MUST in my department because of the key role I had played in its design and given the possibilities for realizing its vision under my direction as chair. We did not anticipate, however, that these two factors might play out differently than expected in the lives of the boundary spanners who served as MUST coordinators and faculty members responsible for developing the partnerships necessary to ensure the success of the program.

The MUST rationale (see Appendix A) focused our work on preparing teachers for urban schools; teaching as research; constructing a critical perspective of schooling; accounting for the effects of race, class, and gender on pedagogy and learning; and stressing the structures of the disciplines as they relate to pedagogy and learning. (Notably, only the last item has been dropped as a program focus, probably because faculty members' theoretical perspectives on teaching and learning are not in accord with this view.) Furthermore, the MUST rationale was based upon the principal's and my notion of a professional development school model, specifically including efforts to

> *… promote continuous renewal of urban university and schools; … model reform efforts and goals; create structures to support renewal; co-teach integrated courses in professional development schools … [and] use reflection, collaboration, and conversation to improve pedagogy and increase student learning. (F. Peterman, personal communication, September 21, 1998)*

As department chair, I was responsible for facilitating program development for MUST, including the hiring of two new tenure-track assistant professors of urban teacher education to serve as program coordinators, as named by the first search committee, which drafted these job descriptions with my guidance. Thus, MUST and the boundary-spanning positions of MUST coordinators were established at CSU. Over the course of the program—six years now—the coordinator job description has changed slightly, marked by differences in the intentions of those who created it and the faculty members who served on later search committees. For instance, in our first advertisement for the two positions, the job duties were designated as follows:

> *Teaching graduate courses in a school-based masters program in secondary teaching; supervising program-related field experiences, including a practicum and student teaching;*

advising students; working closely with supervising teachers and their administrators; developing the masters program; and managing the school partnerships that support the program (F. Peterman, personal communication, October 30, 1998.).

The current coordinators' duties include the following:

> *Supervise program-related field experiences, including practicum and student teaching; co-coordinate the MUST program; manage the school partnerships that support the program; teach graduate courses; conduct research for scholarly publication; participate in university service responsibilities; and advise students. (F. Peterman, personal communication, November 15, 2001.).*

Given that two coordinators left at the end of their first and second years of appointment, and a year passed before their positions were filled, department members expressed concern that the boundary-spanning positions were not desirable enough to attract good candidates. The position is quite demanding, and unless the candidate sees this partnership as an opportunity for research and publication in refereed journals, the job may be too demanding for an assistant professor who must also fulfill his or her tenure and promotion requirements. Therefore, the latest search committee added the following description:

> *This position is related to our Master of Urban Secondary Teaching Program, a 14-month, intensive program for preparing a cohort of secondary teachers for urban settings. The faculty member would work with 25 students, teaching one course in the program each year, supervising practicum and student teaching experiences of several students in the cohort each semester, and collaborating with other full-time faculty who teach in the program. This presents an opportunity for someone who wants to work in urban schools, develop partnerships with one of three settings where students are placed for their field experiences, and play a significant role in the preparation of urban educators. (F. Peterman, personal communication, November 15, 2001.)*

The differences represented in these job descriptions include an initial focus on working with administrators and teachers in partnership schools—an important aspect of our planned professional development school model that, I must admit, sorely lacks any reference to mutually renewing activities and that is simply stated as an opportunity for interested applicants who might want to "develop partnerships." Given the problematic nature of our efforts to both hire and retain assistant professors who were interested in partnership-based, urban teacher preparation, the most recent job description was written to further delineate the school-based work of the faculty member and its potential for research. Again, however, our college and department's lack of experience with developing professional development schools as sites for collaborative renewal is clearly represented in the language used. Furthermore, although the first job description included a "commitment to issues of social justice and equity in education and integration of these issues into teaching and curriculum" as a preferred qualification, the last description did not. It was to the most recent advertisement in fall 2001 that R. D. Nordgren replied. The following is his account of coping with the conflicting demands of sustaining partnerships in urban high schools whose partners are attempting to enact a social justice agenda while simultaneously striving to forge his own record of scholarly activities, teaching classes at the university, and providing service to the university.

R. D.'S WORK AS PROGRAM COORDINATOR

In fall 2002, I began my work as an assistant professor at CSU and a coordinator of the MUST program. My interest in the position was twofold: the program's social justice focus and the opportunity for me to spend time developing partnerships in schools and building the bridge between theory and practice that I found to be lacking in my experiences in Florida.

The job of MUST program coordinator consists of supervising interns during their nine-month field experience, teaching one or two classes each year outside the program, and performing service to the university community, typically in the form of committee work. The administration of the program is quite collaborative in that two other university coordinators (UCs) and I work to set policy with a site coordinator at each of our six partnering high schools and with other university professors teaching within the program. We have also endeavored to include our students, who are referred to as interns, to be as involved as possible. For instance, several of the current interns facilitate the group interview process we use to help select future cohorts of interns. The past two cohorts visited potential mentors at school sites and gave the UCs feedback about these teachers as potential mentors and about their personal preferences for placement.

Collaborative leadership can be time consuming, a great concern for a new tenure-track faculty member who must get accustomed to the demands of the university community and the ever-present pressure to publish. The UCs meet often to discuss specific concerns, most often regarding an intern's field placement and/or progress, and meet monthly with site coordinators and program faculty. Some of us also meet monthly with mentors and with the site coordinator at each partner high school.

Sustaining Partnerships

In addition to program administration, I act as the program and university liaison in one of two partner high schools. One of these schools has been with the program for six years and typically houses six or seven of our interns, as compared to one to three interns at my other high school. I usually supervise all interns at these schools. My supervision load has ranged from 6 to 13 interns, but I have found that seven or eight interns is optimal, considering the other responsibilities of a nontenured faculty member. With most of my interns placed at one school, I naturally spend much more time there than at the other school, and I have attempted to build a professional development school–type partnership there.

As a mentor and teacher at a fledgling professional development school in Florida, I observed our university supervisor observing each intern a couple of times per semester and relied heavily on the judgment of the mentor as to whether or not the intern was a capable beginning teacher and ready to accept a teaching job upon graduation. Though MUST does depend on its mentors for such recommendations, UCs like myself formally and informally see our interns more than once a week, almost every week of the school year.

Thus, we interact regularly with mentors and interns and play a collaborative role in interns' development, even more than I witnessed at the Florida professional development schools. Each semester, I use a Pathwise-based assessment instrument to guide and provide an analysis of four observations of each of my interns; however, I probably visit their classrooms another 20 or so times to interact with interns and mentors alike. As a result, mentors, interns, and their students feel comfortable with my presence in the classroom, and this has created more natural responses from students and interns when I am in the classroom for more formal observations. My frequent presence may also contribute to a high comfort level among my interns, their mentors, and me—a comfort level that allows us to engage in open discussion about daily events in field experiences. Such open discussions frequently curtail potentially problematic situations and allow us to identify and work on particular skill sets and dispositions early in the field experience.

A typical week in the fall and spring finds me at my primary school for about three mornings. My formal observations are followed by postobservation conferences with the interns, usually the next day and often including the mentor. On Mondays, I hold what amounts to half my contractually obligated office hours at my primary school (this is my first year on the school's campus; last year, I was in the district offices). This allows my supervisees and mentors to drop in unannounced, meeting with me in their own territory. One afternoon per week, I meet with a group of the MUST interns. Some discuss their teacher research projects that span the entire 14 months of the program, others discuss their internship experiences. I have been able to meet with these groups at my primary school for the last two years, which is greatly appreciated by the interns, as they do not have to drive to our downtown campus and search for parking, which is both expensive and scarce.

In addition to my supervision of interns, I work with my primary school staff to facilitate their professional development needs and seek funding for their various projects. As a faculty member, I have participated in a number of workshops and presentations at the university campus with my primary school's faculty or at the partnership school site. Three years ago, in one of our partnering districts, I was introduced to a curriculum supervisor with whom I collaborated to write two grants over a two-year period and attended conferences in New York City and Columbus, Ohio, to gain information on the early college–high school model, for which we sought funding. Although neither proposal was funded, the collaboration allowed me to become known throughout the district and in the local community. I have spoken at community meetings and was a member of the interview team for the new small-school principals prior to when my primary school transformed into the schools-within-schools model two years ago.

Partnership takes time, as I have come to find out. Despite the many hours I spend at my primary partnership school (I even get my hair cut in its cosmetology department), I feel that in order to create and sustain a real professional development school partnership—the development of professional development schools is a stated goal of our program and our college—I need to spend even more time at the school and in the community it serves. Up to this point, in describing my role and responsibilities, social justice has been absent from the text. It often remains absent from the demanding schedule and expectations of mentors, interns, and administrators that are not necessarily related to our social justice agenda in discrete ways. How to bring this agenda to the forefront of my work as a UC and our interns' development as teachers is something Fran and I will attempt to unpack in the following sections.

MUST UCS: A BRIEF HISTORY

When the MUST program began in 1999, two newly hired assistant professors of urban teacher education were hired. One, a bright, energetic African American graduate of a nearby state institution was recruited as a Holmes scholar through our interactions at the Holmes special interest group, the Urban Network to Improve Teacher Education (UNITE). A former secondary teacher engaged in partnership work throughout her doctoral program, she seemed to be just right for the job of starting a new program based upon the professional development model. The second faculty member was a social foundations professor who decided to apply because he wanted to be "where the rubber meets the road," and, although he had no school-based teaching or field-based supervision experience, he accepted the position. The dean and I shared concerns about his preparation for this university-school partnership position—not only because of his lack of field experience but also because his interactions in my classroom demonstrated a lack of understanding of who the urban teachers we serve are and how to notice, respond to, and set appropriate boundaries. We also worried about putting together a team—specifically, putting together two faculty members who had never worked together before in a brand new program. What we did not worry about was that I was not only their mentor but also their chair and one of the initial crafters of the MUST program. Although I was inexperienced at being a chair, I was deeply committed to the program's success.

We were trying to build a partnership with (and relationships within) a highly touted high school in the largest urban district in the state when we began implementation of the program, so the first year was filled with question and struggles—basically, figuring things out and establishing procedures as responses to what happened, not necessarily thinking through what might happen. Social justice, though woven into our program plans and texts, appeared as course activities and readings and program outcomes; it was not an integral part of our daily work. For instance, we created roles and responsibilities for interns and their mentors at the mentors' request. "What is it you expect us to do if we serve as mentors?" they asked as placements were being made during the summer. We began a portfolio system by simply asking interns to share standards-related accomplishments in an end-of-the-semester poster fair. (I use the word we *here, because I served as a both a faculty member teaching two courses in the program—educational research in the summer and the teacher research course implemented throughout the fall and spring and culminating in the second summer—and also as the chairperson to whom the MUST coordinators turned for advice and mentoring. Needless to say, in retrospect, I can take responsibility for caring too much about how the program was implemented, probably micromanaging its development in response to requests for assistance and clarification from the faculty members, and simply not being experienced enough as a chairperson to recognize the foibles of the power relationships that existed between me and each coordinator. At times, for instance, I simply overlooked an opportunity for critically analyzing the power of my role as chairperson and its influence on a younger, untenured African American faculty member's decision to leave higher education.)*

Each semester created a new set of challenges and obstacles that complicated the professional lives of the faculty members, who were also worried about tenure and promotion while simply acclimating to a new academic setting. As both a program founder and department chair, I was perhaps too demanding, too direct with expectations, and too involved in program implementation. Coupled with the complexities of the power relationship between an untenured faculty member and his or her chair, the demands of implementing a new program while coming to understand and navigate two institutional settings (the college and the original partnership high school) put a strain on both individuals. At the end of the first year, claiming that she discovered that she wanted to remain involved with schools but was no longer interested in an academic career that required publication, our female faculty member resigned, taking an administrative position in faculty development at the Ohio Department of Education. At the end of the second year, in which a visiting instructor and former district teacher joined him to coordinate MUST, the other professor resigned. During his second year, he experienced the suicide of one of the MUST interns; one principal's disapproval of his ability to serve as a field supervisor and program coordinator; difficulty in managing his teaching load and finding time to write about his real interests, which were outside of teacher preparation; and a significant personal health issue. Given that we were unable to fill the open position, we now had two positions to fill for the fall of 2002. On a trial basis, one of our literacy faculty members, who expressed an interest in urban teacher preparation and whom I recruited from another department to teach the exit course with me—the teacher research project—and a literacy course in the program, co-coordinated the program with me during the 2001–2002 academic year. By the end of the year, he was hooked on boundary spanning and asked to fill one of the open positions and serve on the search committee to select a co-coordinator. That is when R. D. applied for the position—and became the search committee's, department's, chair's, and dean's choice for a candidate who was experienced and most likely to be successful. Although questions were raised again about the competing demands of partnership and publishing research in refereed venues, we believed his enthusiasm for the work and experience in school—especially with professional development school operations and working with interns and mentors—and his doctoral program prepared him well for this position.

THE CHALLENGES FACING THE UC AND THE PROGRAM

To create the MUST program, the dean was able to secure funds to hire two assistant professors whose teaching load would include 12 hours in the program—four hours supervising interns in the fall and eight hours supervising interns in the spring. These positions were initially grant funded by the Martha Holden Jennings Foundation through the COEHS's Center for Urban School Collaboration, which the grant established. During the third year of the program, as MUST was establishing a credible reputation in the community and its enrollment seemed stable and growing, the dean negotiated with the provost to establish two tenure-track positions to serve the program. In the fourth year, to support a Teacher Quality Enhancement Recruitment grant and accommodate an expected enrollment surge, I developed a financial plan for grant cost share that included two visiting instructors to serve as boundary-spanning program coordinators, as well. So, within four years the program was staffed with four full-time faculty members and by the fifth year funds for each of these positions became part of the COEHS permanent budget. Unfortunately, unexpected budget shortfalls in our state budget severely impacted local urban districts—with the Cleveland Municipal School District eliminating 1,400 jobs—and our projected enrollment dropped by 10 interns, so we lost one of the positions to another department, in which enrollment in special education programs had surged.

I realize, however, that the creation and institutionalization of these partnering positions simply is not enough. As evidenced by changes in the job descriptions detailed earlier, little institutional support has been generated for the essence of professional development schools—not only in terms of the mutual renewal of the partnering institutions but also in terms of the roles, responsibilities, and expectations for boundary spanners—or for the critical enactment of a social justice agenda that may or may not be fully embraced by partnering institutions, their leaders, mentors, interns, students, and communities. Competing demands for a UC's time, especially in relation to his or her need to build partnerships while conducting and publishing research to achieve tenure and promotion, can cause undue distress. As chair, because the dean has been unwilling to assign administrative or teaching loads to faculty who develop partnerships (he has stated that it is part of their service), I find myself fudging the workload of the faculty—that is, allowing them more credit for intern supervision than is the norm for the college. One of the UCs, as the new director of the Office of Field Services, is struggling with this issue as well since the dean has directed him to form partnerships with local schools for field placements yet has not provided incentives or workload assignments for such activity. As of this date, we have no plans for institutionalizing the role of the boundary spanners in the college— and conversation about that has been limited even though the expectation to conduct that work has been voiced clearly. In fiscally challenging times such as these—when states limit funding to higher education—the rationale for partnership building should be considered part of a faculty member's service; however, having served in the role and supported new faculty in that role, I realize how difficult the juggling of teaching, researching, and providing service can be. What faculty and administrators have often failed to recognize is that boundary-spanning positions must be established collaboratively—over time. In this case, rarely have we taken the time institutionally to actually define the terms partnership or professional development school, let alone shared meanings for the outcomes set for interns' development—especially those that define our social justice agenda. Instead, we made the road by walking through the responses to daily crises and demands.

SUSTAINING A SOCIAL JUSTICE STANCE

Earlier, I described my challenges with keeping and fostering a partnership between the university and an urban high school. A second challenge is the concept of social justice; that is, enacting this value in my personal and professional lives and, just as important, creating the conditions under which my interns do the same. The social justice agenda of the MUST program initially attracted me; yet, it has been both the most intriguing and frustrating area of my work.

The program, as Fran has pointed out, was founded on the concept of social justice, creating a teacher education program that would enhance the capabilities of its graduates to foster racial, class, religious, and gender equality in urban schools and their communities. Having worked in the program, I cannot help but sense that we have lost this focus. In responding to the complex demands of urban settings—both those of the university and those of our partnering schools and districts—we may be moving unwittingly toward being just another MAT program that uses outcomes as an end, not a means, and that focuses more on meeting outcomes than on how and why we achieve and develop toward them. Worse still, in the process of meeting legislated demands for high-stakes testing and reporting scores, we may simply lose sight of issues of equity and tolerance. We employ a rather complicated portfolio system to assess interns' knowledge and application of the four MUST outcomes that frame our agenda and extend the Interstate New Teacher Assessment and Support Consortium (INTASC) standards upon which our college model is based—namely, social justice; urban teaching; urban schooling and community; and resiliency, resistance, and persistence (see Appendix B). However, I wonder whether our interns' responses to the high stakes of our portfolio assessment have diminished the validity of our criteria—that is, whether they simply mimic the language of assessment rather than deeply examine their performance and professional growth.

First, let me provide a quick overview of the portfolio system. After the end of the first summer semester, the interns meet one-on-one with a UC to explain how each of at least four artifacts from the MUST experience is simply an example of each outcome. At this point, the emphasis is on understanding the outcomes, not on meeting or moving toward them. At the end of the fall semester, interns meet with a different UC to explain four examples of MUST outcomes in other teachers' practices, such as that of their mentors or other teachers at their partner school. Finally, at the end of the spring semester, interns meet with yet another UC to discuss their achievement of each of the four outcomes, presenting at least one artifact of their own practice for each outcome. In this way, the interns' experiences encompass three graduated levels of learning: to know, to be like, and to do.

As a middle school teacher 15 years ago, I worked with colleagues in my Florida school district to develop graduation standards for the year 2001 (this was in response to the Bush I–era Goals 2000). We had to determine what our graduates should know, be like, and do to be successful in the future workforce and society based on literature such as the Secretary's Commission on Achieving Necessary Skills (SCANS; 1992) report. I apply these three levels of understanding and/or application to the MUST program objectives. In MUST, interns use artifacts, supporting documentation, and oral arguments to identify how well they *know* about program standards related to social justice. Through informal and formal observations, UCs and mentors gain a sense of interns' ability to *do* or enact the standards in their teaching. A continuing problem, however, entails interns' abilities to tell us what they *know* in terms used in the assessment rubric—terms that predefine the right answer yet do not require evidence of what interns actually do to enact each standard. An intern can use the language of the rubric without having to *be like* the disposition required by simply taking an artifact (e.g., a lesson plan, book, or student work) and using the script of the standards to describe the performance. Without observing the intern's practice, UCs cannot assess the intern's doing or being like what the standards require in practice. For instance, the social justice standard calls for interns to reflect on and address effects of race, class, gender, linguistic difference, ability, and sexual orientation on their own and their interns' achievement. Just because an intern can write an essay about inequities of race or class that may be represented in an artifact of the high school curriculum and/or uses key words from a rubric to describe an artifact, how do we know that the intern takes action toward addressing the inequities and works toward equitable teaching practices? We want interns to be like or hold certain dispositions upon graduation; we want them to act in socially just ways. Yet, we simply ask for descriptions and reflections on practice without requiring the critical analysis, observation, and enactment of social justice principles inherent in the standards. I am concerned that the current portfolio process promotes talking about practice in specific terms but does not require the kind of critical analysis that would change all of our practices—those of the intern, the mentor, and the UC—while challenging us to act in a principled manner that ensures equity and excellence for all students. Pressured by the need to document interns' meeting standards, we become what Jackson (1986) calls "technobureaucrats," simply disseminating prescribed knowledge rather than actively fostering social change.

CREATING THE CONDITIONS FOR ENACTING
A SOCIAL JUSTICE AGENDA

Partnership is difficult! It is a multilayered ecology (from department to college to university, from classroom to school to district—all embedded in complex, diverse, and impoverished communities) and involves interpersonal relationships that are key to its success. These relationships include combinations among UCs, site coordinators (teachers at each school who coordinate partnership activities), interns, mentors and teachers at the school, and other faculty at the university. These relationships take time to foster, through recognizing the strengths and limitations each of us brings to the table, savoring successes, living through failures, and struggling with the baggage we each bring to the table. Though coordinators' relationships with teachers, administrators, and mentors seem to work well, two key relationships seem to be most problematic: that among the program coordinators and their chair and that between the site coordinator and the boundary spanner assigned to that school. Yet, we rarely talk about how important these relation-ships are or how to develop and maintain them in healthy, productive ways. Too often, I believe, coordinators have simply abandoned the partnership (as in the cases of our first two faculty resignations) or drift away from the problematic relationships rather than work through the difficulties encountered (an artifact of what I call the "nice-nice" prin-ciple at work— that is, in schools and universities, we tend to make "nice-nice" rather than name and work through the conflicts we encounter in professional relationships). Furthermore, as we work in increasingly demanding, more poorly resourced university and school settings, we find ourselves caught up in our tasks—completing assessments, attending professional development activities, and holding office hours—rather than engaged in the healthy, dialogue that is necessary to promote social change. We become part of the problem, walking on egg shells so as not to upturn the apple cart, upset the partner, or stray from the standards-based, critique-free rhetoric of accountability. Though we offer workshops in conflict resolution that deal with teacher-student rela-tionships, we have not institutionalized time and support for building relationships to foster professional development school success based upon shared meaning of key compo-nents of our program and implied by our social justice stndard.

SUGGESTIONS FOR IMPROVING, SUSTAINING, AND REVITALIZING

As we are expanding our partnership efforts throughout all field experiences at CSU, I will suggest that our COEHS executive council (consisting of deans, associate deans, directors, and chairpersons) take the following actions:

- *Develop reasonable timeframes for the development of partnership schools and structures to support ongoing dialogue about the meanings and enactment of social justice standards.*
- *Conduct ongoing dialogues among all partners to define the purpose of our professional development schools, each individual's role and responsibilities in accomplishing partnership goals, and the means by which we enact and assess our progress toward achieving our social justice agenda.*

In particular, we have much to learn from R. D.'s experience in developing our MUST partnerships and others throughout the college.

After four years, I believe the social justice agenda defined in our program outcomes must refocus our partnership development. Therefore, we should examine the following elements of our program:

- the content and purpose of required courses: Do they have a social justice focus? Do they promote collaboration with our partner schools?
- program standards (see Appendix B) and their ability to foster teacher activists;

- the validity of the portfolio assessment process; and
- partnership development, roles, responsibilities, and structures that support ongoing dialogue about program standards and critical analysis of our teaching practices across and within partnering institutions.

Course Content

The COEHS is accredited by the National Council for Accreditation of Teacher Education (NCATE), and its minimum course content is detailed in state-approved syllabi. Although MUST interns take courses as a cohort, the faculty generally sticks to the outcomes delineated in these syllabi, adding some readings that focus on urban teaching yet integrating relatively few assignments and assessments directly related to the program's social justice standards. Given that most of the courses interns take are taught by faculty who are not considered part of the MUST program, it is difficult at best to engage them in revising their courses to reflect these standards, but doing so is essential. As a principal I know in New York once told me, "Effective teaching is a subversive act." Similarly, teaching in the MUST program requires one to be subversive, linking practices to critical analyses of teaching, learning, and schooling in every course that interns attend. The other coordinators and I meet each year with the summer instructors to help coordinate the schedule, room locations, and alignment of major assignments so that our interns are not inundated with work at the end of each summer session, but rarely do we discuss the activities, readings, and assessments in terms of our MUST standards. Long before this meeting, however, UCs and potential instructors might brainstorm ideas through which to refocus our work regarding social justice—not simply the course content and process but also our own teaching practices and those we observe and support in the interns' field experiences. This collaborative, social justice–focused approach is a necessity.

Portfolio Assessment

The current portfolio process relegates a social justice agenda to a set of descriptors found in a rubric, allowing interns, mentors, and UCs to rely on language as a measure of performance rather than performance as a measure of a standard. Some interns simply use the rubric language to describe artifacts in the absence of a critical analysis of the equity of our practices, as was noted previously in this chapter. We must ask: How do these artifacts represent socially just practices and dispositions? What artifacts might we require in each of our courses to reflect interns' enactment of social justice principles represented in the rubric? The collaborative planning of coursework, as previously mentioned, would focus the program and the other faculty teaching courses for the interns on equity, culturally relevant pedagogy, urban schooling and community renewal, resiliency, resistance, and persistence as measured responses to mind- and spirit-numbing accountability efforts at the university and our partnering schools that deter us from examining practice through the lens of social justice.

As Conway and Artiles (Peterman, 2005) suggest, a sociocultural approach to our portfolio assessment would change not only the practices of our interns but also those of our mentors, ourselves, and others engaged in our partnership activities. Such an approach would require our rethinking not simply the artifacts of practice but also how and when interns, their mentors, UCs, and other educators engage in meaningful, ongoing conversations about practice that inevitably and recursively focus on the conditions of teaching, learning, and schooling—especially the equity, hegemony, and injustices inherent in our practices. Rather than simply selecting and presenting reflections upon artifacts, interns would be required to discuss their teaching practice regularly as it relates to their professional learning and the program standards. Participants in such discussions would include other interns, mentors, UCs, content faculty, special education service providers, and other educators at partnering sites. They would take place not only in the traditional fashion following a particular teaching event observed by the UC and/or mentor but also in the university classroom with peers and professor and before or after school in small groups of interns, teachers, and university faculty members who struggle to improve their teaching and their students' learning. They also would be scheduled over time to promote interns' professional growth toward the specific program outcomes that frame our social justice agenda. Participants would be asked to discuss practice—not simply artifacts. These discussions would ask us to look for inequities; to question the relevance of what and how we teach; to engage in community activities that help us define, refine, and renew our urban contexts—schools, universities, and homes, no less; and to ponder to what degree, at which times, and in what manner are resiliency, resistance, and persistence enacted as appropriate responses to the complexities and competing demands of urban settings. All of these are important elements of our social justice agenda as defined in our program standards. Furthermore, such discussions would reinforce the contextual validity of our standards as they would be enacted, questioned, and developed through our collaborative conversations about practice in a particular urban setting.

Partnership School Support: Ensuring That We All Embrace Social Justice

Teacher educators are quick to point out the importance of field experiences for preservice teachers. MUST's nine-month internship, which includes practicum and student teaching experiences, represents our belief in longitudinal, supportive field experience as a means of refining teacher development. Mentors who support our interns one-on-one, five days per week, during these nine months are crucial to the MUST experience. Yet, though our mentors tacitly accept the MUST standards by volunteering to work in the program, the ways in which they enact them have never been discussed. Furthermore, accepting and acting in socially just ways can be distinctly different. Although most teachers accept our outcomes, they rarely model them; and our interns frequently discuss the limited experience they have observing and discussing practices that question and address equity, are culturally responsive, reflect urban school and community reforms, or mirror the types of resiliency and resistance necessary to navigate urban complexities. Though principals support the program and hire our graduates, they generally point to strong teaching skills and content knowledge rather than their enactment of program standards related to social justice as the interns' strengths. Having been a public school administrator, I understand partnership as a representation of awareness and enactment of current teaching practices. That is not to say that teachers and administrators do not support the intent of our MUST standards; they just rarely exhibit them in practice. Accountability measures reinforced in partnering schools—like focusing on standards, not on achieving standards, through relevant and responsive practice based upon theories of learning and culture or simply drill-and-skill pre–standardized test routines—may interfere with educators raising critical questions about teaching, learning, and schooling and with teaching in socially just ways by focusing teaching, learning, and assessing on content and outcomes. Rather, these measures focus the purposes and effects of teaching practices on continuously preparing students for standardized tests rather than for deep understanding. Tests, then, take the front seat in some partnering schools where, without good results reported in the media, vouchers and other market maneuvers can and will threaten their very existence. It is no wonder that our partner schools remain focused on these elements of accountability without thinking critically about the meaning and enactment of a social justice agenda.

Given that four of our six partnering schools are undergoing schools-within-school restructuring, splitting these rather large high schools into four or five small, autonomous schools, it may be unreasonable for us to ask an entire campus with 1,500 to 2,000 students to join us in our enacting our social justice agenda. However, we should consider engaging one small, autonomous, school-within-a-school at each of our partner schools in critical dialogues about equity and excellence, cultural relevancy, urban renewal, and resiliency, resistance, and persistence as viable responses to the complexities and demands of our urban settings. Such an arrangement seems more manageable for the UC and the site coordinator and would also allow for greater support and interactions among mentors, teachers, faculty, interns, and other educators wishing to engage in dialogues about the enactment of social justice principles in practice.

REFERENCES

Jackson, P. W. (1986). *The practice of teaching.* New York: Teachers College Press.

Peterman, F. (Ed.) (2005). *Designing performance assessment systems for urban teacher preparation.* Mahwah, NJ: Lawrence Erlbaum.

The Secretary's Commission on Achieving Necessary Skills (SCANS). (1992). *Learning a living: A blueprint for high performances—A SCANS report for America 2000. Part I.* (DHHS Publication No. 029-000-00439-1). Washington, DC: U.S. Government Printing Office.

APPENDIX A

Note. This rubric was last revised in May 2005.

Table A1. Master of Urban Secondary Teaching Proposal

MEd secondary education	Credits	MUST	Credits
EDB 601: Educational Research	4	EDB 601: Educational Research	4
One of the following: EDB 604: Social Issues and Education EDB 606: Philosophy of Education EDB 608: School and Society in the American Past EDB 609: Comparative and International Education	3	EDB 604: Social Issues and Education	3
One of the following: EDE 600: Psychology of the Adolescent Learner EDE 608: Psychology of Learning and Instruction	3	EDE 608: Psychology of Learning and Instruction	3
EDB 612: Curriculum Theory and Instruction	3	EDC 511: Instructional Design and Delivery (includes Field 1)	3
EDC 501: Diversity in Educational Settings	3	ESE 500: Teaching Students of Varying Abilities	3
One of the following: EDC 512: Instructional Development in Foreign Language Education EDC 513: Instructional Development in English Language Arts Education	4	One of the following: EDS 513: Secondary Language Arts Instruction and Assessment EDS 515: Mathematics Education in the Secondary School	4

EDC 514: Instructional Development in Art Education		EDS 516: Social Studies Education in the Secondary School	
EDC 515: Instructional Development in Mathematics Education		EDS 517: Science Education in the Secondary School	
EDC 516: Instructional Development in Social Studies Education			
EDC 517: Instructional Development in Science Education			
Electives	12 (minimum)	EDB 565: Technology in the Classroom	3
		EDL 503: Reading in the Content Areas	3
		EST 581: Practicum in Secondary Education	3
		EST 582: Student Teaching in Secondary Education	10
		EST 593: Special Topics in Curriculum and Instruction: Teaching as Research	3
Total:	32–36	Total:	42

Note. This program proposal was created on September 21, 1998.

Table A2. Traditional Timeline for Completion of the Master of Urban Secondary Teaching Program

Summer 1a	Summer 1b	Fall	Spring	Summer 2
EDB 608: Psychology	EDB 565: Technology	EDC 511: Instructional Design	EST 582: Student Teaching	EDB 593: Teaching as Research
EDL 503: Reading in Content Areas	EDB 601: Education Research	EDB 604: Social Issues	ESE 500: Varying Abilities	
		EDS 513–517: Secondary Instruction and Assessment EST 581: Practicum		
6 credits	7 credits	13 credits	13 credits	3 credits

Table A3. Master of Urban Secondary Teaching: Rationale and Requirements for Admission

---

Rationale

Prepare teachers for urban schools.

Promote continuous renewal of urban university and schools.

Focus on teaching as research. Should this again be our focus instead of artifacts/portfolios?

Use reflection, collaboration, and conversation to improve pedagogy and increase student learning.

Model reform efforts and goals.

Create structures to support renewal.

Co-teach integrated courses in professional development schools (involving Cleveland State University and school faculty as professors of record).

Construct a critical perspective of schooling, accounting for the effects of race, class, and gender on pedagogy and learning. Admittedly, we do a poor job with this—the schooling part. We're focused on the microlevel (classroom), expecting this to make significant changes in their students' lives.

Stress the structures of the disciplines as they relate to pedagogy and learning.

Requirements for admission

Commitment to urban school teaching and school renewal.

Interest in the principles underlying the program.

Completion of discipline-specific or content area requirements prior to enrollment.

No concurrent employment.

Participation in full-day program during the academic year.

Agreement to complete an independent teacher research project rather than a comprehensive exam.

Agreement to develop professional teaching portfolio.

Agreement to participate in all cohort activities.

Above-average discipline-specific or content knowledge.

Satisfactory score on entry-level interview protocol.

Three positive professional recommendations.

Appendix B. Master of Urban Secondary Teaching (MUST) Outcomes Rubric

	MUST outcomes			
	Social justice	Urban teaching	Urban schooling and communities	Resilience, resistance, and persistence
Assessment	The MUST intern is a reflective, responsive teacher-leader who successfully addresses the effects of race, class, gender, and linguistic difference on student achievement.	The MUST intern promotes students' learning by utilizing culturally relevant and responsive pedagogy.	The MUST intern demonstrates a strong commitment to urban schooling and community activism.	The MUST intern addresses the complexities and demands of urban settings by responding appropriately with resilience, resistance, and persistence.
Proficiencies (as demonstrated by artifacts and reflections by all MUST interns)	1. The MUST intern recognizes and respects his/her own and his/her students' personal, social, and cultural uniqueness and understand how these attributes affect teaching and learning. 2. The MUST intern reflects on and addresses the effects of race, class, gender, linguistic difference, ability, and sexual orientation on his/her own and his/her students' achievement.	1. The MUST intern encourages his/her students to actively participate in creating and governing their own learning experiences and environments, including assessment procedures. 2. The MUST intern relates achievement to teaching by reflecting on strategies and adjusting teaching and assessment practices to meet students' individual and group needs.	1. The MUST intern demonstrates an understanding of the relationship between schools and the community and of the community factors that influence students' learning processes and academic achievement. 2. The MUST intern promotes his/her own and his/her students' abilities to make informed, socially conscious, democratic decisions within the classroom, the local community, and in a wider forum.	1. The MUST intern uses personal and professional reflection to transform challenges related to student achievement into positive learning experiences. 2. The MUST intern devises creative, relevant solutions to planning, classroom management, school, and community challenges.

Appendix B. (continued)

MUST outcomes

Social justice	Urban teaching	Urban schooling and communities	Resilience, resistance, and persistence
3. The MUST intern uses this information to engage students, to promote intrinsic motivation, and to encourage personal, professional risk taking.	3. The MUST intern develops a range of relevant, holistic, learner-centered curricula that utilize available resources and produce authentic results.	3. The MUST intern develops and teaches lessons that are explicitly relevant to the conditions and needs of students' lives and communities (e.g., family concerns, transience, violent events, and poverty).	3. The MUST intern uses personal resources to respond to a lack of school resources.
4. The MUST intern promotes his/her own and his/her students' development of personal, school, and community literacies by using effective, culturally relevant classroom practices.	4. The MUST intern meets intern-selected criteria.	4. The MUST intern incorporates artifacts from students' lives and communities into his/her teaching and utilizes authentic activities and assessments.	4. The MUST intern meets intern-selected criteria.
5. The MUST intern meets intern-selected criteria.		5. The MUST intern meets intern-selected criteria.	

Note. This rubric was last revised in May 2005.

CHAPTER NINE

Teaching What Matters IN THE City: Novice Urban Educators AND Community-Relevant Standards

KRISTIEN MARQUEZ-ZENKOV

Cleveland State University

This chapter describes the broad consideration of educational standards that occurred with a cohort of master's licensure students in public, urban university and high school contexts. This deliberation over standards was initiated in response to the extremely high dropout rates in these future teachers' local school districts, was rooted in the model of standards development presented by these future teachers' licensure program, and called upon this next generation of urban educators to develop community-relevant standards for their own teaching practices. This standards development method first allowed a cohort of teacher candidates to consider the nature and specifics of the current emphasis on standards that is increasingly a part of every educational context. It then provided these preservice city teachers with a process for integrating pertinent community experiences into their teaching practices, for considering specific criteria that might make their teaching responsive to the intense urban conditions of their students' lives, and for developing an expectation that they would operate as teacher activists in the name of promoting their city students' civic engagement with their schools and communities. This chapter reports on the explicitly relevant curricular standards and lesson plans these future city teachers developed prior to their first experiences in urban classrooms.

INTRODUCTION

One cannot peruse the pages of any big city newspaper without encountering at least one report on the state of urban school districts and the challenges they are facing. In my home city, the school district currently confronts the trial of hiring an effective superintendent, stemming the violence that regularly erupts from or outside of its high schools, compensating for the funding shortages caused in part by the local proliferation of charter schools, and working to counter the assessment of the majority of its schools as "failing" according to criteria established by the No Child Left Behind legislation. If we consider this set of challenges as representative of those faced daily by most urban districts, it is reasonable to argue that city schools, teachers, students, and communities are under greater pressures than in any previous time in the history of the United States.

City schools encounter not only these daily trials but also larger structural challenges, including extremely diverse populations, excessively bureaucratic traditions, and poverty-bound and underresourced communities (Peterman, 2005; Shakespear, Beardsley, & Newton, 2003; Weiner, 1999, 2002). These immediate and organizational issues comprise an almost overwhelming array of concerns that every teacher educator and future teacher committed to serving urban schools and communities must consider. In directing an urban-focused teacher licensure program, I have contemplated not only these factors but also three additional related—and perhaps even primary—issues: one, the shortage of qualified, appropriately certified teachers across the subject areas who will *remain* in these urban settings; two, the escalating burden of an ever-increasing range of standards to which all educators are being held accountable; and, three, in my home city, a high school student dropout rate that hovers annually at close to 50%.

Ironically, states', urban school districts', and city universities' responses to these teacher shortages may actually be in danger of exacerbating this scarcity and needlessly obscuring the standards upon which preschool through 12th-grade (P–12) urban educators build their instructional content. Perhaps most destructively, unless these recent licensure program options enhance new urban teachers' capacities for considering the connection between city students' lives and high school education, they may, in fact, worsen the dropout crisis. If these programs, the standards on which they are based, and the curricular objectives toward which they direct city teachers are to confront some of the entrenched problems of urban schools—including this disproportionate dropout rate amongst already at-risk youth—then they need to be explicitly attentive to the specific interests and needs of the communities they are intending to serve. Focusing on one licensure program with this community-relevant orientation (Cleveland State University's Master of Urban Secondary Teaching [MUST] Program), the evidence of this chapter details how urban teacher preparation options might attend not only to the reality of the teacher shortage but also to the factors that have lead to this dearth, supporting future city teachers in identifying how the realities of their students' urban communities can become central components of their subject area curricula.

This chapter introduces a broader definition of *teacher quality* that relies on this notion of community-relevant instruction. It defines some of the outcomes upon which research suggests urban teacher preparation should be founded— explicitly, the idealistic and progressive objectives upon which the MUST program has been focused for the past seven years. The chapter then briefly describes the instructional method employed in the program to assist future urban teachers in their integration of these outcomes into their teaching. My data were collected during the most recent opening sequence of the MUST program's summer courses; findings described illustrate the community-relevant standards and lessons these future teachers chose and created.

Additionally, this chapter reveals how city teachers in the United States might judiciously counter the pressures of the standards movement and answer the difficulty of teaching in urban communities by identifying subject area aims and lessons that are explicitly pertinent to the lives of urban youth. The result might be a generation of urban teachers who engage as curricular activists, formulating standards and lessons that merge mandated objectives with ones they and their student appreciate as significant. As my conclusion suggests, a responsive notion of teacher quality rooted in these high ideals should have a place in this nation's ongoing discussions of who should be teaching our increasingly diverse and disenfranchised city students.

CONTEXTS

Among the myriad factors that the faculty of the MUST program have considered in the program's founding and development, three concerns have been primary: first, the shortage of teachers who are both qualified for and will remain in the teaching profession in urban locales (see chapter 1, by Chou and Tozer, in this volume; Ingersoll, 2002; Levin & Quinn, 2003; Marquez-Zenkov & Stahlman, 2005; National Center for Education Statistics, 2002); second, the explosion of standards that educators across school and university settings must take into account (Blum, 2001; chapter 1, by Chou & Tozer, in this volume; Fritzberg, 2001; Peterman & Sweigard, in this volume) and, third, the extent to which urban communities appear to have rejected the schooling process, best evidenced by high school dropout rates in the program's home and in other cities around the United States (Education Trust, 2003; Federation for Community Planning, 2003; Young,

2003). Though each of these issues might appear to have both straightforward historical causes and practical solutions, none has been addressed effectively by current political and educational systems. Responses in current research literature and educational policies and practices may actually be exacerbating these concerns while failing to recognize the extent to which these issues are related.

Most department of education, district, and university responses to ongoing shortages of qualified urban teachers and disconcerting teacher retention trends (particularly in math, science, and special education) have concentrated on the development of now-commonplace alternative licensure avenues and short-term induction programs. These still-new licensure options include condensed master's degree licensure options—like MUST—and numerous emergency certification avenues—most of which enable school districts to certify as qualified individuals with minimal records of subject area competence and limited-to-nonexistent teaching experience or coursework in pedagogy. Though it would be reasonable to contend that such licensure options are inadequate for preparing teachers for any educational setting—not to mention typically more demanding urban settings— few broad-based support programs exist for helping these teachers persist beyond their first year in the profession. Numerous states and districts organize entry-year teacher programs, yet very few have designed programs specifically for urban teachers, for mentoring and supporting needs beyond the initial year in the profession, or programs that concentrate on more than an orientation to district policies and state licensure requirements. Combined, these alternative licensure options and limited induction efforts are doing little to stem the near-constant need for new city teachers, particularly in content areas where shortages have traditionally existed.

Other factors have contributed to these largely ineffective responses to the challenges of urban teacher shortages and retention. Although the need for teachers who are prepared for and will remain in urban settings would seem to compel city institutions to generate new teachers as quickly as possible, recent federal mandates focusing on a narrower notion of teacher quality and shifting standards for teachers' preparation have become barriers to the preparation and retention of these urgently needed teachers (Darling-Hammond, 2003; Sadaker & Sadaker, 2003). Teacher quality now relies on restrictive concepts of subject area competence, and the primary assessment methods utilized to determine such quality are high-stakes, paper-and-pencil tools (e.g., the Praxis series of tests developed by the Educational Testing Service). Already susceptible to the P–12 testing and accountability pressures imposed by the current Bush administration (Darling-Hammond & Sykes, 2003), underresourced and understaffed urban districts are further burdened by these standards and testing requirements for new and veteran teachers (see chapter 3, by Murrell, in this volume).

The next generation of city teachers must bear in mind standards, objectives, and goals from an ever larger and more vocal array of educational constituents

(Marcello, 1999; Marquez-Zenkov, 2002; Meadmore, 2001; Ohler, 2001; Wise & Leibbrand, 2001). Interestingly, the most popular defense against excessive standards seems to be even *more* standards (see the chapter by Peterman and Sweigard in this volume). Even a passing examination of the content of the current standards profusion reveals that it is as much an attempt by professional and governmental stakeholders of education to keep or augment their pieces of the educational pie. The effect of this outbreak is to shield any core ideas of public school curricula from the apparently detrimental influence of classroom teachers, teacher educators, or community members (Apple, 2001; Johnston & Ross, 2001; Vinson, 1999), while ignoring any explicit connection between subject area content and a community's needs or strengths. In a city context, where school already seems like an irrelevant interruption in students' days, standards that blur constituents' visions of the purposes of formal schooling are veritable death knells for this institution. So, while the nature and quantity of the expectations that teachers and students face multiply, their relationships to the intense urban conditions in which these students and teachers work and live are diminished.

Evidenced by this profusion of standards lists over the past decade, multiple national debates have dramatically shifted the definition of a qualified teacher in the United States. The National Board for Professional Teaching Standards (2002) has provided a heightened focus on teacher quality, offered a model for how to certify teacher quality across national settings, and shifted how teachers are assessed to determine this quality. As well, national subject area organizations (e.g., the National Council of Teachers of English) and professional associations (e.g., the National Council for Accreditation of Teacher Education [2002]) have developed standards to guide the preparation of future teachers. The Bush administration's concept of a highly qualified teacher increases the exclusive emphasis on constricted concepts of P–12 educators' subject area preparation. As well, recent discussions of cultural competence have called upon teachers, teacher education programs, and school districts to consider ways in which knowledge of students' and communities' unique histories and conditions might influence teaching and assessment practices (Irvine, 2003; Lucas & Villegas, 2003; Murrell, 2001; Villegas & Lucas, 2002). Finally, my home state of Ohio has just recently adopted a new set of seven standards for the preparation of teachers.

Yet too few of these definitions, standards, and assessments of teacher quality have considered the goals that the authors of this volume consider most important: the specific activist-oriented qualities that urban teachers must possess and the holistic ways in which urban teachers and students should be evaluated (see chapter 3, by Murrell, in this volume; Irvine & York, 2001; Ladson-Billings, 2000; Reynolds, Ross & Rakow 2002; Zeichner, 2003). In city settings, teachers require not only clear subject area proficiency but also overt abilities to consider how their practices will influence the often oppressive historical conditions of our political, economic, social, and educational institutions. Urban districts and students need teachers who consciously consider both how their practices can promote academic achievement and how these practices can successfully influence city communities' engagement with schools, democratic processes, and the highest ideals of equity.

Urban teachers must possess this broad understanding of the histories of their communities and a sense of urgency about the limited constructive relationship to schooling that their students—and their families—typically have (Chizhik, 2003; Duncan-Adrade, 2005). Though every teacher hears laments from students about the irrelevance of their school texts, assignments, and assessments, in an urban setting, a disinterested student's complaint is more of an aftershock than an actual earthquake—a tiny indicator of a complex problem that started much earlier in a student's schooling life. Furthermore, a single student's objection about an assignment's irrelevance is echoed by the vast majority of city students who do not complete high school. For urban teachers and teacher educators, the message to be heard is not these individual students' laments, but the voices of many generations of these students—who eventually form entire communities—that reject school as an extraneous institution.

In urban settings, it is difficult to determine the origins of high school students' disengagement from school—the chicken was born and the egg was laid simultaneously (Alexander, Entwisle, & Kabbani, 2001; Dorn, 1996; Gallagher, Alvarez-Salvat, Silsby, & Kenny, 2002). Given that many urban high school students are less than half of a traditional generation's length apart from their parents, these parents' rejections of school *are* these students' rebuffs and will very likely be the reasons for their children's eventual dismissals from school (Alexander, Entwisle, & Horsey, 1997; Croninger & Lee, 2001; Fine, 1990; Young, 2003). As a result, both aliteracy and this "unschooling" stance increase at exponential rates (Alvermann, 2001; Brouilette, 1999; Samuelson, 2004). In formerly industrial centers such as Cleveland, this rejection was not previously a concern, as diplomas were not required for entry into the primary economy. Yet, too many analyses of diverse youth, dropout rates, and their general detachment from school fail to consider the broader question of why students are disengaged (Children's Defense Fund, 2001; Federation for Community Planning, 2003; Janisch & Johnson, 2003; Kaufman, Kwon, & Klein, 2000).

THE MUST PROGRAM RESPONDS

In response to this web of teacher shortage and retention, standards movement, and curricular irrelevance concerns, MUST teacher educators have attempted to redefine urban teaching by first redirecting their own program of urban teacher education. Rather than accede to the intensified and underresourced conditions of the urban classrooms, schools, and the university in which it is housed, MUST has made responding to such challenges explicit in its definition of urban teaching and teacher education. Its founders and current coordinators recognize that any successful urban licensure option must continually shift the professions of both urban teacher educators *and* teachers, so they require these educators to take responsibility for addressing intense conditions found in urban universities, schools, classrooms, and communities (see chapter 3, by Murrell, in this volume).

If urban universities and colleges of education are to prepare truly qualified city teachers who are equipped to promote urban students' academic achievement, who will remain in these urban locales, and who will overtly endeavor to improve the conditions of urban students' and communities' lives, then the definition of *quality* must be expanded beyond what current policies propose (Darling-Hammond & Youngs, 2002; Howey, 2000) to include explicit social justice criteria. In sync with the other activist-oriented teacher preparation efforts detailed in this volume, MUST utilizes a broader definition of *teacher quality*: professionals who actively work to make a difference beyond the classroom by considering not only their own classrooms but also the social and political structures in which these classrooms and schools are embedded, and by considering alternative evidence and forms of achievement beyond classroom-level materials, assignments, and assessments. MUST has operated with the assumption that only if city teachers are consciously assessed against these higher principles and evaluated using holistic, performance-based instruments will they achieve the measures of quality that urban schools and communities require. These communities need teachers—and students as future community members—who can work to make school matter in more significant ways, who grow capacity in these communities, and who actively work to improve not just their own but also the very community's well-being.

MUST operates within a professional development school model (Abdul-Haqq, 1998; Darling-Hammond, 1994; Grisham, Berg, Jacobs, & Mathison, 2002; Johnson, 2000; Reynolds, Ross, & Rakow, 2002), with three full-time university-based faculty collaborating with school-based site coordinators and mentor teachers at six Cleveland-area high schools to train approximately 25 new teachers per year. The program is a selective, field-based graduate licensure option that, across its first seven years of existence, has focused on the preparation of secondary English, social studies, math, and science teachers. Students in the program enter as a cohort, take most classes together over a rigid four-semester sequence, and work exclusively with one mentor teacher at a partner high school during a nine-month, unpaid internship. In addition to an Ohio teaching license, graduates earn a master of education degree based on culminating teacher research projects and professional portfolios.

MUST was established using the Cleveland State University College of Education and Human Services framework, which is based on 12 outcomes and a nascent portfolio assessment system. Modeled after both Interstate New Teacher Assessment and Support Consortium (INTASC) and National Council for Accreditation of Teacher Education (NCATE) standards, these norms include standards of communication, assessment, and social foundations (see the Appendix for a comprehensive description of these outcomes). Through the development of this portfolio assessment system (driven, in large part, by an eventually successful NCATE review), all faculty were generally made aware of these foundational objectives. Through the multiyear implementation of the portfolio system, all teacher licensure candidates eventually were called upon to demonstrate proficiency with these outcomes across multiple program checkpoints.

The MUST program's goal is to train thoughtful teacher-activists who will actively address the effects of our nation's oppressive histories on student achievement and communities' well-being. MUST has attempted to transcend the boundaries between city schools and their communities by engaging with these communities in the training of future urban educators, fashioning an additional and unique set of urban- and social justice–oriented teacher licensure standards upon which its students (who are referred to as "interns") would be evaluated through both individual reviews and public exhibitions. Across the program's seven-year existence, these standards have developed into four objectives:

1. Social justice: The MUST intern is a reflective, responsive teacher-leader who successfully addresses the effects of race, class, gender, ability, linguistic difference, and sexual orientation on student achievement.
2. Urban teaching: The MUST intern promotes students' learning by utilizing culturally relevant and responsive pedagogy.
3. Urban schooling and communities: The MUST intern demonstrates a strong commitment to urban schooling and community activism.
4. Resilience, resistance, and persistence: The MUST intern addresses the complexities and demands of urban settings by responding appropriately with resilience, resistance, and persistence.

In an effort to help its graduates remain sensitive to the changing needs of their schools and communities—and persist and be successful in these settings—the MUST outcomes have been consistently modified. Although they were developed based on the program organizers' attentiveness to the factors that their urban constituents were facing, they have been adapted over the past seven years through continuous informal and formal deliberations among program faculty, interns, and mentor teachers. The initial and most significant evolution was the development of a rubric that more specifically delineates what each program objective suggests should occur in community, school, and classroom settings (see Appendix B, Chapter 8).

This commitment to an ongoing evolution has not only helped MUST graduates remain attuned to the pressing needs of their city students; it has also challenged them to recognize the dangers of the current standards movement. Though every new set of objectives for P–12 students or future teachers is introduced with some fanfare by a state body or professional association as the ultimate and newly static set of objectives toward which a given population should be directed, the MUST outcomes have very intentionally remained a work in progress. In some cases, outside factors (e.g., the college's NCATE review or the Ohio Department of Education's reconsideration of teacher education standards) have pressured the program's coordinators to consider changes to these outcomes and rubrics, yet the primary motivation behind this evolution has been a sensitivity to the program's constituents.

The founders of the MUST program also recognized that a performance-based portfolio assessment system was not only a pedagogically credible feature but also the only holistic assessment model consistent with the brevity of such a program (Barton & Collins, 1993; Darling-Hammond & Snyder, 2000; Lyons, 1998; Neill, et al., 1995; Reis & Villaume, 2002; Wolf, 1999). Through its portfolio assessment system, the program has expected its students to demonstrate a commitment to this unique set of urban, social justice outcomes while providing them with a model of assessment that might offer their future high school students the richest opportunities to demonstrate their learning. The program design described an ongoing performance assessment system culminating in a professional teaching portfolio (Campbell et al., 1997; Diez & Hass, 1997; Martin, 1999; Moss, Schutz, & Collins, 1998; Murrell, 1998; Willis & Davies, 2002). Though it was understood that program students would complete a variety of both traditional and nontraditional assessments throughout their college and program coursework, students were expected to collect portfolio artifacts from all coursework and field experiences.

The construction of an intern's MUST portfolio extends across all program experiences and courses but is a focus of several specific classes. It begins in introductory summer courses, including Content Area Literacy, Teaching and Assessment in the Secondary School (a general methods course), and Educational Research. It continues into the fall semester's Practicum in the Secondary School (which includes half-day mentored teaching experiences in urban classrooms for 15 weeks) and concludes during the spring semester's Student Teaching in the Secondary School (which includes full-day mentored teaching experiences in the same city classroom).

Each intern constructs a working portfolio of artifacts gathered from the year's courses, field experiences, workshops, and events. During each of these three semesters, interns gather artifacts representative of their experiences and assess these artifacts as evidence of their proficiency with the MUST outcomes. In general, artifacts gathered during the summer semester focus on community contexts and on interns' definitional understandings of the MUST outcomes, artifacts from the fall semester focus on school settings and mentor teachers' implementation of these outcomes, and artifacts from the spring semester focus on classroom contexts and the interns' implementation of these outcomes in their own teaching. All of these artifacts reflect interns' proficiency with the MUST outcomes and are intended to represent a constructive impact on student learning.

During each semester, interns engage in a formative assessment process around the artifacts they have chosen to address the MUST outcomes. These formative assessment activities are intended to prepare interns for the final, 30-minute summative assessment conference (dubbed the "coordinator review") with a MUST university coordinator at the end of each semester. At the conclusion of each of these three summative coordinator reviews, each intern must be assessed as proficient with each of the four MUST outcomes. If an intern is assessed at any point as not proficient with of any MUST outcomes, she or he has one opportunity to revise the presentation of relevant artifacts, followed by one formal appeal of this assessment. After this revision and appeal, if the intern is not assessed as proficient with all four MUST outcomes, she or he is not allowed to continue in the MUST program the following semester or to finish the program.

Although the MUST program portfolio assessment system is not the focus of this chapter, the description here of the program's outcomes and of the deliberate manner in which interns are assessed against these ideals is intended to illustrate the way in which the program itself models for interns an activist, community-relevant orientation. As evidenced by the MUST program outcomes and rubrics, the founders, coordinators, mentor teachers, and interns of the MUST program have worked to develop a set of teacher education outcomes that are responsive to the broader needs of their urban communities. The program's more important challenge, however, is that pressing practitioner question: How might urban teacher educators who are aware of the dangers of the standards movement help future city teachers to avoid these simultaneously overwhelming and irrelevant tendencies of the standards movement and their curriculum so that they support their students' continued pursuit of a high school diploma?

City students and teachers need sets of standards that are explicitly relevant to their lives if the institutions of school and their curricula are to become pertinent in these communities. Perhaps even more importantly, urban youth and teachers need models of standards development that supply them with the means to revise continually their high school curricula so that they clearly address the changing conditions of their communities and lives. Based on the evolutionary processes of its outcomes and rubric development, the MUST program provides a model of standards and curricula development that, if used by urban teachers, might provide city high school students with a greater appreciation of school.

In the following section of this chapter, I will describe my attempt to provide MUST interns with a mechanism for developing high school subject area standards and curricula that respond to their students' perceptions of school's irrelevance as well as help these high school students become responsible members of their communities. Relying on current, broader notions of *literacy*, I developed a *literacy mapping* project in a content literacy class taught for the most recent cohort of MUST interns. This chapter reports my attempt to integrate this project into my teaching of these future urban educators and on the pertinent curricular standards and lessons these future teachers articulated. The outcomes of this effort and the remaining findings of this case study are twofold: They include (a) the project used to steer these future teachers toward a consideration of their students' lives as germane foundations for their subject area teaching and (b) the community-relevant curricular standards and lessons that MUST interns devised during their pre–field experience courses. The standards and lessons that the MUST interns selected and developed—and that comprise the illustrations of community-relevant secondary level instruction described in this chapter—were also utilized by members of the latest cohort as primary artifacts in their first summative portfolio reviews at the end of the recent summer semester.

URBAN COMMUNITIES, LITERACIES, AND STANDARDS

In the initial weeks of the MUST program's recent introductory summer semester, I asked the new cohort of 30 interns to research and collect the broadest range of standards for teachers and students that they could find—from professional organizations (e.g., the National Education Association), area urban school districts, and state departments of education. I also asked them to consider the core propositions of the National Board for Professional Teaching Standards (2002) and the content standards of their respective subject area associations (e.g., the National Council for the Social Studies). This exploration of standards provided them with an extensive outline of the variety of professional conduct and content-specific ideals that educators currently consider when standards and curricula are discussed. These collections of objectives also gave them a substantial perspective on the chore that building a standards-based curriculum has become and a plethora of objectives from which they might eventually choose for units they would develop in this course or for their own classrooms in the future.

To help these future teachers recognize that the bases for the subject area standards needed to include sources with a direct connection to the urban communities in which they would eventually work, I looked to current notions of literacy for tools through which interns might pay attention to their future students' lives. New and multiple concepts of literacy suggest that teachers should incorporate students' literacies into the existing curriculum to make this content relevant to students' lives (Gallego & Hollingsworth, 2000; Kist, 2002; Moje & O'Brien, 2001). These ideas of literacy suggest that students bring literacies in visual, electronic, and musical media (Au, 1993; Resnick, 2000; Street, 1995), as well as the ample assortment of community and cultural dialects and media that they come across in their countless life experiences (Begoray, 2002; Ben-Yosef, 2003; Cope & Kalantzis, 2000).

City high school students are choosing to read many unauthorized texts (Alvermann, 2001; Gee, 2000, 2002; Hull & Schultz, 2002). They are literate in mobile phone use, hip-hop music lyrics, spoken word poetry, and quick evolutions of youth vernacular—all of which are texts that might be used in school to engage them in more meaningful ways (Newkirk, 2002). Although the realities of most teachers' classrooms—including the pressure to implement mandated curricula and the testing movement—leave little room for preservice teachers to incorporate new literacies, this notion provides a vital mechanism through which detached city youth might reengage with school, specifically through the use of community experiences as valid educational material. Community life can be appreciated as both a text with which today's students are and must be literate and as one of the most promising means for promoting students' development of more traditional subject area and literacy skills.

Utilizing this concept of literacy, I asked MUST interns to begin to record the community experiences of their future students as well as the range of community and personal literacies these students possessed. For the MUST preservice teachers, exploring how the community might affect their subject area standards and lessons started with a thorough visual consideration of the existing conditions of these communities. Using the tools of photography (35 mm and digital cameras) and visual anthropology (Collier & Collier, 1990), each intern created a *literacy map* based on these students' communities that addressed the question, "What are the environments, resources, buildings, homes, and institutions you and students might encounter on the way to and from school?" Based on these visual depictions, interns wrote short *keys*, describing the community literacies that they identified. Eventually, their studies of these photo images and their descriptions of the literacies present in their future students' communities resulted in the creation of unambiguously relevant subject area standards and lessons. Like the MUST program's outcomes, the foundations—or standards—on which these future teachers' curricula depended had to articulate this relevance if these future teachers' high school subject matter was going to possess an urgency that might compel students to remain in school.

Based on this collection of the standards they had researched and the literacies they recognized in these photographs, I asked the MUST interns to begin to select a set of primary objectives that they might use in the teaching of a five-lesson unit in their future classrooms. These standards had to be based in some way on the visual evidence of their students' community literacies and had to engage students in a social justice–oriented activity. Each future teacher eventually selected her or his own set of five to seven standards on which he or she based a series of lessons in a unit that was the final project for this content literacy course. In the following section of this chapter, I highlight examples of the standards and lessons that several interns—at least one each in science, social studies, math, and English—selected, developed, and designed. These examples begin to illustrate the relevance of these standards to city students' lives and the potential for promoting a community-relevant, activist orientation amongst future city teachers and their students.

CITY STANDARDS AND LESSONS

Based on their community mapping and standards research efforts, the MUST interns selected and generated a wide array of subject area standards for their short units. They were able to include professional objectives (related to their relationships with colleagues), personal goals (based on their interests in and beliefs about their subject area), content standards (e.g., school district or Ohio Department of Education aims), and community-relevant issues (related to their schools' city settings). The evidence of these standards and lessons suggests that these future teachers are demonstrating proficiency with elements of the MUST outcomes and enacting this activist-oriented concept of teacher quality.

One preservice science teacher, Janie, emphasized a personal standard: "Students will become educated on biological implications of human resource use in order to make more informed decisions about personal resource use and political debates regarding natural resources." She then reinforced this ideal through an Ohio Department of Education science standard that called for students to be able to "describe ways that human activities can deliberately or inadvertently alter the equilibrium in ecosystems." (Ohio Department of Education, 2002a). Finally, she augmented this standard with her own terms, which called upon her students to "know how to contact appropriate government representatives to promote action." Janie further articulated a goal of one lesson as expanding "students' concepts of the impact of humans on the natural world as well as the injustices of environmental fallout for people of low socioeconomic status," using the students' home county as the basis for this lesson.

Janie's unit called upon students to consider their experiences with the Cleveland Metroparks and to pay attention to the natural environment of their communities, even as they made their ways home from school. She expected her students to engage with one community member as a part of their brainstorming process for a short essay they were to write on how the United States might reduce ozone hole depletion. She planned for students to visit a number of Web sites specific to their home county and to view maps of environmentally unhealthy sites with links to census data about those areas. Her unit culminated in students writing letters to a local, state, or federal representative addressing their concern for any of the environmental issues they had encountered in class, discussing multiple perspectives on the issue, and suggesting at least one solution to the issue.

Most importantly for this study's goal of unambiguously relevant and activist-oriented curricular standards, many of the MUST interns identified educational objectives that accentuated their attentiveness to an association between their students' community lives and school subject matter. A social studies intern, Libbie, articulated the following as an explanation of the relevance of her World War I unit to her students' lives:

> Many students will have family and friends serving in the military and might enter the military upon completion of high school. ... The media is a powerful tool in shaping public opinion. It is imperative that students become savvy, critical media consumers.

Libbie identified an Ohio Department of Education standard for her unit: students will "analyze the struggle for racial and gender equality and its impact on the changing status of minorities since the late (19th century)." (Ohio Department of Education, 2002b). She then related this standard to an activist-oriented MUST program goal: The MUST intern will "encourage students to actively participate in creating and governing their own learning experiences and environments."

One of Libbie's lessons required students to bring to class examples of media propaganda such as a newspaper headline or article, a political cartoon, or a synopsis of a news item presented on TV, and then to explain the intended message, its intended audience, and how the information represented bias. Another lesson utilized actual letters from U.S. soldiers in Iraq as relevant texts and then required students to draft a back story for a soldier whose letter they read. Her goal was to help students understand and engage with the fact that people of lower socioeconomic and minority status are overrepresented in the U.S. military and to consider the role of media, economic, and social injustices in promoting this overrepresentation.

Dirk, a future city math teacher, recognized that his curricula had to deliberately require students to explore the world outside of school and bring this world into the classroom (even through the most basic of concepts in his subject area) through his personal standard that, "students will see that their world and community is flooded with innumerable circles used for all sorts of different purposes." He also realized that students needed to bring these lessons back to their homes and neighborhoods so that they could "see how they can use their knowledge of mathematics and circles to solve real world problems." He made his math curricula relevant to students' lives in one lesson by asking them to consider how "machines, food, objects, school supplies, [and] structures are important in your daily life and which have or relate to circles." He planned to ask students to bring in images of circles in their lives from a variety of sources (e.g., the Internet, a newspaper or magazine, a personal photograph, etc.). Eventually, as a culminating activity for this unit on circles, Dirk planned to have students study menus of local pizzerias to "create a comprehensive solution that maximizes the amount of pizza ordered while staying under $25." His lessons intended to help students appreciate the connections between school and the real world by incorporating such artifacts from their lives and communities into his teaching.

Jerry, a future English teacher, concentrated his unit on students' development of an activist orientation by selecting a popular MUST program expectation as one of his core standards, through which he—like Libbie—would expect his students to "actively participate in creating and governing their own learning experiences and environments." Like Dirk, Jerry also focused on integrating materials from students' lives into his teaching by using photographs of diverse individuals from the school's community who might represent modern versions of characters in *The Canterbury Tales*. Jerry's unit was designed to help students understand how literacy and formal education had not always been accessible to common citizens—the equivalent of those in most of today's urban neighborhoods. His hope was to help students appreciate *The Canterbury Tales* and the opportunities that formal schooling provides. His unit would culminate with students converting translations of the tales into rap songs, through which he expected that they would recognize the universality of literary themes and be able to relate the events of these classic tales to modern day occurrences in their own communities.

Two MUST interns—a future English teacher, Marina, and a future social studies teacher, Antonio—attempted to incorporate and address the issue of violence that dominates much of their city students' lives. Marina articulated a "community-relevant" goal—"I hope students see the benefit of working together"—and then planned to have her students read and discuss as a group *To Kill a Mockingbird*. To promote the seemingly straightforward ability to engage constructively and nonviolently with diverse ideas, she would have them write coauthored persuasive essays, based in part on a simple process of having students use index cards to document their own and their peers' ideas explored in daily group conversations. Similarly, Antonio intended to have his students "consider how civil law affects their everyday lives" by analyzing and interpreting civil wrongs that take place in the community and that are too often addressed through violent means. He crafted a unit that wove together studies of the movie *Hotel Rwanda*, the Cleveland-based novel *Finding Fish* (then a popular movie called *Antwone Fisher*), and a seminal court case on false imprisonment (*McCann v. Wal-Mart*). His intent was to share with students how the tools and power of discussion—in community and legal settings—could be reasonable alternatives to immediate, violent solutions.

Finally, two MUST interns concentrated on larger and more recent events that had lead to major controversies and conflicts in their city settings. A future English teacher, Susanna, hoped to merge the Ohio Department of Education (2001a) standard of having students "apply reading comprehension strategies to understand grade-appropriate text" with the commonly cited MUST outcome of teaching lessons that were explicitly relevant to the conditions of students' communities. She developed a series of lessons through which she helped students see the significance of *Romeo and Juliet* by focusing on the concept of controversial couples. In Susanna's segregated urban setting, the friendships of Black and White students were cause for school unrest. Byron, a preservice math teacher, recognized in the school district's and his own school's building campaign a prime opportunity to address simultaneously an Ohio Department of Education (2001b) math standard ("Students identify, classify, compare, and analyze characteristics, properties, and relationships of one-, two-, and three-dimensional geometric figures and objects") and the MUST outcome of resilience, resistance, and persistence ("Interns will devise creative, relevant solutions to planning, classroom management, school, and community challenges"). In an impoverished urban community, students' engagement as citizens in discussing and diagramming school designs represented a rich, community-relevant exercise.

CONCLUSION

The daily and structural challenges that our city schools encounter are numerous and complex. Though many of these concerns might seem beyond the reach or responsibility of urban teacher educators and teachers, it is imperative that the constituents of urban schools—including teachers in every educational setting from P–12 schools to universities—consider their roles in addressing the broad and immediate needs of these city communities. Those of us most committed to the survival and success of city youth should also sound warnings when the policies of our federal, state, and local governments lead us down paths with popular appeal but negative long-term repercussions. Particularly in urban settings, the significance of standards may be in the community-centered selection process through which educators focus on intelligible, explicitly germane teaching goals. This chapter echoes all of the chapters in this volume: In urban settings, teacher activism is not an *option* but rather an *imperative*.

The founders and current coordinators of the urban, social justice–focused MUST program have most recently paid attention to the ways in which alternative licensure programs and the pressures of the standards movement might serve to drive city youth and new city teachers out of our urban high schools. As documented in this chapter, their responses have been to live and model a process of standards generation that enables future city teachers to recognize, appreciate, and be better prepared to address the literacies—that is, the histories, abilities, challenges, interests, and needs—of their urban communities. The goal of the MUST program is to prepare these teachers for long-term success and retention in our city schools, in part through their intentional, activist-oriented engagement with the realities of urban communities. The program has extended this standards analysis, selection, and development process into the preservice fieldwork of its interns so that they are provided specific and reasonable means through which they can craft curricular standards and lessons with explicit relevance to city students' lives.

In each of the sets of standards and lessons briefly depicted in this chapter, future urban teachers are prioritizing their own and their city students' engagement with community-relevant ideals and with activities that actively connect these students with their future roles as democratic citizens. Each of these future teachers has shared models of how to consider both subject area and community concerns. Each of their units embodies the teacher activist ideals and richer forms of achievement that MUST holds up for them as the standard for urban teaching.

Although the standards and lessons about which this chapter testifies are grounded in limited data taken from future city teachers' planning, they represent evidence of how school subject matter might connect to urban students' lives and involve city high school students in expansive, community-relevant modes of instruction. In urban settings, all curricula might attempt to engage students in this way, and the standards to which teachers hold their own teaching and their students' learning might be ones that are unequivocally applicable to the students and their communities. During the remainder of their MUST program year, these interns have continued to detail the core standards of each of the lessons that a mentor teacher or university supervisor has observed. As a result, the data of these lessons plans and interns' reflections reveal evolving understandings of educational standards as well as a commitment to rethinking the specific standards that guide their preservice teaching. The examples depicted in this chapter and found in lessons from interns' practicum and student teaching experiences suggest a significant shift in their perceived roles in selecting or creating these objectives, and the content of the standards they judge should have prominence in their classrooms. As budding teacher activists, these future city teachers are choosing curricular objectives to which they are professionally and personally committed and that demonstrate an orientation toward relevance to their students' present and future lives.

Follow-up studies on MUST interns' teaching practices will report on the standards these future city teachers have utilized during their year-long internships, as they took increasing responsibility for the planning and implementation of lessons they hoped would be relevant to their urban students' lives. I am currently implementing an online instrument through which I will be able to determine the extent to which MUST program graduates are achieving this social justice–oriented and community-relevant concept of teacher quality in their early years of teaching. In order to understand how to defend against a further narrowing of the standards movement and instead pursue significance to urban students' and their communities, it is important to document how these new educators' understandings and implementations of explicitly germane objectives develop while they are being prepared as teachers and later when they enter the teaching profession.

This chapter illustrates just how urban educators might teach to community—relevant, social justice—oriented ideals—addressing this unique conception of *quality*—without compromising their subject area standards. In some contexts, high school students' complaints about the irrelevance of school is merely bothersome. In settings where many students are provided with external support systems that value formal education, the seeming irrelevance of an assignment may not deter students from meeting their academic responsibilities. But, in inner city classrooms these laments frequently speak to a level of disengagement that our educational system fails to consider adequately. In the city classrooms in which the MUST interns and I work, every message that high school students send is one to take seriously and to respond to with *quality* lessons that clearly matter.

REFERENCES

Abdul-Haqq, I. (1998). *Professional development schools: Weighing the evidence*. Thousand Oaks, CA: Corwin Press.

Alexander, K. L., Entwisle, D. R., & Horsey, C. S. (1997). From first grade forward: Early foundations of high school dropout. *Sociology of Education, 70*, 87–107.

Alexander, K. L., Entwisle, D. R., & Kabbani, N. (2001). The dropout process in life course perspective: Early risk factors at home and school. *Teachers College Record, 103*, 760–822.

Alvermann, D. (2001). Reading adolescents' reading identities: Looking back to see ahead. *Journal of Adolescent and Adult Literacy, 44*, 676–690.

Apple, M. W. (2001). Creating profits by creating failures: Standards, markets, and inequality in education. *International Journal of Inclusive Education, 5*(2/3), 103–118.

Au, K. (1993). An expanded definition of literacy. In K. Au (Ed.), *Literacy instruction in multicultural settings* (pp. 20–34). New York: Harcourt Brace College Publishers.

Barton, J., & Collins, A. (1993). Portfolios in teacher education. *Journal of Teacher Education, 44*, 200–210.

Begoray, D. (2002). Not just reading anymore: Literacy, community and the pre-service teacher. *English Quarterly, 34*(3/4), 39–45.

Ben-Yosef, E. (2003). Respecting students' cultural literacies. *Educational Leadership, 61*(2), 80–83.

Blum, R. E. (2001). Standards-based reform: Can it make a difference for students? *Peabody Journal of Education, 75*(4), 90–113.

Brouilette, L. (1999). Behind the statistics: Urban dropouts and the GED. *Phi Delta Kappan, 4, 4*, 313–322.

Campbell, D., Cignetti, P., Melenyzer, B., Nettles, D., & Wyman, R. (1997). *How to develop a professional portfolio: A manual for teachers.* Boston: Allyn & Bacon.

Children's Defense Fund. (2001). *The state of America's children yearbook. America's children: Key national indicators of well being.* Retrieved April 18, 2004, from http://www.childrensdefense.org/

Chizhik, E. W. (2003). Reflecting on the challenges of preparing suburban teachers for urban schools. *Education and Urban Society, 35*, 443–461.

Collier, J., & Collier, M. (1990). *Visual anthropology: Photography as a research method.* Albuquerque, NM: University of New Mexico Press.

Cope, B., & Kalantzis, M. (2000). Multiliteracies: The beginning of an idea. In B. Cope & M. Kalantzis (Eds.), *Multiliteracies: Literacy learning and the design of social futures* (pp. 3–8). London: Routledge.

Croninger, R., & Lee, V. E. (2001). Social capital and dropping out of high school: Benefits to at-risk students of teachers' support and guidance. *Teachers College Record, 103*, 548–581.

Darling-Hammond, L. (Ed.). (1994). *Professional development schools: Schools for developing a profession.* New York: Teachers College Press.

Darling-Hammond, L. (2003). Keeping good teachers: Why it matters, what leaders can do. *Educational Leadership, 60*(8), 6–13.

Darling-Hammond, L., & Snyder, J. (2000). Authentic assessment of teaching in context. *Teaching and Teacher Education, 16*, 523–545.

Darling-Hammond, L., & Sykes, G. (2003). Wanted: A national teacher supply policy for education: The right way to meet the "highly qualified teacher" challenge. *Educational Policy Analysis Archives, 11*(33).

Darling-Hammond, L., & Youngs, P. (2002). Defining "highly qualified teachers": What does "scientifically-based research actually tell us?" *Educational Researcher, 31*(9), 13–25.

Diez, M., & Hass, J. M. (1997). No more piecemeal reform: Using performance-based approaches to rethink teacher education. *Action in Teacher Education, 19*(2), 17–26.

Dorn, S. (1996). *Creating the dropout: An institutional and social history of school failure.* Westport, CT: Praeger Publications.

Duncan-Andrade, J. (2005). Toward teacher development for the urban in urban teaching. *Teaching Education, 15*, 339–350.

The Education Trust. (2003). *Achievement in America.* Washington, DC: US Department of Education, NCES, National Assessment of Education Progress. Retrieved February 18, 2005, from http://www2.edtrust.org/

Federation for Community Planning & United Way Services of Greater Cleveland. (2003). *Social indicators 2003: Education, employment, and income.* Cleveland, OH: Author.

Fine, M. (1990). *Framing dropouts: Notes on the politics of an urban public high school.* Albany: State University of New York Press.

Fritzberg, G. J. (2001). From rhetoric to reality: Opportunity-to-learn standards and the integrity of American public school reform. *Teacher Education Quarterly, 28*(1), 169–188.

Gallagher, L. A., Alvarez-Salvat, R., Silsby, J., & Kenny, M. A. (2002). Sources of support and psychological distress among academically successful inner-city youth. *Adolescents, 45,* 161–183.

Gallego, M., & Hollingsworth, S. (Eds.). (2000). *What counts as literacy?: Challenging the school standard.* New York: Teachers College Press.

Gee, J. P. (2000). Teenagers in new times: A new literacy studies perspective. *Journal of Adolescent and Adult Literacy, 43,* 1081–1104.

Gee, J. P. (2002). Millennials and Bobos, *Blue's Clues* and *Sesame Street*: A story for our times. In D. E. Alvermann (Ed.), *Adolescents and literacies in a digital world* (pp. 51–67). New York: Peter Lang.

Grisham, D. L., Berg, M., Jacobs, V. R., & Mathison, C. (2002). Can a professional development school have a lasting impact on teachers' beliefs and practices? *Teacher Education Quarterly, 29*(3), 7–24.

Howey, K. R. (2000). *A review of challenges and innovations in the preparation of teachers for urban contexts: Implications for state policy.* Milwaukee: University of Wisconsin–Milwaukee National Partnership on Excellence and Accountability in Education.

Hull, G., & Schultz, K. (2002). *School's out: Bridging out-of-school literacies with classroom practice.* New York: Teachers College Press.

Ingersoll, R. M. (2002). The teacher shortage: A case of wrong diagnosis and wrong prescription. *NASSP Bulletin, 86,* 16–31.

Irvine, J. J. (2003). Educating teachers for diversity: Seeing with a cultural eye. New York: Teachers College Press.

Irvine, J. J., & York, D. E. (2001). Learning styles and culturally diverse students: A literature review. In J. A. Banks (Ed.), *Handbook of research on multicultural education* (pp. 484–497). San Francisco, CA: Jossey-Bass Publishers.

Janisch, C., & Johnson, M. (2003). Effective literacy practices and challenging curriculum for at-risk learners: Great expectations. *Journal of Education for Students Placed at Risk, 8,* 295–308.

Johnson, M. (Ed.). (2000). *Collaborative reform and other improbable dreams: The challenges of professional development schools.* Albany: State University of New York Press.

Johnston, K., & Ross, H. (2001, August 13). Teaching to higher standards—from managing to imagining the purposes of education. *Teachers College Record.* Retrieved from http://www.tcrecord.org/Content.asp?ContentID=10804

Kaufman, P., Kwon, J. Y., & Klein, S. (2000). *Dropout rates in the United States, 1998: Statistical analysis report* (NCES Pub No. 2000-02-00). Washington, DC: National Center for Educational Statistics.

Kist, W. (2002). Finding "new literacy" in action: An interdisciplinary high school Western civilization class. *Journal of Adolescent and Adult Literacy, 45,* 368–377.

Ladson-Billings, G. (2000). Fighting for our lives: Preparing teachers to teach African-American students. *Journal of Teacher Education, 51,* 206–214.

Levin, J., & Quinn, M. (2003). *Missed opportunities: How we keep high-quality teachers out of urban classrooms.* New York: New Teacher Project.

Lucas, T., & Villegas, A. M. (2003). *Educating culturally responsive teachers: A coherent approach.* Albany: State University of New York Press.

Lyons, N. (Ed.). (1998). *With portfolio in hand: Validating the new teacher professionalism.* New York: Teachers College Press.

Marcello, J. S. (1999). A teacher's reflections on teaching and assessing in a standards-based classroom. *Social Education, 65,* 338–342.

Marquez-Zenkov, K. (2002, December). Seeing standards: Schools' built environments and the standards movement. *Mid-Western Educational Researcher,* 15(4), 22–27.

Marquez-Zenkov, K., & Stahlman, J. (2005, Fall). City teachers staying in city schools: New principles of urban teacher education and induction. *Journal of Urban Learning, Teaching, and Research,* 15(4), 22–27.

Martin, D. (1999). *The portfolio planner: Making professional portfolios work for you.* Columbus, OH: Merrill.

Meadmore, D. (2001). The pursuit of standards: Simply managing education? *International Journal of Inclusive Education,* 5(4), 353–366.

Moje, E. B., & O'Brien, D. G. (Eds.). (2001). *Constructions of literacy: Studies of teaching and learning in and out of secondary schools.* Mahwah, NJ: Lawrence Erlbaum Associates.

Moss, P. A., Schutz, A. M., & Collins, K. M. (1998). An integrative approach to portfolio evaluation for teacher licensure. *Journal of Personnel Evaluation in Education,* 12, 139–161.

Murrell, P. C., Jr. (1998). *Like stone soup: The role of the professional development school in the renewal of urban schools.* Washington, DC: American Association of Colleges of Teacher Education.

Murrell, P. C., Jr. (2001). *The community teacher: A new framework for effective urban teaching.* New York: Teachers College Press.

National Board for Professional Teaching Standards. (2002). *What teachers should know and be able to do.* Arlington, VA: Author.

National Center for Education Statistics. (2002). *Characteristics of stayers, movers, and leavers: Results from the Teacher Follow-up Survey, 1999–2000.* Washington, DC: U.S. Department of Education.

National Council for Accreditation of Teacher Education. (2002). *Professional standards for the accreditation of schools, colleges, and departments of education.* Washington, DC: Author.

Neill, M., et al. (1995). *Implementing performance assessments: A guide to classroom, school and system reform.* Cambridge, MA: FairTest.

Newkirk, T. (2002). *Misreading masculinity: Boys, literacy, and popular culture.* Portsmouth, NY: Heinemann.

Ohio Department of Education. (2001a). *Academic content standards for K–12 English language arts.* Columbus, OH: Author. Retrieved August 23, 2007 from http://ode.state.oh.us/GD/Templates/Pages/ODE/ODEDetail.aspx?page=3&TopicRelationID=330&ContentID=489&Content=32574

Ohio Department of Education. (2001b). *Academic content standards: K-12 mathematics.* Columbus, OH: Author. Retrieved August 23, 2007 from http://ode.state.oh.us/GD/Templates/Pages/ODE/ODEDetail.aspx?page=3&TopicRelationID=333&ContentID=801&Content=32581

Department of Education (2002a). *Academic content standards: K-12 science.* Columbus, OH: Author. Retrieved August 23, 2007 from http://ode.state.oh.us/GD/Templates/Pages/ODE/ODEDetail.aspx?page=3&TopicRelationID=334&ContentID=834&Content=32645

Ohio Department of Education. (2002b). *Academic content standards: K–12 Social Studies.* Columbus, OH: Author. Retrieved August 23, 2007 from http://ode.state.oh.us/GD/Templates/Pages/ODE/ODEDetail.aspx?page=3&TopicRelationID=335&ContentID=852&Content=32668

Ohler, J. (2001, March). Education standards as passing fad. *Education Digest,* 66, 4–7.

Peterman, F. (Ed.). (2005). *Designing performance assessment systems for urban teacher preparation.* Mahwah, NJ: Lawrence Erlbaum Associates.

Reis, N. K., & Villaume, S. K. (2002). The benefits, tensions, and visions of portfolios as a wide-scale assessment for teacher education. *Action in Teacher Education, 23*(4), 10–17.

Resnick, L. (2000). Exploring sign systems within an inquiry system. In M. Gallego & S. Hollingsworth (Eds.), *What counts as literacy? Challenging the school standard.* New York: Teachers College Press.

Reynolds, A., Ross, S. M., & Rakow, J. H. (2002). Teacher retention, teaching effectiveness, and professional preparation: A comparison of professional development school and non-professional development school graduates. *Teaching and Teacher Education, 18,* 289–303.

Sadaker, M., & Sadaker, D. (2003). *Teachers, schools, and society* (6th ed.). Boston: McGraw-Hill.

Samuelson, B. L. (2004). "I used to go to school. Now I learn.": Unschoolers critiquing the discourse of school. In J. Mahari (Ed.), *What they don't learn in school: Literacy in the lives of urban youth* (pp. 103–122). New York: Peter Lang.

Shakespear, E., Beardsley, L., & Newton, A. (2003). *Preparing urban teachers: Uncovering communities. A community curriculum for interns and new teachers. Evaluation report from Jobs for the Future.* Boston: Jobs for the Future.

Street, B. (1995). *Social literacies: Critical approaches to literacy in development, ethnography and education.* London: Longman.

Villegas, A. M., & Lucas, T. (2002). Preparing culturally response teachers: Rethinking the curriculum. *Journal of Teacher Education, 53,* 20–32.

Vinson, K. D. (1999). National curriculum standards and social studies education: Dewey, Freire, Foucault, and the construction of a radical critique. *Theory and Research in Social Education, 27*(3), 296.

Weiner, L. (1999). *Urban teaching: The essentials.* New York: Teachers College Press.

Weiner, L. (2002). Evidence and inquiry in teacher education: What's needed for urban schools. *Journal of Teacher Education, 53,* 254–261.

Willis, E. M., & Davies, M. A. (2002). Promise and practice of professional portfolios. *Action in Teacher Education, 23*(4), 18–27.

Wise, A. E., & Leibbrand, J. A. (2001). Standards in the new millennium: Where we are, where we're headed. *Journal of Teacher Education, 52,* 244–255.

Wolf, K. (1999). *Leading the professional portfolio process for change.* Arlington Heights, IL: Skylight Professional Development.

Young, B. A. (2003). *Public high school dropouts and completers from the common core of data: School year 2000–2002 (statistical analysis report).* Washington, DC: National Center for Education Statistics.

Zeichner, K. (2003). The adequacies and inadequacies of three current strategies to recruit, prepare, and retain the best teachers for all students. *Teachers College Record, 105,* 490–519.

APPENDIX

CLEVELAND STATE UNIVERSITY (CSU) COLLEGE OF EDUCATION OUTCOMES

1. Personal philosophy: The CSU teacher education student articulates a personal philosophy of teaching and learning that is grounded in theory and practice.
2. Social foundations: The CSU teacher education student possesses knowledge and understanding of the social, political, and economic factors that influence education and shape the worlds in which we live.
3. Knowledge of subject matter and inquiry: The CSU teacher education student understands content, disciplinary concepts, and tools of inquiry related to the development of an educated person.
4. Knowledge of development and learning: The CSU teacher education student understands how individuals learn and develop and that students enter the learning setting with prior experiences that give meaning to the construction of new knowledge.
5. Diversity: The CSU teacher education student understands how individuals differ in their backgrounds and approaches to learning and incorporates and accounts for such diversity in teaching and learning.
6. Learning environment: The CSU teacher education student uses an understanding of individual and group motivation to promote positive social interaction, active engagement in learning, and self-motivation.
7. Communication: The CSU teacher education student uses knowledge of effective verbal, nonverbal, and media communication techniques to foster inquiry, collaboration, and engagement in learning environments.
8. Instructional strategies: The CSU teacher education student plans and implements a variety of developmentally appropriate instructional strategies to develop performance skills, critical thinking, and problem solving, as well as to foster social, emotional, creative, and physical development.
9. Assessment: The CSU teacher education student understands, selects, and uses a range of assessment strategies to foster the physical, cognitive, social, and emotional development of learners and gives accounts of students' learning to the outside world.
10. Technology: The CSU teacher education student understands and uses up-to-date technology to enhance the learning environment across the full range of learner needs.
11. Professional development: The CSU teacher education student is a reflective practitioner who evaluates his/her interactions with others (e.g., learners, parents/guardians, colleagues, and professionals in the community) and seeks opportunities to grow professionally.
12. Collaboration and professionalism: The CSU teacher education student fosters relationships with colleagues, parents/guardians, community agencies, and colleges/universities to support students' growth and well-being.

CHAPTER TEN

New Teacher Induction AND Professional Development THROUGH A Video Technology Mentoring Program

BRIAN YUSKO

Cleveland State University

This chapter documents how the Video Technology Mentoring Program (VTMP), a school-based urban teacher induction and professional development program, was developed and implemented to give classroom teachers greater control over their professional development by developing a community of practice for reflecting on teaching. The project used video technology to combine a school-based induction program with activities to promote experienced teachers' inquiry into practice. The chapter provides an overview and rationale of the program, and it highlights successes and challenges in the effort to develop new roles, new processes, and new tools for teacher learning. The chapter concludes with reflections on the challenges and possibilities of the VTMP in urban settings.

ACTIVISM THROUGH PARTICIPATORY PROFESSIONAL DEVELOPMENT

The traditionally dominant approach to professional development has involved the development of formal programs to help teachers implement specific innovations faithfully—what Fullan (1991) calls the "fidelity perspective" (p. 38). From this perspective evolved the familiar practices of one-shot workshops on in-service days as the dominant form of teacher professional development. Although most current researchers of professional development characterize these as weak interventions unlikely to promote significant change (Hawley & Valli, 1999; Little, 1993; Lord, 1994; Putnam & Borko, 2000), the format persists. In large urban school districts where the centralization of power often "results in top-down mandates for standardized curriculum, instruction, and assessments" (see chapter 1, by Chou and Tozer, in this volume), workshops offer the illusion of effectively implementing district-mandated reforms faithfully on a large scale.

Within the last 15 years, there has been a trend away from the fidelity approach toward a bottom-up approach that views teachers as tinkerers (Tyack & Cuban, 1995) or bricoleurs (Huberman, 1993), who actively decide which ideas to use and how to use them in their classrooms. From this perspective, change in teaching involves the gradual interweaving of new practices into the fabric of existing practices. Teacher learning for this kind of change calls for teachers to identify their own learning needs and work in school-based settings "where participants struggle along with others to construct meaningful local knowledge and where inquiry is regarded as part of larger efforts to transform teaching, learning, and schooling" in context-specific ways (Cochran-Smith & Lytle, 1999, p. 278).

Although widespread support exists for such approaches, they do not fit easily into reform initiatives that treat teachers as cogs in the machine of systemic change. Urban districts whose students perform poorly on high-stakes tests are under great pressure to demonstrate rapid progress, and this pressure often leads to more prescriptive reforms such as providing teachers with strict pacing charts, carefully scripted curriculum materials, or more frequent district-wide student assessments mirroring state tests. Such reforms require teachers to be good team players who adopt and faithfully implement the latest district reform, but they undermine the value of having teachers identify their own learning needs or incorporate context-specific changes into existing practices. At their worst, such reforms view any variation from the master plan as insubordination.

I worked in one large urban district with administrators and teachers at Linus Elementary School[1] to develop a school-based program—the VTMP— designed to honor the teachers as learners. Intended to increase teacher retention and provide ongoing professional development for experienced teachers, the VTMP involved teachers in a form of participatory democracy (see chapter 4, by Shirley, in this volume), with teachers setting professional goals, observing and videotaping in one another's classrooms, and reflecting collaboratively on their progress toward these goals. The VTMP is an example of activism that attempts to disrupt the power imbalance of top-down approaches to mentoring and professional development. By providing teachers with resources—new roles, tools, and processes—the VTMP sought to enrich the Linus professional community and promote change by institutionalizing opportunities for thoughtful reflection, resulting in modified instruction and optimal student learning.

This chapter uses data collected during the first three years of the VTMP to address two questions:

1. How did the VTMP challenge prevailing norms of professional development opportunities to foster a community of practice that engaged in consistent and systematic appraisal of teaching practice?
2. What challenges specific to the urban context were faced by the program designers and program participants in the implementation of the program?

These research questions provide an opportunity to examine the successes as well as the challenges inherent in such projects.

Urban Context

Linus Elementary is located in a large midwestern city facing problems similar to those of other urban areas (see chapter 2, by Peterman and Sweigard, in this volume). The city ranked last among other comparable large cities for children's overall quality of life, as measured by the percentage of children living in poverty, the teenage birth rate, the percentage of children living in single-parent families, the delinquency rate, the lead-poisoning rate for children younger than six years of age, and the high school dropout rate (Mazzolini & Davis, 2003). These problems manifested themselves in the schools as well. In 2003, its school district was considered by the state to be in a condition of "academic emergency," with an average of only 46% of fourth graders passing each part of the state proficiency test (Ohio Department of Education, 2003).

In contrast to these dismal statistics about the city and district, the Linus principal and faculty reported that Linus was a generally successful school where teachers were happy to work. Linus is a diverse school compared to many in the district, with 25% African American students, 17% Hispanic students, 50% White students, and a significant Middle Eastern student population. The principal, in her third year at Linus, was proud of her success in securing grants and raising student achievement as measured by proficiency test scores. Despite these accomplishments, the school faced problems with teacher retention, which approaches 50% within five years in urban settings (Fideler & Haselkorn, 1999; Weiner, 1999). In 2001, Scott and van Lier (2001) reported that almost half of the new teachers in the district were considering leaving. Teacher transience was evident at Linus as well. Twenty-three of 50 teachers during 2002–2003 school year either had fewer than five years of experience or were experienced teachers newly transferred to the building. Two new teachers who had not passed the state teaching examination were working without a license.

Before the VTMP, Linus's new teacher support system consisted of one-hour monthly meetings among new teachers and administrators. The school assigned curriculum support teachers as mentors, but no formal meeting schedule, special training, or support for mentors existed. In a separate program, the district provided mentors from outside the building who were trained in the Educational Testing Service's (ETS) Pathwise model (ETS, 2001) to help new teachers pass state performance evaluations for licensure. No mentors were provided for second-year or transferred teachers. The teachers had access to standard district-wide professional development offerings but no formal opportunities for teachers to reflect on their teaching together. Linus's principal nonetheless valued thoughtful reflection on teaching, and she wanted to make opportunities for reflection available to *all* the teachers in her building—new teachers, veteran teachers newly transferred to the building, struggling veteran teachers, and teachers exploring new teaching strategies.

Program Design

The program designers, of which I was one, planned to assemble a group of new and experienced teachers as a professional community or "circle of co-practice" (see chapter 3, by Murrell, in this volume) to support teacher learning and student achievement. We recruited experienced teachers (i.e., those with two years of experience or more) through an open invitation to the Linus faculty and special invitations from the principal to outstanding faculty members. New teachers included teachers with less than five years of experience as well as those who had transferred to the school within the past five years, regardless of teaching experience. We partnered new teachers and experienced teachers together to match grade level wherever possible to create teacher pairs.

At the beginning of the year, every participant—both new and experienced—identified two goals using Danielson's (1996) framework for teaching: one from domain B—managing a learning environment—and one from domain C—teaching for content. Teachers were scheduled to visit and videotape a lesson in one another's classrooms once per month. Teacher pairs would capture these videotapes onto classroom computers and use Pinnacle Studio video-editing software to produce 5- to 10-minute video teaching cases that illustrated successes and challenges related to their goals. These teaching cases were then shared and discussed during biweekly meetings of the whole group using a standardized case-discussion protocol (Yusko, 2004). All participants had the opportunity to earn graduate credit: one credit for attending all meetings, two credits for producing at least one video case, and three credits for producing a video case with an accompanying reflective paper describing what they learned.

In the following sections, I describe and analyze the new mentoring roles, new technological tools, and new collaborative processes that were inherent in the design of the VTMP.

New Roles: Mentoring as Partnership

Almost all induction programs offer support by pairing new teachers with experienced ones to provide mentoring—that is, direct classroom assistance, psychological support, and, sometimes, assessment (Feiman-Nemser, Carver, Schwille, & Yusko, 1999). From a fidelity perspective, mentors are seen as expert teachers who know and can teach others all the best teaching practices; new teachers are expected to absorb mentors' wisdom and incorporate recommendations immediately. Instead of a unidirectional transmission of teaching knowledge, the program leaders and I sought to adopt a more bottom-up approach that acknowledged the need for all teachers to be involved in a constant process of professional reflection and modification of teaching.

To reflect this approach, we opted for the title *partner teacher* rather than *mentor teacher* to emphasize that partner teachers and new teachers were working together to analyze and improve their teaching, functioning "as fellow learners and researchers rather than experts" (Cochran-Smith & Lytle, 1999, p. 278). In selecting program participants, we did not seek only the most accomplished teachers or those with the most experience; we chose teachers at all levels of experience who expressed a desire to improve their own teaching. By requiring all teachers to set professional goals, we highlighted the fact that everyone in the group was involved in professional development. Finally, to move beyond a dyadic approach to mentoring that emphasized the transmission of knowledge from mentor to novice toward a more distributed view of teaching knowledge, we created opportunities for the whole group—partner teachers and novices alike—to engage in shared inquiry. As I discuss in the following sections, it was extremely difficult for these teachers to embrace these new mentoring roles and view themselves as partners in one another's learning.

Conceptions of mentoring. The program called on partner teachers to initiate and facilitate conversation about teaching through editing videotapes of one another's teaching. During a summer workshop, partner teachers watched videotapes of teaching, practiced giving descriptive (rather than evaluative) feedback, and asked probing questions about the lessons they watched. I hoped these activities would prepare them to facilitate similar conversations while editing videos; however, I saw no substantial evidence that they embraced the task of engaging the new teachers in shared inquiry. Rather, they tended to view their responsibilities to new teachers, even at the end of the first year, as mentoring by providing teaching tips and strategies or assisting with school policies and procedures. Some partner teachers felt hesitant to provide teaching advice because they had little or no more experience than some new teachers.

The distinction between partner teachers and new teachers was exacerbated by the strategies used for recruiting teachers to participate. Most partner teachers joined because they were interested in technology. New teachers felt pressured to attend, and several indicated that they had been "assigned" to this "committee," even though they had requested to serve on other school committees. Letters requiring them to attend the first meeting were placed in their mailboxes with little explanation of the program or the reasons why they were being required to participate. The following comments illustrate one participant's surprise and feeling of pressure to participate:

> Well, basically there was a flyer … that was put in my mailbox and stuff about basically participating in it, that it's going to start, when it was going to start and I was basically going to be involved in it. … I didn't know what was going to be involved in it basically and I guess how much time it was going to take. … I guess I was just kind of surprised in getting it. (Teacher A-3, new)

This sense of coercion was exacerbated when new teachers with several years of teaching experience expressed neither desire nor need for mentoring as they perceived it. Although the school facilitator and I tried to downplay the power differential between partner teachers who had volunteered and new teachers who were required to participate,[2] the difference in status was always clear.

At the end of the first year of the program, none of the completed teaching cases had been produced jointly by a pair. Partner teachers did not arrange meetings with new teachers to discuss video or to produce video cases; they waited for new teachers to request assistance. Given that many new teachers were unsure why they had been forced to participate and did not feel they needed assistance, they never requested meetings. Instead, participants worked alone on the videotaping and editing process. Almost every participant cited support from the school facilitator—videotaping, substituting in their classroom to videotape their partner, capturing video, or helping them edit—as a catalyst for progress at some point. The participants most interested in technology saw the production of cases, rather than the collaborative editing process, as the goal, so they typically experimented with the software and produced video cases independently.

These partner teachers' persistent view of mentoring demonstrates the entrenched view of the fidelity perspective, which deems mentors to be vehicles for disseminating district policies and recommended teaching practices and ensuring that new teachers comply. Helping teachers understand and adopt new roles calls for a radical shift in thinking.

Time. The challenge of adopting new roles was complicated by the ever-present challenges of finding time for participants to complete VTMP activities together. Observations of and reports from successful participants indicated that it took them approximately five hours to produce a video teaching case: videotaping, capturing video, dividing video into scenes, selecting and trimming scenes, and adding titles and transitions. However, it took much longer for someone new to the process. Many participants who did not produce videos or left the program cited problems with time:

> The taping—that was minimal, but after that, putting the tape together and looking at it and all. Yea[h], those factors is what takes more of the time (Teacher A-3, new)

> How do you eat an elephant? One bite at a time, right? Well, I forgot that. I tried to eat the whole elephant at once and that found me a little bit, whoa what am I getting into here? (Teacher C-1, partner)

Participants with less interest in technology spent little time exploring the technology and never became proficient. The pairs did not meet regularly, so partner teachers were unable to assist the new teachers with technology.

Part of the problem was the challenge of making time for pairs to visit one another's classrooms or meet for editing. This challenge arose from problems specific to the urban context. Due to budget concerns, teachers could not remain in their classrooms more than 30 minutes after the end of the school day, so that the school could cut custodial expenses. Even though all the pairs shared a common planning or lunch period, they opted to use these times for planning lessons rather than editing video. Although the program had money available to pay substitutes for release time, the bureaucracy of this urban district's substitute policy made it nearly impossible to arrange for substitutes in advance. Teachers relied on building substitutes who were only available when no other teachers were absent that day. Demonstrating resiliency and persistence (see chapter 2, by Peterman and Sweigard, in this volume), participants explored alternate strategies to solve this problem for over two years with varying success. One teacher asked students to videotape, and others used tripods. Another commandeered student teachers placed in his classroom to videotape. These strategies allowed teachers to videotape successfully but defeated the goal of having teachers visit one another's classrooms. Occasionally, teachers divided up their students and sent them into neighboring classrooms so that they could go and videotape someone else, but this raised concerns about whether the payoff of having a videotape in hand was worth sacrificing students' learning time, thus undermining the whole purpose of the project in promoting student learning. Sometimes, the group was able to trick the system by having multiple members call for substitutes on the same day, in the hopes that the district would send at least one.

District policies were not the only problem. Some new teachers explained that the VTMP did not mesh with their other responsibilities in and out of school, such as school committees, the demands of teaching, graduate courses, and family commitments. Their reasons appeared plausible; however, partner teachers who successfully produced videos also cited conflicting responsibilities. For example, three of the five teachers who successfully produced final videos were fourth-grade teachers who tutored students after school from January through March to prepare students for the state proficiency exam. Tutoring responsibilities took precedence over the VTMP during this time, so they did not attend meetings, but they still produced video cases. The fourth-grade teachers' success suggests that a high level of interest and commitment can override the challenges of finding time for the work.

By the end of the first year of the program, five participants successfully produced at least one video case, but none of these were new teachers. Participants who continued into the second year were devoted and enthusiastic, but—with one exception—these continuing teachers were all partner teachers. All but one of the new teachers lost their teaching positions, left teaching, or chose not to continue the program.

Challenges and possibilities of new roles. Developing new roles for teachers to collaborate in one another's professional development represents a challenge to existing school structures. First, designers of programs like the VTMP challenge the individualistic culture of teaching. Context-specific teacher learning has been limited mostly to mentoring as a one-way transmission from one who knows to one who does not. If teachers do not need immediate assistance about a specific issue, they may see little need for discussing problems of teaching with one another. This problem is complicated by teacher autonomy without shared visions of effective teaching. Altering mentor-novice power relationships requires more than making semantic distinctions between a *mentor* and a *partner* or introducing teachers to new processes. Collaborative professional development that fosters the learning of new and experienced teachers demands that programs like the VTMP draw on the strengths of both new and experienced teachers, so that all teachers understand and experience the potential benefits of such arrangements.

Second, program designers need to ensure that participants' concerns about time are addressed. This means challenging or working around school or district policies that make it difficult or impossible for teachers to meet together to institutionalize regular, predictable meeting times. However, it also means helping all program participants value the collaborative nature of the work. For new teachers especially, program leaders must eliminate or minimize the distraction of other school responsibilities and offer direct intervention to help teachers juggle VTMP responsibilities with other commitments.

New Tools: Video Technology

"Records of practice" (Ball & Cohen, 1999) are useful for promoting meaningful conversations about teaching. In a study of teacher change, Yusko (2000) found that seeing teaching through "a second set of eyes"—being observed, observing fellow teachers, or observing oneself on videotape—produced powerful professional development. As video technology has become more simple and affordable, teacher educators have begun to embrace it as a teacher education tool (Lampert & Ball, 1998; Tochon, 1999; Wang & Hartley, 2003). As Tochon (1999) points out, video can be fun, and the surprising ease of producing high-quality video on a computer is alluring. Wang and Hartley (2003) note that video technology allows the documentation of rich, complex, teaching and learning situations. Video allows for a common experience of a lesson, so that teachers can focus conversations on observed actions rather than recollections. By allowing participants to see classrooms from different perspectives—capturing student behaviors and responses missed during the frenetic pace of teaching, zooming in on small group interactions while the teacher works with other groups, or focusing on individual students and work samples—video provides excellent material for shared observation and collective reflection.

In urban settings, video may be particularly useful. In any school, but in urban schools in particular, teachers may tend to focus on problems within the setting, such as challenging students, ineffective parents, meddling or overzealous administrators, inefficient bureaucracies, or unreasonable district policies. By making videotapes of teaching the center of the conversation, video can contextualize and focus a discussion on one teacher and her students during a single lesson. Using video as a focus for inquiry and shared reflection allows teachers to interpret classroom events through multiple lenses.

Working with captured video on computers adds even more possibilities for teacher reflection. Once video is captured onto a computer, teachers can easily slow down the action and reflect systematically by viewing parts of a lesson multiple times. They can choose how to represent their teaching by selecting relevant scenes through video editing (Lampert & Ball, 1990). This process can be enhanced by having teachers view captured videos together and discuss how segments relate to professional goals. Once videos are edited, they can be used to promote conversation among groups of teachers. Edited videos stored on CDs or DVDs allow for quick access to any point on the video and facilitate viewing and reviewing specific scenes.

Enthusiasm for technology. All of the VTMP partner teachers indicated a keen interest in technology. Two partner teachers wanted to use video with their students, but most were interested in the technology for themselves:

> I was always tied into technology—at Linus, anyways—from when I first came on board. ... I ran a scientific learning program, so I've always been tied into the technology component. (School Facilitator)

> I wanted to learn the technology and then I went upstairs and asked the other fourth grade teachers and they were all doing it, so we all said yes. (Teacher B-1, partner)

> I liked the idea of incorporating the technology in the classroom. I thought that would be a real good idea. I had just finished, well not just finished, like the year before I had taken a tech class at [a local university]. Oh god, it was great! So, I figured this would be really cool to do too. (Teacher C-1, partner)

The school facilitator explained that the district "has lots of expensive things, but we don't always use them right." The program exposed teachers to technologies they might have never explored or even imagined. The participants who completed video cases and continued with the group were the most interested in technology. These teachers all enjoyed producing the video cases and commented on how much fun they had sprucing up their videos with transitions and background music. One VTMP participant allowed his students to use the video camera to tape classroom activities; it would only be a short leap to involve his students in editing video as an instructional tool.

Video cases as records of practice. At the beginning of the first year of the program, some participants asked what the teaching cases should include. I explained that the cases should illustrate both successes and challenges related to goals, so that the video was not just a showcase of best practices but also a tool to stimulate conversation about challenges that all the teachers faced in their teaching. I wanted to focus on the *process* of creating cases, and I hoped that the process would yield different visions of how a *product* might look. Ultimately, viewing the finished cases was valuable for both the participants who produced video cases as well as those who simply watched others' cases.

Each participant identified one management-related goal and one instruction-related goal. Participants' management goals included giving effective directions, managing routines and transitions, and instructing groups. Their instructional goals included the structuring and pacing of lessons, making content comprehensible to students, and implementing more hands-on activities and less lecture. The completed products took a range of forms. One teacher created a highly polished video case explaining and demonstrating features of her mathematics instruction to explain her methods to parents and other teachers. Another teacher produced a video case comparing the engagement of his students during lecture and hands-on science instruction. A third teacher, who used the project for her master's degree culminating project, completed a literature review on effective reading instruction and produced a video demonstrating the new practices she had studied.

Several participants reported the value of seeing things on their own or others' videos that led them to think about their own teaching:

> I don't like seeing myself on TV or anything, but it does help, you know in how you deal with the discipline and how much you miss when you turn your back. What the kids are doing behind you and they knew the camera was on, but they still did it anyway. (Teacher A-1, partner)

> As I went through [the video], now I was more aware of the students. What their reactions were, what they were doing during class because when I saw the lecture part and then I went to the hands-on part it was two whole worlds. You know, so how can I make the lecture brief and at the same time be effective with something they can touch. That's what I needed to do. (Teacher E-1, partner)

> [As I watched another person's video], I don't know what the outcome was supposed to be or I don't know what the standard was. ... That little clip said, "Wow, am I making sure that I introduce everyday what the standard is or what the kids are supposed to learn and what are you supposed to do at the end." It got me to think to myself, "Wow, I hope I tell my kids what they're supposed to be doing before an assignment." (Teacher B-3, partner)

> When I teach a science topic, if it's new to them, I have a problem with bringing myself down to their level. So, I have a tendency to give them too much information ... and I saw that on the tape in the beginning, the blank stares and just like, "Oh I don't get this." But, then as I moved and changed the lesson I saw how they got actively involved in it. (Teacher E-2, partner)

The videos allowed teachers to see things they could not have seen while teaching—student behavior while their backs were turned, students' independent work, and group interactions. Videos enabled teachers to watch and listen closely to student responses. These new views of their classrooms led them to consider new ways to present information and new ways to manage classroom activities.

Technology access and support. Although the grant provided all the necessary hardware and software to prepare the teachers' classroom computers for this project, the bureaucracy of the urban context presented additional challenges. Except for one teacher who functioned as the building technology representative (for which there was no release time), all technology support came from a central district technology office. The hardware and software could only be installed by district technology staff, since the teachers had no access to the Windows Control Panel on their classroom computers. Although we requested the installations in early September, district technology staff could not complete the installations until the end of October. When there were problems with the installation, participants sometimes waited weeks for technology support staff to troubleshoot, and they could not begin editing until December. Since there was no one in the building with expertise in the software, teachers stopped working whenever they encountered a problem and waited until the next group meeting. The grant only provided one video camera, and the district's technology expenditures were frozen due to budget shortfalls. Since people needed the camera for both videotaping and capturing video, access was a regular concern.

Challenges and possibilities of new tools. The completed cases demonstrate how teachers can use video cases to reflect on multiple goals and to represent their teaching for a variety of audiences. Requiring teachers to focus on management and instructional goals ensured that they went beyond reflection on discipline and management techniques to examine what and when their students were learning. The teachers' enthusiasm over producing and watching one another's cases highlights the value in using video tools to stimulate teacher reflection.

These benefits do not come without a cost. In large, poorly funded, bureaucratized systems, availability and access to technology make it difficult for teachers to use new technological tools. The VTMP shows that as little as $10,000 can provide the necessary materials, but, without access and expertise, program leaders and participants are at the whim of district technology staff who may already be stretched too thin. Participants with intrinsic interest in technology have enough motivation and knowledge to complete VTMP videotaping and editing in the face of these obstacles, but, to reach teachers with less of an interest in technology, program leaders must struggle to overcome these obstacles.

New Processes: Joint Inquiry Into Teaching

Little (1982) reported that teachers in well-functioning schools "teach each other the practice of teaching." Lord (1994) argued that teacher development is enriched by "critical colleagueship" when teachers engage in sustained, concrete talk about their teaching. Our goal was to develop a community of practice that went beyond sharing stories of teaching to engage in a "consistent and systematic appraisal of practice" (see chapter 3, by Murrell, in this volume) by creating a formal structure and opportunity to engage in such discussion. One way to foster such discussion is through case discussion, which has become a popular tool for teacher educators (Shulman, 1992; Sykes & Bird, 1992). Case discussion approaches allow groups of people to examine teaching situations from multiple angles and to engage in reflection—connecting theory to practice, reflecting on underlying causes of situations, and generating and engaging in problem solving (Carter, 1988; Doyle, 1997; Merseth & Lacey, 1993). Although case methods have predominantly been used in preservice teacher education, such methods may also be useful for practicing teachers, as demonstrated by activities like Japanese lesson study (Shimahara, 1998).

Improvement of teaching through collegiality. The VTMP offered teachers opportunities that did not exist anywhere else in their professional lives. Successful participants demonstrated that busy teachers, despite the obstacles, can complete VTMP activities if they are motivated and see their value.

Both partner teachers and new teachers felt that the program provided valuable opportunities to discuss teaching with a group in the hope of improving their teaching. The VTMP provided a forum to share teaching ideas, as well as concerns. Some were looking for feedback about their teaching:

> Unless the principal comes in here or something, you really don't get any feedback from anyone else. So, I mean it was good to be paired up and you can kind of work with each other. And you each can help each other with the taping and all that and learning how to do that. (Teacher A-3, new)

> I mean, you're on the right track … it's a non-supervisory person talking to this person giving them hints. We all need that! … Teaching is a lonely profession; you need to talk to other people, run ideas off them if nothing else, get ideas from them. They talk about the Japanese collaborating all the time and look at their education system, so we could learn some things. (Teacher C-1, partner)

The teachers all enjoyed discussing teaching with their school colleagues:

> I think pairing up with somebody is better because … four eyes are better than two. I think it's important because it gets you talking, you learn from everybody. I mean I could sit there myself and say the same thing over and over again. So, I think it is beneficial. (Teacher A-1, partner)

> I liked talking to adults. … We don't have a chance in the building to get around and say, "You know what? I'm having trouble with this particular behavior. What do you guys have?" I mean usually you go to the same person over and over and they've already … tried and dealt with that kid and they're done. … Or even ideas for a different lesson. I enjoyed that. I enjoyed even just going into someone else's room, I know that sounds silly, but to just kind of look around. And I like how relaxed it was. (Teacher B-3, partner)

Despite some initial trepidation about being videotaped, the partner teachers enjoyed videotaping their teaching and sharing their cases with the whole group. Even though none of the pairs produced their video cases collaboratively, the watching of the cases still turned out to be a learning experience. Some teachers commented on how pleasantly surprised they were by what they saw on their videotapes:

> I saw the kids that were listening, that were doing what I asked them to do. I know that it is working in some areas; there's just some kids who need more influence. (Teacher A-1, partner)

> It was kind of neat to see, you know, "Gee, that lesson really went as well as I thought it did." (Teacher C-1, partner)

Others gathered new ideas from watching others teach:

> One of my goals was to try to get more effective classroom discipline. And that was a goal that I had in mind for myself and I wanted to see how this peer grouping could help me by watching other teachers modeling how behavior can be dealt with. (Teacher C-2, new)

> I always enjoy talking about teaching and I enjoyed watching other teachers. You know I remember watching Teacher B-4 a couple of times. It's just helpful. So much of the time as teachers we are alone with the kids and so for a chance to have adult conversations about what it is we are trying to do every day is so beneficial to me. I just don't get tired of it and I'm always looking for new ideas and more examples and suggestions. (Teacher D-1, new)

Talking about teaching, visiting one another's classrooms, and watching one another's video cases provided valuable opportunities that these teachers did not get from any other sources. These interactions provided the teachers with new ideas, caused them to raise new questions, and offered validation for their teaching.

Faculty transience. Unfortunately, the VTMP was difficult to sustain, in large part because of challenges posed by low teacher retention in an urban school district (see chapter 2, by Peterman and Sweigard, in this volume; and chapter 1, by Chou and Tozer, in this volume). The VTMP had been instituted partly to increase teacher retention by cultivating a professional community at Linus where teachers would want to stay. Ironically, outside influences made it impossible for the VTMP to achieve this goal. After the first year, four participants left the school—two because they had failed to earn their teaching licenses and two for personal reasons. The facilitator, who had been released from classroom duties to oversee the program, had been instrumental in fostering participants' progress. Budget cuts during the second year of the program forced her to teach full-time, which made it difficult to maintain the same level of involvement. At the end of the second year, the district failed to pass a major levy, resulting in massive budget shortfalls and teacher layoffs. Over two years, 7 of the original 14 participants were either laid off or transferred to new buildings. Three years after the initial launch of the VTMP, only three teachers (one of whom had left the VTMP after the first year) remained employed at Linus.

The loss of teachers from the VTMP serves as a reminder that the problem of retention is not simply one of recruiting and retaining teachers. Research on intensive group-oriented professional development activities, such as the VTMP, suggests that it takes several years of consistent involvement by the same participants to realize significant learning opportunities through breakthroughs in levels of disclosure about one's teaching and specificity of conversations (Beasley, Corbin, Feiman-Nemser, & Shank, 1996; Featherstone, 1998). In a district where teachers are moved regularly from building to building as if they were interchangeable, and when layoffs based on seniority result in only the most veteran teachers staying employed, long-range projects like the VTMP are nearly impossible to sustain.

Challenges and possibilities of new processes. During our goal-setting sessions, all of the VTMP teachers shared high goals for student learning, frustrations at not being able to accomplish all of these goals, and a desire to improve their teaching. Many also expressed a lack of opportunities for sharing their concerns with other teachers, for receiving direct feedback on their teaching, and for exchanging teaching ideas. The participants' enthusiasm for these opportunities was convincing that the program's efforts to overcome the challenges were worthwhile. Unfortunately, the transience of the participants due to personal circumstances and district budget crises provided the main challenge to getting teachers to work together.

WHERE THERE IS A WILL, THERE MUST BE A WAY

The VTMP faced multiple challenges, some resulting from its design and others from its implementation in an urban setting. Requiring teachers to set teaching goals and work collaboratively to produce and analyze their own video cases represented a radical departure from centralized, workshop-based professional development opportunities. Giving teachers more control over their own professional development can be empowering, but it can also be intimidating. Treating the mentoring relationship as a partnership within a collective of partnerships challenged dominant views of mentoring. Observing and videotaping in colleagues' classrooms and watching and editing videotapes involved a higher level of scrutiny than teachers had ever received, even from evaluating principals.

The urban context added more layers of complexity. Our method of informing the new teachers of their participation unwittingly undermined our attempts to empower the teachers and sent a message that the VTMP was just another example of district-mandated professional development, another responsibility heaped onto their already full plates. Inefficient systems for providing substitute teachers made it nearly impossible to make time for partners to visit one another's classrooms. Budget shortages aggravated this problem by preventing teachers from meeting after school, halting the purchase of additional equipment, and transferring or laying off valuable participants. Despite these multiple challenges, the evidence suggests that the potential rewards are worth the hard work. In this section, I propose some ways to engage in the kind of activism that is required to sustain such a program.

First, program leaders must maximize conditions for participants' intrinsic motivation. Some teachers are intrinsically motivated by technology, others are motivated by opportunities for collegial interaction, and still others are motivated by the search for new teaching strategies. Participants with the least involvement in the program were those who felt coerced to participate, had little interest in technology, or were uncomfortable with technology. Program leaders should make efforts to minimize coercion and provide experiences matched with participants' motivations. Teachers fearful of being taped might begin by taping other teachers who have already been taped. New participants could join in case discussions to witness the benefits for those whose cases are being discussed. Experienced participants' openness to the process would help new participants feel less intimidated, and everyone would still benefit from watching and discussing the video cases. Pairing teachers teaching a similar grade level or sharing similar goals also ensures that teachers will be motivated to meet and discuss their progress. To ensure that the teachers work on editing, at least one partner should be enthusiastic about technology.

Second, teachers must have the necessary time built into their work day. Ideally, partner teachers should have common planning time before, during, or after school. Specifying a regular day and time to work on editing would relieve both members of the pair from the responsibility of arranging meetings, which could be viewed as nagging by experienced teachers or advice seeking by new teachers. Developing a schedule of manageable, short-term goals would ensure that the work moves forward. For new teachers especially, the program should not conflict with other school responsibilities or schoolwide initiatives, since they are most likely to be overwhelmed with the tasks of teaching. Additional responsibilities make it unlikely that they will complete the VTMP activities.

Third, there must be program support within the building. All technology should be in place before the program begins to eliminate frustration in waiting for technology to be installed or fixed. All participants should have easy access to a computer and video camera in a quiet place. The school should have an on-site facilitator with at least two hours per week per pair to devote to the program. The facilitator should assist with scheduling release time for videotaping and editing and should make sure that all participants have appropriate access to equipment when needed. The facilitator should also have technology proficiency to provide technical assistance when necessary and should have personal experience creating a video case to scaffold pairs' conversations during editing conversations.

These conditions are ideal, but they provide a goal for school-level activists. Many situations outside school-level control will affect the ability to realize these conditions. Personnel decisions made by district or regional offices mean that teacher assignments are never ensured, particularly in districts where budget shortages result in teacher layoffs, reduced access to the school building, unavailability of technology support, and lack of substitute teachers or release time. Inefficient bureaucratic systems, such as those for allocating substitute teachers, are unlikely to change quickly. The VTMP will always function within a complex and shifting terrain of new district-wide initiatives (see chapter 1, by Chou and Tozer, this volume). As activists, VTMP teachers and program leaders must be committed, flexible, and willing to engage in creative problem solving as they challenge systemic norms in pursuit of optimal teacher learning. Arming teachers with new roles, new tools, and new processes, the VTMP fosters teacher autonomy that prepares teachers to take greater responsibility for their collective professional development.

NOTES

1. School and participant names are pseudonyms.
2. None of the participants were required to participate in the research portion of the program, but all program participants chose to sign consent forms.

REFERENCES

Ball, D. L., & Cohen, D. (1999). Developing practice, developing practitioners: Toward a practice-based theory of professional education. In L. Darling-Hammond & G. Sykes (Eds.), *Teaching as the learning profession* (pp. 3–32). San Francisco: Jossey Bass.

Beasley, K., Corbin, D., Feiman-Nemser, S., & Shank, C. (1996). Making it happen: Teachers mentoring one another. *Theory Into Practice, 35,* 158–164.

Carter, K. (1988). Using cases to frame mentor-novice conversations. *Theory Into Practice, 27,* 214–222.

Cochran-Smith, M., & Lytle, S. (1999). Relationships of knowledge and practice: Teacher learning in communities. In A. Iran-Nejad & P. D. Pearson (Eds.), *Review of Research in Education* (Vol. 24, pp. 249–306). Washington, DC: American Educational Research Association.

Danielson, C. (1996). *Enhancing professional practice: A framework for teaching.* Alexandria, VA: Association of Supervision and Curriculum Development.

Doyle, W. (1997). Heard any really good stories lately? A critique of the critics of narrative in educational research. *Teaching and Teacher Education, 13,* 93–99.

Educational Testing Service. (2001). *Praxis topics.* Princeton, NJ: Educational Testing Service.

Featherstone, H. (1998). Studying children: The Philadelphia Teachers' Learning Cooperative. In D. Allen (Ed.), *Assessing student learning: From grading to understanding* (pp. 66–83). New York: Teachers College Press.

Feiman-Nemser, S., Carver, C., Schwille, S., & Yusko, B. (1999). Beyond support: Taking new teachers seriously as learners. In M. Scherer (Ed.), *A better beginning: Supporting and mentoring new teachers* (pp. 3–12). Alexandria, VA: Association for Supervision and Curriculum Development.

Fideler, E., & Haselkorn, D. (1999). *Learning the ropes: Urban teacher induction programs and practices in the United States.* Boston: Recruiting New Teachers.

Fullan, M. (1991). *The new meaning of educational change.* New York: Teachers College Press.

Hawley, W. D., & Valli, L. (1999). The essentials of effective professional development: A new consensus. In L. Darling-Hammond & G. Sykes (Eds.), *Teaching as the learning profession* (pp. 127–150). San Francisco: Jossey Bass.

Huberman, M. (1993). *The lives of teachers.* New York: Teachers College Press.

Lampert, M., & Ball, D. L. (1990). *Using hypermedia technology to support a new pedagogy of teacher education* (Issue Paper 90-5). East Lansing, MI: National Center for Research on Teacher Education, Michigan State University.

Lampert, M., & Ball, D. L. (1998). *Teaching, multimedia, and mathematics: Investigations of real practice.* New York: Teachers College Press.

Little, J. W. (1982). Norms of collegiality and experimentation: Workplace conditions of school success. *American Educational Research Journal, 19,* 325–340.

Little, J. W. (1993). Teachers' professional development in a climate of educational reform. *Educational Evaluation and Policy Analysis, 15,* 129–151.

Lord, B. (1994). Teachers' professional development: Critical colleagueship and the role of professional communities. In N. Cobb (Ed.), *The future of education: Perspectives on national standards in education* (pp. 175–204). New York: College Entrance Examination Board.

Mazzolini, J., & Davis, D. (2003, July 20). City far behind comparable communities in quality-of-life measures, analysis finds. *The Plain Dealer,* pp. 1, 6.

Merseth, K. K., & Lacey, C. A. (1993). Weaving stronger fabric: The pedagogical promise of hypermedia and case methods in teacher education. *Teaching and Teacher Education, 9,* 283–299.

Ohio Department of Education. (2003). *Proficiency test results.* Retrieved July 25, 2003, from http://www.ode.state.oh.us

Putnam, R., & Borko, H. (2000). What do new views of knowledge and thinking have to say about research on teacher learning? *Educational Researcher, 29*(1), 4–16.

Scott, C., & van Lier, P. (2001, August/September). Mid-year survey: Half of new teachers considered leaving. *Catalyst Cleveland,* 4.

Shimahara, N. K. (1998). The Japanese model of professional development: Teaching as craft. *Teaching and Teacher Education, 14,* 451–462.

Shulman, J. (Ed.). (1992). *Case methods in teacher education.* New York: Teachers College Press.

Sykes, G., & Bird, T. (1992). Teacher education and the case idea. *Review of Research in Education, 18,* 457–521.

Tochon, F. V. (1999). *Video study groups for education, professional development, and change.* Madison, WI: Atwood Publishing.

Tyack, D., & Cuban, L. (1995). *Tinkering toward Utopia: Reflections on a century of public school reform.* Cambridge, MA: Harvard University Press.

Wang, J., & Hartley, K. (2003). Video technology as a support for teacher education reform. *Journal of Technology and Teacher Education, 11*, 105–138.

Weiner, L. (1999). *Urban teaching: The essentials.* New York: Teachers College Press.

Yusko, B. (2000). *"Constellations" of professional development for promoting attentiveness to students.* Unpublished doctoral dissertation, Michigan State University, East Lansing, MI.

Yusko, B. (2004). Promoting reflective teaching conversations: Framing and reframing the problem. *Teaching Education, 15*(4), 363–374.

CHAPTER ELEVEN

The Fragility OF Urban Teaching: A Longitudinal Study OF Career Development AND Activism

KAREN HUNTER QUARTZ

University of California, Los Angeles

BRAD OLSEN

University of California, Santa Cruz

JEFF DUNCAN-ANDRADE

San Francisco State University

Teacher educators at the University of California, Los Angeles (UCLA), have been struggling over the past decade—guided by a strong commitment to social justice—to make their work responsive to the needs of high-poverty urban schools. Their intention is to prepare teachers as change agents who will work with local communities to help improve the conditions of schooling. In this chapter, we describe the creation and development of UCLA's Urban Teacher Education Program at Center X[1]. Specifically, we focus on its effort to partner with local communities to create alternative sites of learning for novice teachers. We then share a story of Center X graduates working in one Los Angeles elementary school in order to set the stage for our research question: Under what conditions do highly qualified urban teachers remain committed to a career as a social justice educator? We report interim retention data from a longitudinal study of Center X graduates and explore the issue of how professional learning communities emerge in urban schools. The chapter closes with an analysis of the fragility of urban teaching.

CENTER X: WHERE RESEARCH AND PRACTICE INTERSECT FOR URBAN SCHOOL PROFESSIONALS

Center X was first conceived in 1992 as a result of the upheaval and self-examination stemming from Los Angeles's Rodney King–verdict uprisings. In 1994, Center X began as an integrated, experimental, two-year urban teacher preparation program in the Graduate School of Education and Information Studies at UCLA (Oakes, 1996). Previously, UCLA's teacher education program was a highly regarded but conventional one-year master of education (M.Ed.) program that prepared teachers by emphasizing constructivism and practitioner reflection. The newly formed Center X—named as such to highlight experimentation and the intersection of theory and practice—put forward an activist commitment to social justice, grounded itself in sociocultural learning theory, and embedded teacher apprenticeship inside urban school community partnerships. Teacher preparation was reconceptualized as dialogical inquiry and guided social practice about what it means to be a transformative social justice educator in urban Los Angeles—consonant with the view espoused by Shirley in chapter 4 that participatory democracy holds the most promise for reforming urban schools.[2]

The new program recruited diverse groups of faculty and teacher candidates interested in social change, put students and instructors in small learning teams, and extended the MEd program through a scaffolded, resident year of full-time teaching after the novice year. Center X began small, graduating 90 teachers in each of its first two years, and has slowly grown to twice that size. The Center X curriculum stresses views of inequity as structural, activism as necessary, multiculturalism as central, and the critical study of race and society as crucial in order to prepare teachers to teach successfully for social justice in urban schools. The program rejects purely technical, social efficiency models of teaching and learning in favor of culturally relevant pedagogy, sociocultural learning approaches, and moral-political dimensions of teaching. Such an approach parallels the contextually responsive standards for urban teaching that Peterman and Sweigard discuss in chapter 2 of this volume. Teacher candidates at Center X engage around notions of sociocultural theories of learning (Lave & Wenger, 1991; Vygotsky, 1978), asset mapping (Kretzmann & McKnight, 1993), funds of knowledge (Moll, 1988, 1998), language acquisition (Cummins, 1996) and cultural identity (Tatum, 1997). Candidates participate in inquiry sessions, curriculum design and teaching projects in schools, classrooms and community centers with groups of peers, kindergarten through 12th grade (K–12) students, professors, and veteran teachers—building the sort of professional learning community described by Murrell in chapter 3 of this volume. This set of ideas and practices has become the program. For the sake of our discussion here, we have selected three Center X perspectives to illustrate the program. These perspectives echo the framework presented in the introductory chapters of this book and exemplify the goals of Center X:

- An emphasis on social justice.
- A social theory of learning.
- Teacher preparation as an integrated whole, occurring over time, in context.

An Emphasis on Social Justice

Center X is committed to preparing teachers as agents of social change. Given this mission, the program foregrounds social justice. Ideas and readings from the following related domains informed the creation of the program and continue to guide the program's practices: multiculturalism (Banks, 1994; Darder, 1998; Nieto, 1999), critical pedagogy (Freire, 1970; Giroux, 1992; Hooks, 1994; McLaren, 1997), culturally responsive teaching (Cochran-Smith, 1997; Ladson-Billings, 1994; Oakes & Lipton, 2003; Sleeter, 1993), and community organizing (Alinsky, 1989). Center X has adopted a view of teaching that moves participants outside traditional frames of classrooms into larger examinations of societal inequity and conditions of schooling. The program links macroperspectives of society (coming from sociology, cultural anthropology, and political science) to microanalyses of students, schools, and classrooms (including student motivation, tracking, and curriculum design). Through participation in team seminars, candidates use theory and research to create curricula that integrate learning goals with students' homes and communities. The goal of these curricula is to raise students' awareness and therefore empower K–12 students to identify and challenge inequity at the same time that they learn the skills and academics of their school's official curriculum.

Center X also attempts to build partnerships with urban school communities and decided early on to partner only with particular urban schools—high-poverty, hard-to-staff schools that are most in need of highly qualified teachers. As Chou and Tozer explain in chapter 1 of this volume, defining what constitutes an *urban* school is wrought with complexity. Center X attempts to take on the distinctive urban challenge of size, heterogeneity, and cultural politics within Los Angeles and the massive Los Angeles Unified School District. Teams often hold their seminars at the local schools, not on the university campus. As part of the coursework during their first year, candidates complete a community project in which they form groups to investigate the particular community where they will student teach: They identify and map community assets; interview parents and other community members; research the history, demographics, and culture of the neighborhoods; and present findings in portfolios, community presentations, and action plans. Second-year students—now full-time teachers—enter partner schools in pairs or small groups and work closely with veteran teachers and Center X faculty to continually embed social justice in their practice.

These community partnerships are still a work in progress and represent one of the center's toughest struggles. It has proved difficult to dislodge vestiges of the traditional hierarchy of university-school (or expert-subject) relations; full buy-in from communities and district administrators has proved elusive; Center X personnel can be constrained by holding perspectives that are different from schools and communities; charges of ivory tower elitism linger; and many Center X teachers report a wide gap separating university conceptions and Los Angeles school realities, finding it hard to build pedagogical bridges between them.

Finally, Center X attempts to guide its own practice with social justice principles. With varying success, the program recruits diverse groups of students and faculty. By no means perfectly democratic, Center X favors collaborative decision making, a flattened hierarchy, and governance by committee. These components allow the program to try and remain self-renewing and responsive to students' needs and the needs of the school communities.

A Social Theory of Learning

Center X embraces sociocultural learning perspectives that view learning as embedded in students' and teachers' social interactions and contexts (Cummins, 1996; Lave & Wenger, 1991; Moll, 1988, 1998; Tharp & Gallimore, 1988; Vygotsky, 1978). Many in Center X believe that learning is largely acculturation (Oakes, 1996) and, as such, emerges from the multiple identities, interpretations, purposes, prior experiences, and combined perspectives on which any group of people relies in a collective endeavor like schooling. Given this cultural and community view, Center X faculty attempt to merge pedagogy with relationships through collaborative learning, apprenticeship models of teaching, and assessment that is embedded inside authentic activities. Faculty try to locate teacher development not in the university lecture hall but in the schools and communities in which their teachers work. This stance leads Center X to instruct its own candidates in the same ways it urges candidates to conduct their own teaching: in teams and using inquiry and dialogue as primary pedagogical tools. Because purposefully thoughtful teachers need a firm grounding in the research and theory that guide their pedagogies, learning theory is a cornerstone of the curriculum. To evaluate candidates, the program relies on authentic forms of assessment, such as collaborative projects, portfolios, ongoing conversation, and field supervisors as teaching coaches. Candidates participate in inquiry-based courses, such as Cultural Identity and Social Foundations and Cultural Diversity in American Education, and they choose one of three cultures of emphasis (African American, Latino, or Asian American) for an inquiry group linking culture, curriculum, and pedagogy.

The sociocultural principles that prepare teachers for classroom work also guide Center X efforts to create teacher learning communities in schools. Center X often recruits its new faculty from partner districts. Center X maintains close working relationships with like-minded teachers and administrators from the schools with whom Center X partners, using those relationships to recreate schools as productive places of collaboration and inquiry toward social change. However, as Lane, Lacefield-Parachini, and Isken (2003) have reported, it has sometimes been difficult to find large numbers of school personnel whose education philosophies match that of Center X.

Teacher Preparation as Integrated Whole, Occurring Over Time, in Context

Because Center X takes a holistic view of teachers and teaching, the program stresses teacher preparation as the simultaneous development of teacher identities and supportive teacher communities. Preservice teachers learn their craft and professional dispositions within this holistic environment of teachers, teaching, and communities. Center X is a collection of several undertakings that support urban teacher development: the Subject Matter Projects (a set of statewide professional development centers), the Teacher Education Program, and several research and outreach efforts that link empirical analyses of urban schooling with attempts to widen and deepen the center's work. These units are more or less independent of one another, but significant coherence results from their subscribing to a common Center X perspective.

Students remain in the same team (of usually 18 candidates) for two years and typically have the same faculty advisor as team leader for both years. This enables team leaders and students to develop relationships that personalize the preparation process and attend to frequently neglected aspects of professional development, including moral, political, social, and affective dimensions of becoming a career urban educator. The faculty tends to place the daily exigencies of classroom challenges (pedagogy, student-teacher-classroom relationships, curriculum, etc.) in the context of open themes like the social justice implications of practice; the teacher's respectful participation in helping students construct knowledge; the unspoken, ignored, or unintended lessons about themselves and society that students learn; and so on. Students (and faculty) are often frustrated to find that these dialogues do not produce firm answers—that it is the constructive participation itself that may ultimately be most liberating and productive. That said, however, such practices can be deeply unnerving (Bird, Anderson, Sullivan, & Swidler, 1993).

The program has adopted an iterative view of teacher development, believing that its preservice candidates and in-service graduates should continually revisit the principles of practice that Center X promotes. During the novice year, students grapple with the perspectives and issues (already described) that the program foregrounds. During the resident year, Center X faculty guide residents in another cycle of reflection on these notions, which are now embedded in their full-time teaching practice. These investigations take place as the teachers continue to meet in teams and prepare their master's degree portfolios. Once they graduate, the beginning teachers are invited into the Urban Educator Network (UEN)—a series of professional development opportunities, inquiry groups, and networks created in order to establish additional sites of collaborative practice for teachers within the school-university partnerships. For example, one component of the network is the Consortium of urban schools Involved in Renewal and Committed to Leadership in Education (CIRCLE), a set of district-based groups of teachers, administrators, university faculty, and community leaders who meet quarterly to strategize ways to better integrate school, district, and university. Another UEN effort, Critical Teacher Inquiry Groups for Growth and Retention, brings activist-minded teachers from a school together to collaborate on ways to continually embed social justice in their teaching practice. This UEN effort is featured next in this chapter.

Although those who participate in UEN activities find them helpful, often invaluable (Quartz & TEP Research Group, 2003), only a few dozen teachers participate regularly. And, even though some non-Center X teachers participate, the groups are sometimes perceived as closed-door UCLA enclaves. Moreover, as Center X was growing, its view of professional development for graduates has had to change. With over 900 graduates, the goal of reaching all graduates has been replaced with the more research-oriented goal of understanding how best to establish successful and continual professional development in urban schools. At their best, these development structures act as collective apprenticeship. In this way, Center X attempts to support urban teachers to build activist communities at their teaching sites; consider themselves school leaders and coalition builders, as well as teachers; and work to become public intellectuals. The program does not always succeed, but it remains committed to trying.

We turn now to one example of teachers struggling together to find hope and energy amid the considerable challenges they face each day. This example is not intended to represent the complexity or richness of teaching in urban schools. Instead, it provides a context for the type of meaningful professional development and classroom practice that is possible in urban schools.

THE SOCIAL JUSTICE EDUCATORS AT POWER ELEMENTARY[3]

Today was an almost unbearably sad day at school … not sure if you've heard … interesting in light of our email exchange yesterday: according to my students (all of which were SOBBING this morning when I arrived) two young men (Black) were sitting in a car yesterday afternoon. … some men in a car rolled up, got out and shot one in the eye (his head exploded) there was a 3-month old in the back seat (she was left "unharmed") the other got out and ran (they call him "baby" Marcus) the guys ran after him and shot him in the back and then more when he fell. … both men dead, the perpetrators (known by the way) got away, drove around doing donuts in front of folks' homes, and laughing about the incident. … the nephew of one is in my class, the brother of the other is in Mr. [R's] class. This is a close community so word spread pretty rapidly yesterday. I called for a community circle this morning, and for an hour and a half the kids all just talked and cried. I felt ill-equipped to handle a crisis like this (on such a grand scale) but, we got through it. … I said as little as possible, I cried with the kids, we all consoled each other, and others began sharing different stories of violence and loss. … in the end, I did what I thought (and hope) was best … tried to empower them with the belief that they must work to become the warriors who combat the senseless violence and madness on the streets. I also gave them some "street lessons": walk against traffic, don't sit in parked cars chillin' with your friends, be vigilant, check your surroundings, etc. etc. We're making cards, and going to send a little money to the families … and the kids all seem to feel a little better. … how would you handle this? It looks as if many teachers didn't say or do much. … feeling a bit weary today … (Ms. Grant)

This email correspondence reveals just one of the challenges facing teachers in high-poverty urban schools. One way UCLA has tried to support teachers facing challenges like this is through critical teacher inquiry groups like the one based at Power Elementary School in Watts, a community in South Central Los Angeles. The group came together to support colleagues committed to developing as social justice educators (Oakes & Lipton, 2003). Seven teachers participated in the seminar, at least one from every grade except for the first grade. A UCLA teacher educator facilitated the group, which met twice a month after school in Mr. Roberts's classroom to discuss a set of shared readings on social and educational theory (see the Appendix for a syllabus of course readings), review and offer critical feedback on video from their classroom practice, and organize long-term objectives for the group. The selection of readings, and the discussions that emanated out of them, were in keeping with the spirit of critical pedagogy

(Freire, 1970; Shor, 1992) and critical education theory (Darling-Hammond, 1998; Morrow & Torres, 1995; Valenzuela, 1999).

Ms. Grant

One example of the power resting in this kind of teacher development group came in December, 2002, during the group's discussion of long-term goals. Ideas floated around about designing professional development seminars on social justice, forming vertical teams, and organizing a youth activists' group on campus. The teachers seemed to have equal interest in each of the ideas. At Ms. Grant's turn, she produced a *Los Angeles Times* article titled, "City Declares War on Gangs" (Garvey & Winton, 2002), the abstract of which reads,

> Mayor James K. Hahn and Los Angeles Police Chief William J. Bratton declared an all-out assault on the city's street gangs Tuesday, saying they will use the same tactics that crippled the Mafia to pursue gang leaders and members. Bratton on Tuesday called gang activity "homeland terrorism," warning that the city's street gangs are "the head that needs to be cut off."

She summarized the article and the intent of the new Los Angeles police chief to use profiling techniques to crack down on suspected gang members before they engage in violent behavior. This response from the police chief came at a time when Los Angeles was in national headlines with the nation's highest number of murders. The murder rate had surpassed 600 in 2002, with most deaths occurring in South Central Los Angeles. At one point in late November, there were 12 straight days during which at least one person was shot and killed within an eight-block radius. Much of this killing was attributed to gang warfare, and much was occurring in the neighborhoods surrounding Power Elementary School. The teachers in the group were acutely aware of the impact of these "ghettoized conditions" (Anyon, 1997; Tabb, 1970) on their students. They also realized that the school failed to address the neighborhood's effects on students. Faculty were upset that the district-mandated strict adherence to state standards, a culturally irrelevant scripted reading program, and overemphasis on Stanford Achievement Test, ninth edition (SAT-9) testing preparation did little to correct the school's long history of failing its 100% African American and Latino student population.

Ms. Grant explained that she had distributed copies of the article to her fourth-grade students, so that they could read it and discuss it as a class. The class discussion revealed that her students were unaware of the policies being put in place as measures to stop the violence. Ms. Grant was particularly concerned that the larger school community would be negatively affected by profiling measures that would become legally justified causes for police harassment. She was equally concerned that it was people who lived outside of the community who were designing the response to the murders. This was, she thought, a recipe for police insensitivity, increased tensions, and hostility. Ultimately, Ms. Grant believed that these policies would have a negative impact on her students and the school. Having grown up in East Palo Alto in the mid-1980s, when it was dubbed the "murder capital" of the nation, she witnessed the harmful impact of similar policing measures aimed at curbing violence. By sharing her childhood experience, she helped the group to understand that, oftentimes, the remnants of such policies are feelings of increased disenfranchisement shared among equally disempowered groups of people hermetically sealed inside impoverished communities.

The group was intrigued by her analysis and pushed her to share her intentions for using the article in her class. Ms. Grant explained the process of sharing and discussing the article about the killings and the response of elected officials to the situation as culturally relevant critical pedagogy:

> We have to think of it like Freire for kids. We have to help our kids name their oppression first, before we can expect them to seek out liberation in any shape or form. So, to start talking about the killings in this way, to talk about how it's going to affect them and their families in ways like just them going to the corner store, is important here.

It was clear that, for Ms. Grant, the process of critical pedagogy was not limited to issues inside the walls of her classroom. To accomplish this process of critical inquiry, she first engaged students in a lengthy discussion about the article and the impact such policies would have on their lives. Then, they wrote expository papers on gangs, offering alternative methods for combating the proliferation of gangs and gang violence (such as community policing and community-led strategizing sessions to revisit the 1992 South Central gang truce).

As Ms. Grant finished an impassioned discussion of the unit and her politics of pedagogy, it was clear that the dynamics of the discussion had been dramatically altered. Effectively, she had insisted that the group deal more explicitly with the larger social environment in which they were being asked to teach. Her colleagues responded enthusiastically with discussions about their own pedagogical efforts. These discussions revealed that four of the six participants had already been engaging their students in similar discussions about the killings, but all were unaware of their colleagues' efforts. This type of critical professional discussion acts as a key component for urban teachers collaborating as *compañeras/os* (sisters and brothers in struggle), pursuing an authentically caring (Valenzuela, 1999) and empowering critical pedagogy (Shor, 1992).

The group decided that one project emerging from their community of practice would be a quarterly, thematic newspaper showcasing their students' work. The first issue would focus on critiquing popularized notions of gangs and gang members. They talked about lessons using this theme that would teach grade-level standards and empower students to produce humanizing narratives about gang members, as well as counternarratives about their community. All six teachers present agreed to have their class take on at least one aspect of the production. Ms. Grant suggested that her class could take the lead on the newspaper, acting as the editors for submissions from any class in the school. Mr. Kinsman and Ms. Olson said that their third-grade classes would provide editorial submissions, along with translation services, so that the paper's message could also reach Spanish speakers.

Ms. Mok

Ms. Mok was already dealing with similar issues with her second graders because of recurring violent episodes in her students' lives. She shared this class discussion: A Latino boy was having trouble focusing and often drifted off. Another child said that the class needed to go into community circle[4] to discuss a pressing issue. When Ms. Mok invited students to talk about gunshots fired in their neighborhoods, roughly three-fourths of the class said that they heard shots from their homes; two said that their homes had been shot into. When asked, nearly all of the students knew someone who had been a victim of similar events. Through the community circle, the particularly troubled and distracted boy shared that his house had been sprayed with bullets a few nights before and now he was afraid he might die. In response to this conversation, the class developed a survey for other students about school and community safety. Students used their math time to tally their findings and analyze the data.

These events provided scaffolding for Ms. Mok's students when she decided to follow Ms. Grant's lead and use the *Los Angeles Times* article as a discussion piece with her class as well. This dovetailed into larger class discussions about the politics of public portrayals and stereotyping, culminating in Ms. Mok's class writing letters to the mayor, requesting that he rethink policies that promote profiling as a police practice. These letters received a quick response letter along with an autographed picture from the mayor, both of which were displayed in the main office.

Mr. Truong and Mr. Ballesteros

Mr. Truong's fifth-grade class partnered with Mr. Ballesteros's kindergarten class to address issues of profiling in the community. Mr. Ballesteros began his unit by having his students draw portraits that represented their ideas of gang members. On a later day, he asked students to draw self-portraits. Many of the images were similarly stereotypical of urban youth (portraits of dark-hued characters with baggy clothes and beanies or baseball caps on sideways), except for the weaponry that was often attached to their images of gang members. To further emphasize the power of stereotyping, Mr. Ballesteros asked students to describe the attire that gang members could be expected to wear. Students shouted out similar descriptions to those found in their drawings of themselves, many of which could easily be ascribed to large numbers of urban youth (baggy jeans, baggy shirts, baseball caps, and sneakers). To problematize his students' thinking, Mr. Ballesteros brought two students who regularly served as peer tutors, one Chicano male and one African American male, from Mr. Truong's class to the front of the room. Mr. Ballesteros and Mr. Truong recounted what happened next:

> MR. BALLESTEROS: So, I asked my students, "Are these two young men gang members?" And my students yelled out, "No!" So, I asked them to look back at their descriptions of gang members, and pretty much all the things they listed off—baggy jeans, big t-shirts, baseball hats—were on your two students. Then some of them started to change—I mean, to say "yes" that they were gang members.
>
> MR. TRUONG: Yeah. man, they [my two students] were pissed off. They came back to my class saying how messed up it was that kids thought they were in gangs.
>
> MR. BALLESTEROS: Yeah, but it's weird because my kids were really stuck. I mean they knew that they weren't gang members, but then they fit the description.

Mr. Ballesteros saw clear value in asking kindergartners to question dominant narratives. For the two fifth graders in Mr. Truong's class, the experience provided two powerful moments for sharing their perspectives on dominant images of urban males of color. One of these moments came when they described the experience to their own peers in Mr. Truong's class; the other moment came when they returned to Mr. Ballesteros's kindergarten class to tell students how they were personally hurt by their stereotypes.

FROM SUPPORT TO RETENTION—A NATIONAL CRISIS

Many urban teachers experience the kind of painful consequences of poverty and violence that Ms. Grant shared in her e-mail. Few, however, have the necessary support to deal with these consequences in the constructive, educative way that Ms. Grant proposed to her colleagues. Together, these social justice educators helped one another see their practice as an integrated, coherent whole. Together, they engaged students across grade levels and classrooms in critical, probing analyses of an important social issue. Together, they read and discussed social theory and the values that ground culturally relevant critical pedagogy. Together, they were creating a professional culture that rewards collegiality and promotes challenging discussions about matters relevant to effective teaching in high-poverty schools. Creating this culture should be a natural extension of the work of rigorous preservice programs—like Center X—that are committed to furthering social justice. With supportive learning communities, teachers in high-poverty schools have a shot at beating the one-in-five odds that they will abandon their school or teaching completely at the end of the year.[5]

Teacher retention—as opposed to the teacher shortage—has been called "a national crisis" (National Commission on Teaching and America's Future, 2003). It is a crisis most acutely felt in urban, high-poverty schools where the annual turnover rate is almost a third higher than the rate for all teachers in all schools (National Commission on Teaching and America's Future, 2003). High attrition within these *hard-to-staff* schools—as this book's introductory chapters point out—is perpetuated by abysmal working conditions; high percentages of new, inexperienced, often uncredentialed, teachers; and revolving leadership. As the National Commission on Teaching and America's Future (2003) advocates, we have the best hope of breaking this cycle of urban teacher attrition by "finding a way for school systems to organize the work of qualified teachers so they can collaborate with their colleagues in developing strong learning communities that will sustain them as they become more accomplished teachers" (p. 7).

As this chapter introduced at the outset, Center X seeks to set these strong learning communities in motion through its urban teacher education program. When they graduate, Center X–educated teachers have reported the following programmatic emphases as very valuable: viewing practice through the lens of theory, creating supportive networks of like-minded peers, and viewing cultural and linguistic diversity as strengths not deficits. Overall, graduates leave the program feeling very confident in their abilities to become effective teachers, enact socially just practices, teach empowering curricula, and design appropriate and challenging lesson plans. As Figure 1 illustrates, Center X graduates are also considerably more diverse than the teaching workforce, which, in general, bears little resemblance to the characteristics of urban students.

RESEARCH CONTEXT

As a research sample, the Center X graduates represent the population of highly qualified, diverse, and committed urban educators for which most reformers clamor. If these teachers cannot be retained, who can? In our initial analysis

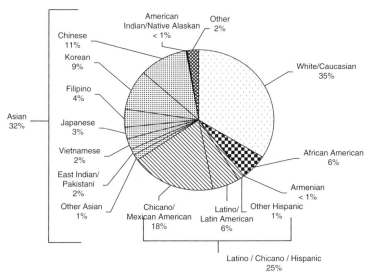

Figure 1. Ethnicity of Center X Students/Graduates, 1995–2003 (N = 913)

of Center X's graduates (Quartz & TEP Research Group, 2003), we wondered whether our retention figures would confirm research findings that early career teachers considered by many to be "the best and the brightest" are the ones most likely to leave. Several studies, for instance, show that the majority of those who leave early include individuals with higher IQs, grade point averages (GPAs), and standardized test scores and those with academic majors or minors along with an education degree (Darling-Hammond & Sclan, 1996; Murnane, 1996; Sclan, 1993). Moreover, teachers who have earned advanced degrees within the prior two years leave at the highest rates (Boe et al., 1997). Our sample, however, is unique. Though Center X graduates all earn advanced degrees, complete subject-based undergraduate degrees, and have high test scores, they also define themselves as urban educators. Nationally, fewer than 6% of all education graduates express a desire for inner-city placements (National Partnership for Excellence and Accountability in Teaching, 2000), yet, for Center X graduates, teaching in such schools explicitly defines their professional identity. They also receive specialized training to teach in these schools. Perhaps, therefore, we should not be surprised if Center X graduates are retained; we should instead be disturbed if they leave.

The story unfolds after graduation, when these highly qualified, social justice educators disperse; by 2002, Center X's 417 graduates had taught at more than 140 schools across and beyond Los Angeles. We are in the midst of a longitudinal study to track these graduates and their career development. At the end of the study, we will have nine cohorts of graduates, in their first through 10th years of teaching, enabling us to better understand the conditions under which these graduates are retained in urban schools. At this point, however, our preliminary findings help frame the current policy debate surrounding urban teacher retention.

As expected, Center X graduates stay in teaching at higher rates than the national average, but many do leave. To better capture the career trajectories of graduates, we distinguish in our survey data between leaving the classroom and leaving education. Typically, attrition is defined as leaving teaching.[6] Although we agree that it is crucial to track the retention of full-time classroom teachers, we also think it is important to expand the definition of retention to include those educators who have left full-time classroom teaching for other professional roles in education. Interestingly, as Table 1 summarizes, the move to leave education seems to stabilize after four years, while the exodus from the classroom accelerates. What lies between these two pathways may help explain part of the puzzle of retaining urban teachers.

Looking across Center X's first five cohorts of graduates, 94% remain in education, and, of these educators, 86% are still full-time classroom teachers. The remaining 14% take on a variety of roles, as displayed in Figure 2.

Looking at the Educator (Inside K–12) category, we find an interesting variety of roles, including beginning teacher support and assessment (BTSA) coordinator, college counselor, instructional math coach, Title VII/dual immersion specialist, literacy coach, educational therapist, afterschool coordinator, and others. Educators working outside the K–12 system include a museum educator, UCLA field supervisors, an educational media consultant, doctoral students, an education nonprofit coordinator, college professors, and others. Interestingly, when we used the same categories to probe graduates' future plans, none of the retained educators anticipated leaving education, but, as Figure 3 demonstrates, it is clear that many see their role extending beyond the classroom.

Table 1. Beginning Teacher Attrition: Center X Graduates Compared to National Averages

Length of Time Spent Teaching	Center X Graduates (1997–2001)		Nationwide Schools and Staffing Survey (2000–2001)
	Left Classroom	Left Education	Left Teaching
After two years	3%	1%	24%
After three years	5%	1%	33%
After four years	21%	11%	40%
After five years	24%	12%	46%
After six years	37%	10%	—

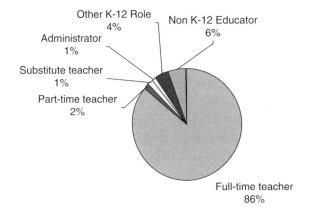

Figure 2. Primary Role of Retained Educators

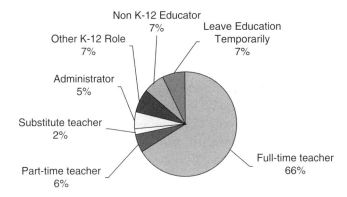

Figure 3. What Will You Be Doing in Five Years?

SEEKING PROFESSIONAL COMMUNITIES: THE MULTIPLE ROLES OF URBAN EDUCATORS

In 2002, we asked the incoming class of Center X students to look ahead to their own retention: 78% anticipated that they would be full-time classroom teachers in five years—a figure that comes close to our cohort-based 24% five-year attrition rate. Interestingly, however, when asked, "Do you envision your career as primarily rooted in the classroom or in multiple roles extending beyond the classroom?" approximately 7 out of 10 (68%) chose "multiple roles" as their answer. Moreover, those students who see themselves engaged in multiple roles beyond the classroom describe the reasons they entered teaching in different terms. Compared to their classroom-rooted peers, these students attach a higher level of importance to changing the world, furthering social justice, and working in a low-income community as reasons to become a teacher. Not surprisingly, envisioning oneself engaged in multiple roles is also related to viewing teaching as a stepping stone to leadership positions in public service. These intake data make clear a pattern we also see in our graduate data: Most highly qualified urban educators define their professional identities in multiple ways that extend beyond the classroom.

We asked graduates to identify not just their primary roles in education, but also the roles that they took on in addition to these primary roles. What emerges is a portrait of active, professionally engaged urban educators. Across the board, Center X graduates report taking on an array of commitments beyond their classrooms. More than half of the educators take university courses and participate in observational visits to other schools. Eighty percent are involved in regularly scheduled collaboration with other teachers on issues of instruction, and 95% attend workshops, conferences, or trainings. Additionally, 44% of the educators report involvement with individual or collaborative research, 25% are part of a mentoring program, 20% participate in activist organizations, and 17% participate in a network of teachers outside of their schools. In addition to these professional development roles, a smaller percentage of graduates also takes on leadership roles. These include department or grade-level chair (8%), mentoring other teachers (11%), administrators (2%), staff developers (13%), coaches (7%), activists (7%), coordinators (13%), or some other leadership role (22%). Overall, graduates report an average of five professional development and leadership roles in addition to their primary job responsibilities.

Are these roles enabling educators to develop strong learning communities that will sustain them as they become more accomplished professionals and enabling their schools to improve over time? Perhaps. Educators with more roles report that they stay in education, because they find teaching to be a fulfilling and challenging career, and because they have good relationships with colleagues. They are also more satisfied with their opportunities for professional advancement and report a higher degree of perceived respect from society. But embedded in this issue is the very definition of an education professional. Is the push to take on more and more professional roles and responsibilities outside the classroom a positive one—one that will ultimately benefit students and improve schools? Or is it a half-step move toward leaving the classroom in favor of other work inside urban education? The repercussions of framing classroom teaching as a stepping stone to something larger, more important, and more respected are clearly problematic, and significant efforts are underway to frame teaching as a profession rooted in the classroom (Olsen & Anderson, in press).

As Johnson (2001) suggests, the National Board for Professional Teaching Standards (NBPTS) could lead to teaching as a staged career, with multiple levels of accomplishment depending upon individual interest, energy, and ambition, all while retaining the teachers within the classroom. Harmon (2001), NBPTS's director of research, envisions creating new leadership roles, such as teaching university classes and mentoring preservice teachers; designing and presenting professional development programs; and creating flexible administrative structures that allow teachers to take on new roles without leaving the classroom, such as pairing two teachers to teach a single class, thereby providing time for each to pursue professional activities. Efforts to professionalize teaching, however, such as NBPTS, will have to address the unique conditions of urban schools, where the creation of professional learning communities is exacerbated by higher rates of teacher turnover and greater percentages of new teachers, as well as greater percentages of underqualified teachers. Finding a professional foothold—a mentor teacher, a teaching team, space for reflection—is especially challenging in these settings. Add to these challenges the typically poor working conditions and lack of resources in urban schools discussed in earlier chapters, and much of the retention crisis is explained. To escape this vicious cycle, we must better understand the conditions under which urban teachers—like the faculty at Power Elementary—manage to stay connected to their profession and the students about whom they care.

THE FRAGILITY OF URBAN TEACHING:
HOW HOPEFULNESS DAMPENS OVER TIME

Ms. Grant closed her e-mail with the lament, "feeling a bit weary today." Another pattern emerging from our retention data is a gradual dampening of idealism, hopefulness, and commitment to changing the world through teaching. When asked about their reasons for teaching, 71% of those entering Center X said it was extremely important to them to change the world and further social justice as a teacher. And, for 64%, it was extremely important to help kids in low-income communities. As Table 2 summarizes, over time, these commitments wane. We also asked respondents to indicate how strongly they agreed with the following statement: "I am hopeful that my school/workplace will improve over time." Perhaps predictably, responses are related to years in education and plans to stay or leave the profession. The educators who express the least hope for school improvement are those who have been working the longest and those who plan to leave the profession.

This disheartening trend illustrates the fragility of teaching in urban, high-poverty schools. Despite their stellar and specialized urban teacher preparation and the fact that they all started with a strong commitment to teaching in urban high-poverty schools, approximately one-third of each graduating cohort remains

Table 2. Why Do You Stay in Education?

Number of years in education	"I stay in education because I feel my work helps change the world and further social justice." (rating = extremely important)	"I stay in education because I'm committed to working in a low-income community." (rating = extremely important)
Two	57%	50%
Three	47%	30%
Four	41%	30%
Five	49%	31%
Six	39%	23%

undecided about whether to stick with teaching as a career. Despite the fact that every Center X graduate taught in an urban, high-poverty school for his or her first year of teaching, there has been a steady move away from these contexts. For example, within Center X's first cohort, only 69% of those who had stayed in education for six years remained in high-poverty schools. Others had left the profession altogether. When asked why, the most important reasons that surfaced were dissatisfaction with working conditions and feeling "overwhelmed and emotionally drained." If we expect teachers to work with students who are regularly traumatized by poverty and violence, we must support them in meaningful and powerful ways. We must help schools answer Ms. Grant's question, "How would you handle this?" We must also learn from teachers like the ones at Power Elementary. As Nieto frames the enterprise, we must ask, "What should we know about effective, caring, committed, persevering teachers, and how can we use this knowledge to support all teachers and in the process support the students who most need them?" (Nieto, 2003, p. 2). We continue our research on Center X graduates to answer just these questions.

NOTES

1. Support for the research reported in this chapter was generously provided through grants from the Stuart Foundation and Atlantic Philanthropies. We wish to acknowledge the contributions of our colleagues Joanna Goode, Kimberly Barraza Lyons, Andrew Thomas, Eileen Lai Horng, Stella Bruno, and Martin Lipton in the preparation of this paper.

2. In this chapter, social justice educators is meant to refer to teachers who see their work as part of a broader agenda for social change and justice—one that embodies activism and active engagement with communities.

3. For a fuller analysis of this data, see Duncan-Andrade (2004).

4. Community circle brings students in Ms. Mok's class together in a circle to discuss issues and problems pertinent to their lives.

5. This figure is based on National Center for Education Statistics (NCES) 2000-01 School and Staffing/Teacher Follow-up Survey (SASS/TFS) annual teacher turnover data, as reported in Ingersoll (2001).

6. This category certainly includes full-time classroom teachers, but it may also extend beyond the classroom to capture teachers on special assignments, coordinators, or others. We are currently investigating how other retention studies define a retained teacher.

REFERENCES

Alinsky, S. (1989). *Rules for radicals: A practical primer for realistic radicals*. New York: Vintage Books.

Anyon, J. (1997). *Ghetto schooling: A political economy of urban educational reform*. New York: Teachers College Press.

Banks, J. (1994). *An introduction to multicultural education*. Boston: Allyn and Bacon.

Bird, T., Anderson, L., Sullivan, B., & Swidler, S. (1993). Pedagogical balancing acts: Attempts to influence prospective teachers' beliefs. *Teacher and Teacher Education, 9*(3), 253–267.

Boe, E. E., Bobbitt, S. A., Cook, L. H., Whitener, S. D., & Weber, A. L. (1997). Why didst thou go? Predictors of retention, transfer, and attrition of special and general education teachers from a national perspective. *The Journal of Special Education, 30*(4), 390–411.

Cochran-Smith, M. (1997). Knowledge, skills and experiences for teaching culturally diverse learners: A perspective for practicing teachers. In J. Irvine (Ed.), *Critical knowledge for diverse teachers and learners* (pp. 27–88). Washington, DC: American Association of Colleges for Teacher Education.

Cummins, J. (1996). *Negotiating identities: Education for empowerment in a diverse society*. Los Angeles: CABE.

Darder, A. (1998). Teaching as an act of love. In J. Fredrickson (Ed.), *Reclaiming our voices: Emancipatory narratives and critical literacy, praxis & pedagogy* (pp. 25–42). Ontario, Canada: CABE.

Darling-Hammond, L. (1998). Unequal opportunity: Race and education. *Brookings Review, 16*(2), 28–32.

Darling-Hammond, L., & Sclan, E. M. (1996). Who teaches and why: Dilemmas of building a profession for twenty-first century schools. In J. Sikula (Ed.), *Handbook of research on teacher education* (2nd ed., pp. 67–101). New York: Simon & Schuster.

Duncan-Andrade, J. (2004). Preparing for the urban in urban teaching: Toward teacher development for retention and activism. *Teaching Education Journal, 15*(4), 339–350.

Freire, P. (1970). *Pedagogy of the oppressed*. New York: Continuum.

Garvey, M., & Winton, R. (2002, December 4). City declares war on gangs; Hahn and Bratton say they'll go after leaders and members with the same aggressive tactics that worked against the Mafia on the East Coast. *Los Angeles Times*, p. A1.

Giroux, H. (1992). *Border crossings: Cultural workers and the politics of education*. New York: Routledge.

Harmon, A. E. (2001). A wider role for the National Board. *Educational Leadership, 58*(8), 54–56.

Hooks, B. (1994). *Teaching to transgress: Education as the practice of freedom*. New York: Routledge.

Ingersoll, R. (2001, Fall). Teacher turnover and teacher shortages: An organizational analysis. *American Educational Research Journal, 38*, 499–534.

Johnson, S. M. (2001). Can professional certification for teachers reshape teaching as a career? *Phi Delta Kappan, 82*(5), 393–399.

Kretzmann, J., & McKnight, J. (1993). *Building communities from the inside out: A path toward finding and mobilizing a community's assets.* Chicago: ACTA Publications.

Ladson-Billings, G. (1994). *The dreamkeepers: Successful teachers of African American children.* San Francisco: Josey-Bass.

Lane, S., Lacefield-Parachini, N., & Isken, J. (2003). Developing novice teachers as change agents: Student teacher placements "against the grain." *Teacher Education Quarterly, 30*(2), 55–68.

Lave, J., & Wenger, E. (1991). *Situated learning.* Cambridge, UK: Cambridge University Press.

McLaren, P. (1997). *Life in schools: An introduction to critical pedagogy in the foundations of education.* New York: Addison Wesley Longman.

Moll, L. (1988). Some key issues in teaching Latino students. *Language Arts, 64*(5), 465–472.

Moll, L. (1998, February 5). *Funds of knowledge for teaching: A new approach in education.* Keynote address presented at the Illinois State Board of Education, Springfield, IL.

Morrow, R., & Torres, C. (1995). *Social theory and education: A critique of theories of social and cultural reproduction.* New York: SUNY Press.

Murnane, R. J. (1996). Staffing the nation's schools with skilled teachers. In E. A. Hanushek & D. W. Jorgenson (Eds.), *Improving America's schools: The role of incentives* (pp. 241–258). Washington, DC: National Academy Press.

National Commission on Teaching and America's Future. (2003). *No dream denied: A pledge to America's children.* Washington, DC: Author.

National Partnership for Excellence and Accountability in Teaching. (2000). Revisioning professional development. *Journal of Staff Development, 21*(Suppl. 1), 1–19.

Nieto, S. (1999). *The light in their eyes.* New York: Teachers College Press.

Nieto, S. (2003). *What keeps teachers going?* New York: Teachers College Press.

Oakes, J. (1996). Making the rhetoric real: UCLA's struggle for teacher education that is multicultural and social reconstructionist. *National Association of Multicultural Education Journal, 4* (2), 4–10.

Oakes, J., & Lipton, M. (2003). *Teaching to change the world* (2nd ed.). Boston: McGraw-Hill.

Olsen, B., & Anderson, L. (in press). Courses of action: A qualitative investigation into urban teacher retention and career development. *Urban Education.*

Quartz, K. H., & TEP Research Group (2003). Too angry to leave: Supporting new teachers commitment to transform urban schools. *Journal of Teacher Education, 54*(2), 99–111.

Sclan, E. M. (1993). The effect of perceived workplace conditions on beginning teachers' work commitment, career choice commitment, and planned retention. *Dissertation Abstracts International, 54,* 08A. (UMINo. 9400594)

Shor, I. (1992). *Empowering education: Critical teaching for social change.* Chicago: University of Chicago Press.

Sleeter, C. (1993). How white teachers construct race. In C. McCarthy & W. Crichlow (Eds.), *Race, identity and representation in education* (pp. 157–171). New York: Routledge.

Tabb, W. (1970). *The political economy of the black ghetto.* New York: W. W. Norton & Company.

Tatum, B. (1997). *Why are all the black kids sitting together in the cafeteria?: And other conversations about race.* New York: Basic Books.

Tharp, R., & Gallimore, R. (1988). *Rousing minds to life: Teaching, learning and schooling in social context.* New York: Cambridge University Press.

Valenzuela, A. (1999). *Subtractive schooling: U.S.-Mexican youth and the politics of caring.* New York: SUNY Press.

Vygotsky, L. (1978). *Mind in society.* Cambridge, MA: Harvard University Press.

APPENDIX

A Teacher Seminar on Powerful Teaching Through Critical Research Pedagogy 2002–2003 Syllabus

Introduction: Accountability With Some Bite

ACLU of Southern California. (2002). *Landmark education case will hold state to promise of equal education* [Press release]. Retrieved from http://www.aclu-sc.org/News/Releases/2000/100195/

Institute for Democracy, Education and Access (IDEA). (2002a). *California's education crisis—FAQs*. Los Angeles, CA: Author.

Institute for Democracy, Education and Access (IDEA). (2002b). Educational court cases: Questions and answers. *Teaching to Change LA, 2*(1–10). Retrieved from www.idea.gseis.ucla.edu/publications/utec/wp/pdf/01.pdf

Institute for Democracy, Education and Access (IDEA). (2002c). *The crisis in California's public schools*. Los Angeles, CA: Author.

Quality Counts 2002. (2002). *Education Week*. Retrieved from http://www.edweek.org/sreports/qc02/templates/state.cfm?slug=17ca.h21

School Accountability Report Card. (2002). *Jordan High School, Locke High School, and 99th St. Elementary*. Retrieved from http://search.lausd.k12.ca.us/cgi-bin/fccgi.exe?w3exec=sarc0

Tools for Making Our Voices Heard

A-Plus Communications. (1999). Reporting results: What the public wants to know. *Education Week*. Retrieved from http://www.edweek.org/sreports/qc99/opinion/aplus1.html

California Department of Education. (2002). *Sample School Accountability Report Card template*. Retrieved from http://www.cde.ca.gov/ta/ac/sa/templates.asp

Institute for Democracy, Education and Access (IDEA). (2002a). School report card #1: Facilities. *Teaching to Change LA, 2*(1–10). Retrieved from http://tcla.gseis.ucla.edu/rights/resources/reportcard1.html

Institute for Democracy, Education and Access (IDEA). (2002b). School report card #2: Learning materials. *Teaching to Change LA, 2*(1–10). Retrieved from http://tcla.gseis.ucla.edu/rights/resources/reportcard2.html

Using Social Theory to Analyze Inequality

Darling-Hammond, L. (1998a). New standards, old inequalities: The current challenge for African-American education. In L. A. Daniels (Ed.), *The state of Black America* (pp. 109–171). New York: Urban League.

Darling-Hammond, L. (1998b). Unequal opportunity: Race and education. *Brookings Review, 16*(2), 28–32.

Lemert, C. (1993). Introduction: Social theory, its uses and pleasures. In C. Lemert (Ed.), *Social theory: The multicultural and classic readings* (pp. 1–3). Boulder, CO: Westview Press.

Oakes, J., & Lipton, M. (2003). *Teaching to change the world* (chap. 1, pp. 2–35). Boston: McGraw-Hill.

Using Social Theory to Read the World

Freire, P. (1997). First letter: Reading the word/reading the world. In P. Freire, *Teachers as cultural workers: Letters to those who dare to teach* (D. Macedo, D. Koike, & A. Oliveira, Trans.) (pp. 17–26). Boulder, CO: Westview Press.

Engaging Young People in Research

Cook-Sather, A. (2002). Authorizing students' perspectives: Toward trust, dialogue, and change in education. *Educational Researcher*, 31(4), 3–14.

Olson, L. (2002, September 11). Critical voices. *Education Week*. Retrieved from http://www.edweek.org/ew/ewstory.cfm?slug=02fine.h22

The Right to Learning Materials

Finn, P. (1999). *Literacy with an attitude: Educating working class children in their own self interest* (pp. 9–26). New York: SUNY Press.

Harris, L. (2002). A survey of the status of equality in public education in California. *Public Advocates*. Retrieved from www.edfordemocracy.org/tqi/Harris%20Poll%20-%20Equality%20in%20Schools.pdf

Williams, P. J. (2002, April 8). Diary of a mad law professor: Tests, tracking and derailment. *The Nation*. Retrieved from http://www.thenation.com/doc.mhtml?i=20020422&s=williams

The Right to Quality Teaching

Corbett, D., & Wilson, B.. (2002, September). What urban students say about good teaching. *Education Leadership*, 18–22.

Scherer, M. (2001, May). Improving the quality of the teaching force: A conversation with David C. Berliner. *Educational Leadership*, 58(8), pp. 6–10.

Valenzuela, A. (2001). Subtractive schooling: What happens when schools disrespect students' cultural heritage and when teachers fail to listen to the students. *Rethinking Schools*, 15(2), 1–8.

Viadero, D. (2002, September 18). Studies say students learn more from licensed teachers. *Education Week*. Retrieved from http://www.edweek.org/ew/ewstory.cfm?slug=03teach.h22

The Right to Relevant Learning and Assessment

Meier, D. (1995). *The power of their ideas: Lessons for America from a small school in Harlem* (chap. 9, pp. 161–173). Boston: Beacon Press.

Morrell, E., & Duncan-Andrade, J. (2002, July). Promoting academic literacy with urban youth through engaging hip-hop culture. *English Journal*, 88–92.

Oakes, J., & Rogers, J. (2002, October 6). Diploma penalty misplaces blame. *Los Angeles Times*. Retrieved from http://www.latimes.com/

Schrag, P. (2000, August). High stakes are for tomatoes. *The Atlantic*. Retrieved from http://www.theatlantic.com/issues/2000/08/schrag.html

Tomlinson, C. (2002, September). Invitations to learn. *Education Leadership*, 6–10.

The Right to a Safe and Democratic School Environment

Noguera, P. A. (1999, November 11). Listen first: How student perspectives on violence can be used to create safer schools. *In Motion Magazine*. Retrieved from http://www.inmotionmagazine. com/pnlist1.html

Quality Counts 2002: California's data. (2002). *Education Week*. Retrieved from http://www.edweek. org/sreports/qc02/templates/state_data.cfm?slug=17qcca.h21#standacct

Conclusion: Situating Teacher Education IN Social Activism

JAMES FRASER

New York University

As the reader who has gotten to this conclusion already knows, *Partnering to Prepare Urban Teachers: A Call to Activism* is more than the title suggests and, indeed, more than the sum of its parts. The various chapters in this volume are certainly a call to activism, but they are also a road map through what Afra Hersi and Dennis Shirley properly call the "messy realities" of urban teacher preparation. As someone who has become increasingly suspicious, indeed downright weary, of calls to activism that do not give the reader any tools for the activism, I found *Partnering to Prepare Urban Teachers* a refreshing change. For those of us whose professional lives are immersed in the preparation of urban teachers, this book is an invaluable guide. It is both a call to action and a repository of examples of good curriculum and best practices. And, for anyone who cares about the teachers in the city schools of the 21st century—be they teacher educator, teacher, parent, policy maker, or concerned citizen—the passionate yet practical call to activism embedded here is essential reading.

Among the major themes of this volume are three key ones, all included in the title—urban, teachers, and activism or social justice. At this concluding point of the volume, each of these themes is worth one more reminder of its importance.

URBAN

As Victoria Chou and Steven Tozer wisely note, the word *urban* means many things and "is often a coded marker" for many more. Sometimes, urban means the Census Bureau's definition of "a population density of at least 1,000 people per square mile" (as quoted in chapter 1, by Chou and Tozer, in this volume). More often, certainly when used in education circles, urban is code for poor and not White. Indeed, as Chou and Tozer note, urban often really means poor and racially segregated. And, as many educators know, this reality quickly translates into preparing teachers who will be asked to do much with far too few resources and, at the same time, preparing teachers who, in too many cases, will not share the experiences of racism and poverty that have shaped the lives of their students in essential ways.

Reading through the chapters, one is reminded of Jacqueline Jordan Irvine's warning that:

> when teachers ignore their students' ethnic identities and their unique cultural beliefs, perceptions, values, and worldviews, they fail as culturally responsive pedagogists. Color-blind teachers claim that they treat all students "the same," which usually means that all students are treated as if they are, or should be, both White and middle class. (Irvine, 2003, p. xvii)

Happily, one comes away from this volume with a strong sense that there are teacher education programs in this country that do not fall into this fatuitous approach to "color-blind" teaching. As Francine Peterman and Kristy Sweigard write,

> To be best prepared for urban settings, we posit, teachers must meet not only generic standards for professionally planning, teaching, reflecting, and collaborating but also contextually responsive standards that represent the distinguishing characteristics of urban communities, schools and classrooms, and their students.

It is this focus on contextually responsive standards that sets this volume apart from many others.

TEACHERS

When Karen Hunter Quartz, Brad Olsen, and Jeff Duncan-Andrade describe the University of California, Los Angeles's (UCLA's) highly respected Center X as taking "a holistic view of teachers and teaching," they note the importance of the "simultaneous development of teacher identities and supportive teacher communities." A theme that runs through this volume is that, in the field of teacher preparation, as in any other field, what Paulo Freire called the "banking" model of education is an utter failure. We cannot pour knowledge, sensitivity, or the best of antiracist and procommunity attitudes into aspiring teachers as if they were empty vessels waiting to receive our wisdom, even when our wisdom is terribly important.

On the contrary, Peter Murrell, Jr., in his chapter in this volume, describes the importance of situating learning practice *for* urban schools *in* urban schools by creating new professional learning communities. This is not just a matter of moving the location of teacher education instruction from the university to the schoolhouse. It is certainly not the development of an uncritical apprenticeship program where aspiring teachers are taught "the tricks of the trade" by seasoned— and sometimes cynical—veterans. Rather, it means preparing what Murrell (2001) has elsewhere called "community dedicated teachers" by providing the opportunities for critical engagement, reflection, self-criticism, and growth as part of an induction process, a process in which new teachers join a community not only of teachers but also of parents and community activists in a common effort to build a more just future.

Only the more difficult and sustained opportunities for aspiring teachers to grow and mature the personal, professional, and activist sides of themselves will produce the kinds of teachers for which this volume ultimately calls. Not too long ago, I was in a meeting in which a deeply committed friend of the schools reflected on what he was hearing. In summarizing a presentation we had heard about one city's schools, he said, "I think what I have heard is that there's nothing wrong with the schools except that all the teachers are disengaged and all the students are disengaged." Tameka, interviewed by Mark Storz and Karen Nestor, would have replied to this, "To get a good education, you need teachers that care and students that care. Teachers that care about their students, and the students, they care about themselves." This volume offers a series of guides—some quite wonderfully specific—to the production of such teachers who will then have the knowledge, skill, and commitment to transform the cynicism and boredom that today are so rampant in both the schools and the profession designed to serve them.

SOCIAL JUSTICE

Calling for the preparation of a new generation of teachers who will be actively committed to social justice is at the very core of this volume. Quartz, Olsen and Duncan-Andrade describe their program at UCLA as "committed to preparing teachers as agents of social change." As described by Kristien Marquez-Zenkov, the Master of Urban Secondary Teaching (MUST) Program at Cleveland State University begins with a focus on social justice: "The MUST intern is a reflective, responsive teacher-leader who successfully addresses the effects of race, class, gender, ability, linguistic difference, and sexual orientation on student achievement." All the other chapters and the programs they describe reflect the same commitment.

A focus on social justice has become quite common in the teacher preparation literature of late, partly as a response by many teacher educators to an overly rigid and oppressive testing and standards-driven approach to schooling and students that is too dominant in the United States today, to say nothing of the broader lack of social justice in the nation. But the term *social justice* has been used so often in education schools, sometimes for quite modest concerns, that it has been trivialized. There is something all too rare in the approach to social justice in this volume. Future teachers are not merely asked to hold the values of social justice. The chapters here describe programs in all parts of the country that create the contexts for aspiring teachers in which they can grapple with the meaning of social justice and the means of being effective agents of social change in a way that too few other advocates of the same words actually offer. The difference is the difference between teaching aspiring teachers how to give lip service to some catch phrases and offering them life-changing engagement with the ways to begin to build a more just and inclusive society in the classrooms of urban schools and in the body politic of the United States.

SOME QUESTIONS FOR THE FUTURE

I leave *Partnering to Prepare Urban Teachers: A Call to Activism* with a sense of gratitude for what the authors have offered but also a sense that they have raised a number of new questions that can be veins for future research, reflection, and collaborative discussions. For me, among the most prominent questions raised by this book are those related to one of the major players in the partnership—the university itself. If we teacher educators are to design new programs that reflect a more truly mutual and engaging partnership between university-based programs and community and school partners, then we also need to spend some time reflecting on the strengths and, equally, the weaknesses that the university as an institution and as a home to teacher preparation brings into that partnership.

University-based teacher preparation programs are not—to put it far too mildly—highly respected today. Indeed, Labaree (2004) is right in saying that "the ed school is the Rodney Dangerfield of higher education: it don't get no respect" (p. 2). We need to understand the reasons for this low standing. At the same time, I believe that we need to resist an apprenticeship model of teacher preparation that is becoming more and more popular. Merely preparing teachers in schools, on the job, inevitably means that a host of critical political, pedagogical, and philosophical questions about the nature of teaching and the link between teaching and social justice are not likely to be asked. On the other hand, we need a hard and careful look at the problems that make the university a sometimes difficult partner in collaborative efforts aimed at teacher excellence or social justice. Let me suggest three reasons that those of us who are teacher educators based in universities need to continue our own internal reform efforts as well as our partnership activities:

- *The triumph of constructivism.* When Labaree writes thoughtfully of *The Trouble With Ed Schools* (2004), he notes that there is today too often a major disjunction between what those of us in schools of education seem to value and what many in the larger public—including not just political leaders but also the parents and community residents in the urban communities that are the focus of this book—really want schools to accomplish. Citing a study by the Public Agenda, Labaree writes of "a professoriate [in education schools] preparing teachers for an idealized world that prizes 'learning how to learn' but disdains mastery of a core body of knowledge and gives short shrift to fundamentals such as class-room management," while, on the other hand, many in the public want to see schools, and the teachers who are prepared to teach in them, "to emphasize the basics: reading, writing, and mathematics, taught in orderly and disciplined classrooms" (p. 136). Of course, it is easy to dismiss this public critique as either a right-wing diatribe or the product of simple-minded thinking. Certainly, many critics of progressive education are less than fully informed about what it means, and the Right has been brilliant at casting all proponents of progressivism in education, especially education school professors, as suffering from "the tyranny of low expectations." Just because reactionary voices have been critical of us does not mean that we can dismiss all these concerns, however. Indeed, if we simply brush concerns about content knowledge and discipline away, we will alienate many parents and community residents and many teachers who ought to be our closest allies and push them into the happily waiting arms of the reactionaries. Parents have a right to want their children to be able to read, write, and do mathematics and to do so at a high level, not just think about how to do it. Parents, especially parents in poor and marginalized communities, have a right to want order and discipline in the classrooms of their children, knowing, as they do, how disorderly and undisciplined the larger world can be. We need not abandon our own views about how knowledge is constructed, but we need to be every bit as prepared to enter into conversations with urban parents and community members about these issues as we are about the ways to prepare teachers who will actively fight for justice for their students.
- *The irrelevance of much of the arts and sciences curriculum.* With Peter Murrell, I have worked long and hard to engage arts and sciences

faculty in the teacher preparation enterprise; and I have been delighted that so many of my former arts and sciences colleagues at Northeastern University, led by that college's dean, responded with so much enthusiasm to the challenge of building a new teacher preparation program focused on preparing community-dedicated teachers who were also the products of an academically rigorous curriculum. But, if one looks at universities across the United States, especially the most elite research universities, one cannot help but conclude that, at its core, the arts and sciences curriculum is fundamentally committed to irrelevance. What Freeland (2004) calls "practice-oriented education," an educational experience linking classroom-based learning with real-world experiences by students in schools, business, or the community, is often fiercely resisted. At tenure and promotion time, it is not just faculty who spend time on practical matters but even faculty whose research has a practical or applicable side, who are penalized because practical application detracts from so-called pure research. Perhaps most seriously, far too many undergraduate majors in the academic disciplines are organized with only one purpose: to prepare students for graduate research in the same discipline, leading ultimately to a doctor of philosophy (PhD) degree based on a dissertation that focuses with narrow precision on a very narrow topic. Though I have long advocated the need for arts and sciences majors for all teachers, and I still do, the arts and sciences major offered in many college campuses today is not the sort of undergraduate major needed by effective urban teachers. Indeed, it is not the sort of major needed by any teacher or by a student using an arts and science major as a springboard to a dozen other professional fields. Until our arts and sciences colleagues join us in a fundamental rethinking of their enterprise—the reward structures, the research focus, and, most of all, the curriculum of the undergraduate college—we will not be preparing teachers or citizens with the knowledge and skills that they need.

- *The real ethical crisis of the university.* Do many readers of this book really believe that a majority of the faculty of their own college or university or many administrators in their own or any other university would not sacrifice the whole social justice mission for a two-point jump in the *U.S. News & World Report* rankings? The problem here is not merely the increasing corporate domination of universities, though that is certainly a problem. The larger problem is one that has been developing since at least the end of World War II: what Riesman (1956) so long ago described as the "institutional homogenization" of higher education in the United States. Half a century ago, Riesman wrote of "a snake-like procession" in which universities are forever trying to catch up with each other and, in the process, are becoming more and more alike as they seek to assume—more thoroughly than their neighbors and more thoroughly even than their role models—the attributes of a kind of "one best system" (pp. 21, 43). Only conformity, it seems, will give the modern university the boost in the various rankings and the prestige that will attract better faculty, better students—meaning those who have higher scores on a culturally biased set of tests and grades—and better access to the dollars that inevitably follow prestige. The places where a commitment to social justice will hold its own with the focus on those ever-present ranking systems that so dominate academic life in the United States today are too few. And I worry about the fate of social justice initiatives within universities in this context.

These perhaps dyspeptic musings on the current status of the modern university—that university that we seek to make a major partner with the community in teacher preparation—are, however, the subject of another volume, one that is inspired by and builds on this one. In the meantime, there is nourishment for every teacher educator in the volume now in hand.

Although this volume certainly leads at least this one teacher educator to think soberly about problems facing our field in the future, such thoughts are far from the dominant sense with which one concludes a reading of this book. On the contrary, as one who is quite thoroughly convinced that people like Haycock (1998) and her colleagues at the Education Trust are right that "good teaching matters ... a lot," I find in *Partnering to Prepare Urban Teachers* a terrific guide to some of the best ways to prepare a city teacher whose impact will indeed matter ... a lot. Haycock elaborates on her own assertion: "A number of large-scale studies provide convincing proof that what we do in education does matter. Schools—and especially teachers, it turns out—really DO make a difference (p. 2)."

At one time, especially in light of some of the research done by James Coleman and Christopher Jencks in the late 1960s and early 1970s, it became fashionable and easy for too many teachers and teacher educators to claim that, no matter what they did, schools could not do much to impact poverty and racism in the lives of their students. If such conclusions were ultimately true, then there would be little value in efforts to struggle with the best ways of preparing urban teachers. But more recent research points in a very different direction. As Haycock (1998) notes, "Earlier educational researchers just didn't have very good ways of measuring the variables" (pp. 11–12). But it is now long past time for those of us in teacher education to stop clinging "to dog-eared copies of the Coleman Report" (p. 2) and say that we are off the hook since we cannot make any difference anyway.

Once we have come to the point of owning our own responsibility as teacher educators, the next obvious question is, "What are we going to do about it?" For those of us who take that sobering question truly seriously, there are few better starting points in seeking practical and philosophically coherent answers than this volume.

REFERENCES

Freeland, R. M. (2004). The third way. *The Atlantic, 294*(3).

Haycock, K. (1998). Good teaching matters: How well-qualified teachers can close the gap. *Thinking–K16, 3*(2).

Irvine, J. J. (2003). *Educating teachers for diversity: Seeing with a cultural eye*. New York: Teachers College Press.

Labaree, D. F. (2004). *The trouble with ed schools*. New Haven: Yale University Press.

Murrell, P. C., Jr. (2001). *The community teacher: A new framework for effective urban teaching*. New York: Teachers College Press.

Riesman, D. (1956). *Constraint and variety in American higher education*. Garden City, NY: Doubleday.

Contributors

Jeffrey Michael Reyes Duncan-Andrade is an assistant professor of Raza Studies and education administration and interdisciplinary studies and co-director of the Educational Equity Initiative at San Francisco State University's Cesar Chavez Institute. Duncan-Andrade's research interests and publications span the areas of urban schooling and curriculum change, urban teacher development and retention, critical pedagogy, and cultural and ethnic studies.

Maria Alburquerque Candela is an educational psychologist, specializing in children and teenagers with behavioral problems and learning disabilities. From 1992 to 1995, she studied elementary education at the School of Education at the University of Cordoba, Spain. She graduated as an educational psychologist from the University of Cordoba in 1998. In 2003, she obtained her Ph.D. in Critical Literacy and Critical Pedagogy at the University of Cordoba. Her research interest lies in gender and feminism.

Victoria Chou has served as dean of the College of Education at University of Illionis at Chicago since 1996. She earned her Ph.D. in Curriculum and Instruction at the University of Wisconsin-Madison. Prior to her deanship, she was a classroom teacher, a reading specialist, and reading researcher. Currently, her energies are dedicated to developing a college that prepares excellent teachers and school leaders for students in Chicago's historically under-served neighborhood schools.

James W. Fraser is an historian of education and professor at the Steinhardt School of Culture, Education and Human Development at New York University (NYU). His most recent book is *Preparing America's Teachers: A History*

(Teachers College Press, 2007). Earlier works include *A History of Hope: When Americans Have Dared to Dream of a Better Future* (Palgrave-Macmillan, 2002), *Between Church and State: Religion & Public Education in a Multicultural America* (Palgrave-Macmillan, 1999), and *Reading, Writing, and Justice: School Reform As If Democracy Matters* (State University of New York Press, 1997) as well as articles in several journals. At NYU Steinhardt Fraser teaches courses in the history of education, religion and public education, and Inquiries into Teaching and Learning (the foundational course for all teacher preparation students for which he is the lead instructor). He is also engaged with the partnership with the New York City public schools and serves as NYU liaison to New Design High School in New York City. Prior to coming to NYU he was professor of History and Education and founding dean of the School of Education at Northeastern University in Boston, Massachusetts. He has also taught at Lesley University, the University of Massachusetts at Boston, Boston University, Wellesley College, and Public School 76. Fraser holds a Ph.D. from Columbia University. He is also an ordained minister in the United Church of Christ and was, for twenty years, the part-time pastor of Grace Church Federated in East Boston, Massachusetts.

Afra Ahmed Hersi is an assistant professor in the School of Education at Loyola College in Maryland. Her research interests focus on the areas of literacy, bilingual education, critical multicultural education, teacher education, and parent engagement in urban schools. Hersi earned her Ph.D. from Boston College in 2007.

Kristien Marquez-Zenkov is associate professor of literacy education in the Department of Teacher Education at Cleveland State University, where he serves as the co-director of the Master of Urban Secondary Teaching (MUST) program and coordinates partnerships with five local high schools. He has published on the impact of the standards movement on city teachers and students, urban professional development school partnerships, literacy, and urban students' academic engagement and success. In support of these urban school and teacher education commitments, he also co-teaches a 10th grade English class at a Cleveland-area high school.

Eugene Matusov is an associate professor of education at the University of Delaware. He was born in the Soviet Union. He studied developmental psychology with Soviet researchers working in the Vygotskian paradigm and worked as a school teacher before emigrating to the United States. He uses sociocultural and dialogic approaches to learning, which he views as transformation of participation in a sociocultural practice.

Cris Mayo is an associate professor in the Department of Educational Policy Studies and the Gender and Women's Studies Program at the University of Illinois at Urbana-Champaign. Her research interests include philosophy of education, gender and sexuality studies, and contemporary race theory. Her publications include articles in *Educational Theory, Philosophy of Education, Gay and Lesbian Issues in Education, Philosophical Studies in Education, Gay and Lesbian Quarterly* and a book, *Disputing the Subject of Sex: Sexuality and School Controversies* (Rowman and Littlefield, 2004).

Peter C. Murrell, Jr. is a professor of urban education at Northeastern University in Boston, Massachusetts, where he also directs the Center for Innovation in Urban Education. He is a teacher and researcher in human learning, cognitive development, urban pedagogy and the social-cultural contexts of human performance and school achievement. He is a member of several national initiatives on teacher assessment, including membership on the board of examiners for the National Council for Accreditation of Teacher Education and the International Recognition in Teacher Education, and the National Commission on High Stakes Testing. Dr. Murrell is the author of *Like Stone Soup: The Role of The Professional Development School in the Renewal of Urban Schools* (American Association of Colleges for Teacher Education Press, 2008), *Community Teachers: Teacher Preparation for the Renewal of Urban Schools and Communities* (Teachers College Press, 2001) and *African-Centered Pedagogy: Creating Schools of Achievement for African American Children* (State University of New York Press, 2002). Dr. Murrell's research focuses upon: (a) learning environments—qualitative studies of human learning in cultural and community contexts; (b) achievement performance—learning achievement in urban-focused professional development schools; (c) practice-oriented education; and (d) cultural and racial identity development and their relationships to school achievement.

Karen R. Nestor has been a classroom teacher, teacher educator, professional development specialist, and curriculum consultant in Chicago, Philadelphia and Cleveland. Most recently she worked with the Institute for Educational Renewal at John Carroll University to create comprehensive school improvement partnerships in urban schools. These partnerships combined graduate work in curriculum with in-school classroom work to encourage collaborative leadership, effective teaching and learning strategies, and positive school culture to ensure student achievement. This work led to her ongoing research interest in the voices of students, teachers and parents as agents of school change. Her recent book, *They Call Us to Justice: Responding to the Call of the Church and Our Students* (National Catholic Education Association, 2007), coauthored with Dr. Mark Storz, uses student voice to promote teachers' reflection on their classroom practice. Karen has led a team that is developing and implementing an innovative curriculum for St. Martin de Porres High School in Cleveland, which is part of the national Cristo Rey Network. Karen has also been a leader in youth and community development efforts for a wide variety of non-profit organizations. She holds an M.Ed. from Clevland State University.

R. D. Nordgren is interim department chair of Counseling, Administration, Supervision, and Adult Learning at Cleveland State University and is an associate professor of urban education. Nordgren is a former co-coordinator of the Master of Urban Secondary Teaching (MUST) program, supervising interns in Cleveland-area high schools. After earning a B.S. in English Education, Nordgren was an assistant principal at both the high school and middle school levels while earning an M.Ed. in Educational Leadership, and a Ph.D. in Curriculum and Instruction at University of South Florida. Nordgren is also a former middle and high school English teacher in Florida where he resided for 17 years. His research interests include democratic learning environments, and urban school reform. Nordgren is the author of *Making Schooling Relevant for the Global Age: Fulfilling Our Moral Obligation* (Rowman Littlefield, 2003) and is co-authoring a case study in curriculum and a instruction book and a teaching methods/educational psychology textbook.

Brad Olsen is an assistant professor of education at the University of California, Santa Cruz. His teaching and research focus on teachers, teaching, and teacher development (with emphases on knowledge and identity); critical pedagogy; English education; and sociolinguistics.

Francine Peterman is a professor in the Department of Curriculum and Foundations at Cleveland State University and has served as an urban teacher educator since attaining a Ph.D. at University of Arizona in 1991. Peterman writes about urban teaching and teacher preparation, standards for urban teacher education, inquiry-based teaching and learning, and the invention of cultures and practices that support renewal that is socially just. Her roots in teaching in Miami, Florida for 12 years and partnering with local Cleveland schools keep her grounded in her work in schools, where she prepares educators for the complexities and demands of urban teaching.

Karen Hunter Quartz is assistant director for research at the Institute for Democracy, Education, and Access where she conducts research on the career development of urban educators as part of the University of California, Los Angels's Urban Teacher Education Collaborative. Dr. Quartz is also Co-director of the Los Angeles Small Schools Collective, a professional learning community of small democratic high schools. In addition to several presentations and articles, Quartz co-edited (with Jeannie Oakes) *Creating New Educational Communities* (University of Chicago Press, 1995) and co-authored (with Jeannie Oakes, Steve Ryan and Martin Lipton) *Becoming Good American Schools: The Struggle for Civic Virtue in Education Reform* (Jossey Bass, 2000), the recipient of the 2001 American Educational Research Association's Outstanding Book Award.

Dennis Shirley is professor of Teacher Education at the Lynch School of Education at Boston College. Shirley has published in the history, sociology, and philosophy of education and his research has been translated into Spanish, French, and German. He raised $7 million from the United States Department of Education to lead the Massachusetts Coalition for Teacher Quality and Student Achievement from 1999 to 2005. In his role as department chair of Teacher Education at the Lynch School, he led the university's recent successful efforts to acquire a $5 million Carnegie-funded Teachers for a New Era grant. Shirley's current research efforts focus on teacher leadership; the harmonization of short, medium, and long-term educational change initiatives; and the diverse modalities of urban school reform. He holds a Ed.D. from the Harvard Graduate School of Education.

Mark Smith is a doctoral candidate in education at the University of Delaware. He is interested in dialogic education and collaborative settings for learning, both in school and in out-of-school contexts. His dissertation research explores the relationship between teacher authority and dialogue, and the degree to which teacher authority helps, hinders or destroys possibilities for dialogue in education.

Mark Storz is an associate professor in the Department of Education and Allied Studies at John Carroll University where he oversees initial licensure programs at the graduate and undergraduate level. He teaches courses at the undergraduate level in middle childhood philosophy and instruction and social studies methods and at the graduate level in educational research, urban education, and learning theory. His research interests focus on the perspectives of students, teachers and parents regarding the types of schools, teachers, and pedagogical practices that help urban young adolescents be successful in school.

Prior to his work at the university, Mark was a teacher and administrator in middle and secondary schools. He earned his Ph.D. in Urban Education in 1998 at Cleveland State University.

Kristy Sweigard is a first grade teacher on leave from an urban school based in Chicago, Illinois with previous experience in early childhood special education. While working for her M.Ed. at Cleveland State University, she had the privilege to closely work with the editor of this book, conducting research regarding the term "urban" that helped develop the framework of their chapter. She works each day to renew a cycle of hope for today's urban youth. She believes and acts as if we *can* make a difference.

Steve Tozer is a professor in the College of Education at the University of Illinois at Chicago and founding coordinator of the UIC Ed.D. Program in Urban Education Leadership. He is past president of the American Educational Studies Association (2005-06) and the Council for Social Foundations of Education, (2001-04). His research interests have focused on social context knowledge in teacher preparation. In journals such as *Educational Foundations, Educational Studies, Teachers College Record,* and *Educational Theory,* he has explored the origins of the field of social foundations of education at Teachers College Columbia in the 1930s and 1940s. He is currently associate editor of *Educational Theory.* He has co-authored or co-edited five books on the social contexts of schooling, including a textbook for teachers, *School and Society, Historical and Contemporary Perspectives* (McGraw Hill, 2005), now in its fifth edition. His collaborations in reform of the professional preparation and development of teachers and school leaders have been funded by MacArthur Foundation, McDougal Family Foundation, Chicago Community Trust, Joyce Foundation, Chicago Public Education Fund, and Stone Family Foundation, among others. He is past recipient of the Stevenson Award from the Association for Teacher Educators for leadership and dedication to the education profession.

Brian Yusko is an associate professor in the Department of Curriculum and Foundations at Clevland State University. Dr. Yusko completed his Ph.D. in Teaching, Curriculum, and Educational Policy from Michigan State University. He has a M.Ed. in English Education and a B.A. in Philosophy from Fordham University. Dr. Yusko teaches graduate and undergraduate courses in curriculum and instruction, with an emphasis on middle grades teaching in urban settings. His research focuses on teacher learning, specifically on professional development opportunities that help teachers learn to design and deliver student-centered instruction. Since coming to Cleveland State, he has been involved with several grants. As a participant in the MIMIC grant, he designed Video CD-ROM's for instructional materials in undergraduate teacher education courses. He worked on the design of a virtual curriculum for an early methods course for students intending to teach in urban settings as part of a Great Cities Universities grant. He is currently designing and researching a video technology mentoring program for new teachers at a Cleveland elementary school with a grant from the Center for Urban School Collaboration.

Index